Building Facebook Applications For Dummies

Cheat Sheet

Common API Calls

Methods	Description
events.get	Returns events matching specified criteria
events.getMembers	Returns members of an event
feed.publishTemplatizedAction	Publish a mini-feed story to a user and news feed stories to friends and fans
fql.query	Evaluates an FQL query
friends.areFriends	Checks to see whether users are friends with each other
friends.get	Gets a list of friends of the specified user
friends.getAppUsers	Gets a list of friends of user who are signed up with the application
groups.get	Gets groups based on specified criteria
groups.getMembers	Gets members of a group
notifications.get	Gets outstanding Facebook notifications for user
notifications.send	Sends a notification to one or more users
notifications.sendEmail	Sends an e-mail to one or more users of the application
profile.getFBML	Gets the FBML markup that is currently set for a user's profile
profile.setFBML	Sets the FBML for a user's profile, including the content for the profile box, profile actions, and the mobile device profile box
users.getInfo	Gets user-specific information
users.getLoggedInUser	Gets the current user ID
users.isAppAdded	Checks to see whether the logged-in user has added the calling application
users.setStatus	Updates a user's Facebook status (unofficial at time of writing)

Common FBML Elements

Groups	FBML Elements	Description
User and group	fb:name	Outputs the name of the specified user.
	fb:grouplink	Outputs the name of the specified group.
	fb:user	Specifies that the contained content is owned by the specified user.
	fb:pronoun	Outputs a pronoun for the specified user.
	fb:profile-pic	Displays the specified user's profile picture.

(continued)

Building Facebook™ Applications For Dummies®

Cheat Sheet

Common FBML Elements *(continued)*

Groups	FBML Elements	Description
Profile	`fb:wide`	Displays contained content only when profile box is in the wide column of the user's profile.
	`fb:narrow`	Displays contained content only when profile box is in the narrow column of the user's profile.
	`fb:profile-action`	Displays a link on the user's profile underneath their photo.
	`fb:subtitle`	Specifies the subtitle for the profile box.
	`fb:action`	Displays an action link on the right-hand side of a profile box or dashboard.
Request forms	`fb:request-form`	Defines a request form.
	`fb:multi-friend-input`	Renders a tabular display of friends in a request form (or, if `condensed="true"`, displays a condensed list).
	`fb:request-form-submit`	Displays a submit button for condensed request forms.
	`fb:req-choice`	Defines a button at the bottom of a user's request page.
Page header and navigation	`fb:dashboard`	Renders a top dashboard.
	`fb:action`	Displays an action link in a dashboard.
	`fb:create-button`	Adds a Create button to the dashboard.
	`fb:help`	Adds a Help link to the dashboard.
	`fb:header-title`	Provides a title for a media header.
	`fb:owner-action`	Specifies an action link inside of a media header.
	`fb:tabs`	Defines a tabset for page navigation.
	`fb:tab-item`	Defines a tab link.

For Dummies: Bestselling Book Series for Beginners

Building Facebook™ Applications

FOR

DUMMIES®

by Richard Wagner

WILEY

Wiley Publishing, Inc.

Building Facebook™ Applications For Dummies®

Published by
Wiley Publishing, Inc.
111 River Street
Hoboken, NJ 07030-5774

www.wiley.com

WILEY

About the Author

Richard Wagner is an experienced Web designer and developer as well as author of several Web-related books. These books include *Professional iPhone and iPod touch Programming, XSLT For Dummies, Creating Web Pages All-in-One Desk Reference For Dummies, XML All-in-One Desk Reference For Dummies, Web Design Before & After Makeovers,* and *JavaScript Unleashed* (1st, 2nd ed.). Before moving into full-time authoring, Richard was vice president of product development at NetObjects. He was also inventor and chief architect of the award-winning NetObjects ScriptBuilder. A versatile author with a wide range of interests, he is also author of *The Myth of Happiness* and *C.S. Lewis & Narnia For Dummies.*

Dedication

To my top Facebook friends, Kim, Jordan, Jared, and Justus.

Author's Acknowledgments

For this book, I was blessed with a terrific editorial team at Wiley. Thanks go to Christopher Morris for his steady, flawless management of the book project. Thanks also go to Christopher McCulloh for his close attention to all technical details and helpful suggestions on the coding examples. Further, thanks to John Edwards and Linda Morris for their keen editing eyes.

Publisher's Acknowledgments

We're proud of this book; please send us your comments through our online registration form located at www.dummies.com/register/.

Some of the people who helped bring this book to market include the following:

Acquisitions, Editorial, and Media Development

Sr. Project Editor: Christopher Morris

Acquisitions Editor: Katie Feltman

Copy Editors: John Edwards, Linda Morris

Technical Editor: Christopher McCulloh

Editorial Manager: Kevin Kirschner

Media Development Project Manager: Laura Moss-Hollister

Media Development Assistant Producer: Angela Denny

Editorial Assistant: Amanda Foxworth

Sr. Editorial Assistant: Cherie Case

Cartoons: Rich Tennant (www.the5thwave.com)

Composition Services

Project Coordinator: Katie Key

Layout and Graphics: Stacie Brooks, Carl Byers, Reuben W. Davis, Alissa D. Ellet, Ronald Terry, Christine Williams

Proofreaders: Laura Albert, Debbye Butler, David Faust

Indexer: Lynnzee Elze

Publishing and Editorial for Technology Dummies

> **Richard Swadley,** Vice President and Executive Group Publisher
>
> **Andy Cummings,** Vice President and Publisher
>
> **Mary Bednarek,** Executive Acquisitions Director
>
> **Mary C. Corder,** Editorial Director

Publishing for Consumer Dummies

> **Diane Graves Steele,** Vice President and Publisher
>
> **Joyce Pepple,** Acquisitions Director

Composition Services

> **Gerry Fahey,** Vice President of Production Services
>
> **Debbie Stailey,** Director of Composition Services

Contents at a Glance

Table of Contents

Introduction

*I*f you have spent much time developing Web apps over the past couple of years, you've probably heard the term *social network* so many times that you hear it ringing in your ears while you sleep. (Talk about nightmares.) Until Facebook released its platform, one could understand the nightmares, because social networking seemed far more important to teenage girls on MySpace than to serious Web developers. However, when the Facebook Platform was announced by Facebook, social networking suddenly became a buzzword worth dreaming about for the Web development community. A whole new breed of Web application was born — a social network–enabled application.

If you are interested in developing a Web application that taps into the social networking heart of Facebook, you've found the right book.

About This Book

Building Facebook Applications For Dummies serves as your no-nonsense guide to creating and designing Facebook applications. I focus on providing the essentials that you need to know to be successful. You'll explore how to do many tasks in this book, such as these:

- ✔ Seamlessly integrate with Facebook.com using the Facebook API

- ✔ Make sense of Facebook Platform technologies, including Facebook Markup Language (FBML), Facebook Query Language (FQL), and Facebook JavaScript (FBJS)

- ✔ Migrate your existing Web application to a Facebook app

- ✔ Tap into core Facebook services, such as the News Feed and Wall

- ✔ Create mobile apps for Facebook

- ✔ Get your app noticed by Facebook users

You can create Facebook apps using many Web programming languages — including PHP, Java, ASP.NET, ASP, ColdFusion, C++, C#, Python, Ruby on Rails, and more. Because it is impossible to fully cover each of these languages in any book, this book focuses on PHP in the examples. However, many of the Facebook technologies (FBML, FQL, and FBJS) are language neutral and will be implemented the same way regardless of the language used. And, in cases in which you need to call the Facebook API, you can follow along by translating the API calls into your language of choice.

Foolish Assumptions

In *Building Facebook Applications For Dummies,* I don't assume that you have experience with Facebook or the Facebook Platform. However, I do assume that you have some working knowledge of Web client technologies (HTML, JavaScript, and CSS) and a Web programming language.

Conventions Used in This Book

In spotting the heading for this section, I was all set to tell you about the conventions that you can read about in this book at the Javits Center in New York or the Las Vegas Convention Center. But then I realized that you are probably far more interested in the set of rules that I use in the book. These conventions are as follows:

- ✔ **Text formatting:** As you read through the book, you'll see that I *italicize* terms that I am defining. **Bold text** is used to indicate specific commands that you are to perform. Finally, URLs and programming code stand out from normal text with a `monospaced font`.

- ✔ **Markup terminology:** In this book, you will often be working with markup style languages, including Hypertext Markup Language (HTML) and Facebook's own Facebook Markup Language (FBML). Here's how the terminology works: A markup language consists of many *elements,* each of which has a *start tag, end tag,* and *content* in between. For example:

```
<h1>My First Facebook App</h1>
```

The `<h1>` is the start tag, `</h1>` is the end tag, and `My First Facebook App` is the content. The entire piece of code is called the `h1` element or tag.

What You Don't Have to Read

I am confident that you will find this book's narrative to be so compelling and thought-provoking that you can't help yourself but digest each and every word. However, you can feel free to avoid a couple of modules in the book if you like without missing the information you absolutely need to know:

- **Text marked with a Technical Stuff icon:** This icon warns you that certain paragraphs provide technical details that are interesting, but not essential.
- **Sidebars:** You'll discover shaded sidebars popping up here and there throughout the book. These sections provide interesting info, but it is not directly part of the discussion at hand.

How This Book Is Organized

This book is carved up into four parts. Following is a summary of these parts.

Part I: Getting Friendly with the Facebook Platform

Before diving into Facebook technologies, you should first get a solid overview of Facebook and its platform and Facebook's "social graph." These discussions are designed to be particularly helpful for Web developers who are new to Facebook. After that discussion, you will be ready for a walk-through of creating your first Facebook application.

Part II: Poking the API

The Facebook Platform consists of several interrelated technologies, including the Facebook API, FBML, FQL, and FBJS. In Part II, you dive into each of these and understand how to work with them to create apps. You also explore the issues of using the API versus FQL. Finally, you will explore the suite of developer tools available for working with the Facebook Platform.

Part III: Developing Facebook Applications

If Part II is about discovering the individual Facebook Platform technologies, Part III is all about effectively applying them so that you can build apps. In addition to architecting Facebook apps, I also talk about how to design apps that look and feel like a native part of Facebook itself.

Part IV: The Part of Tens

David Letterman may have his wimpy "Top Ten Lists," but this book has something much more insightful (albeit less funny) — The Part of Tens. In this final part, I round out the discussion by looking at various tips, tricks, and tidbits on the Facebook Platform.

Icons Used in This Book

Just like a legend provides assistance on a road map, so too do icons throughout this book. You'll find these four icons:

The Remember icon indicates a paragraph that is particularly amazing, vital, or significant to the future of the world. Okay, perhaps that's a little over-board, but the icon does show you info that is especially important for your understanding of the Facebook Platform.

The Tip icon highlights important programming tips that you should take note of.

The Warning icon alerts you to snags and pitfalls that can occur if you are not careful.

As I mention in the "What You Don't Have to Read" section, the Technical Stuff icon points out technical but nonessential info. These paragraphs are meant to feed that little geek inside everyone.

Where to Go from Here

Now that you've made it this far, you are ready to begin your odyssey into the Facebook Platform. You don't have to read this book sequentially, so here's a road map that will help point you in the right direction:

- ✔ To explore Facebook and the Facebook Platform, turn the page and begin reading Chapter 1.
- ✔ To discover what a social network is, check out Chapter 1.
- ✔ To create your first Facebook application, skip over to Chapter 2.
- ✔ To dive headfirst into Facebook Platform development, head over to Part II.
- ✔ To begin working with Facebook development tools, read Chapter 7.

Sample Files for This Book

This book comes with samples files that can be downloaded from the Wiley Web site at the following URL:

```
www.dummies.com/go/facebookappsfd
```

Part I
Getting Friendly
with the Facebook
Platform

"These are the parts of our life that aren't on Facebook."

In this part . . .

Whether you are a socialite or socially awkward, you are ready to dive into creating "social networking" applications for Facebook. Get the scoop in Part I, where I introduce you to Facebook and its developer platform. I then explore the social graph, Facebook's social network. Finally, you roll up your sleeves and code your first Facebook app.

Chapter 1

Introducing Facebook and the Facebook Platform

*W*e hear all of the time about "platforms" in various walks of life. Political parties put their policies and agendas into documents called *platforms*. An Olympic diver performs a perfect dive off of a 10 meter *platform* on the way to a gold medal. Heck, *platform tennis* is a form of tennis that people play with paddles.

Facebook too has its own platform — cleverly called the Facebook Platform. Fortunately for your coworkers, it is a platform that you don't need a swimsuit or a paddle to use. You do need to know a Web programming language such as PHP or Java, however.

Facebook gained popularity because of its structured environment and social network, but its Facebook Platform is proving to be a critical means of preventing it from becoming the latest "flavor of the month." Because of third-party applications, Facebook now offers a compelling reason for users to invest themselves in Facebook.com in a way that they were never really able to do with social networking sites like MySpace. In fact, upon the Platform's release, it was only a matter of weeks before users began to see thousands and thousands of Facebook-inspired applications from all sorts of developers — from major corporations to hobbyists working in their basements.

In this chapter, I introduce you to the basics of Facebook and its development platform. If you are an application developer just coming to this social networking site as a newcomer, I get you up to speed by surveying the core concepts and components of Facebook itself. Next, I survey the Facebook Platform and its various parts and show you how they work together to form a cohesive solution.

Get your platform shoes on and let's take a hike!

Discovering Facebook

MySpace and Friendster may have been the early "go to" places for online social interaction, but Facebook has overtaken them as the fastest growing social networking site on the Web. Its structured environment, enjoyable user experience, and expandable platform for third-party applications have helped it gain this level of importance and popularity.

Before you begin to develop applications for Facebook, you should get to know all of the ins and outs of Facebook itself to ensure you fully understand the potential of how your application can tap into its platform.

If you are a newcomer to Facebook, you need to get your arms around two important concepts: the *News Feed* and the *profile*.

News Feed

After you are logged in to Facebook, the Facebook home page (`www.face book.com`) displays the News Feed, as shown in Figure 1-1. Think of the News Feed as your own personalized news channel — something like a FNN (Friends News Network), if you want to get clever.

The News Feed contains a live list of announcements or stories about the activity of your network of friends on Facebook — whom they befriended, what apps they added, what their Status is. For example, if my friend Jared Allen became friends with Ally Horinsky, I would receive the following story:

```
Jared Allen and Ally Horinsky are now friends.
```

Facebook compiles this list of news stories based on several factors — the activity of your friends, your preferences of story types, frequency settings on specific friends, the privacy levels of your friends, a user's opinion on the quality of a story (known as "thumbs up" and "x" votes) — all mixed together into a behind-the-scenes, super-secret algorithm. A user can determine the frequency of certain news stories, but Facebook ultimately retains control over what is placed on the News Feed. Facebook also places social ads inside of the News Feed.

In this book, you discover how your application can add news stories to the News Feed.

The News Feed

Figure 1-1:
The
News Feed
contains a
list of news
stories
about your
network of
friends.

Requests and notifications

The Facebook home page devotes the right sidebar column to listings of requests, notifications, birthday reminders, pokes, status updates, and more. You can use this space to quickly glance through items requiring your attention. You can also access these notifications through the profile.

Profile

Each Facebook user has an individualized profile page, such as the one shown in Figure 1-2. A profile page is a user's "real estate" on Facebook.com, a home page for the user, friends, and others. Users decide what information to show or restrict based on who the visitor is.

Left Nav

Profile box

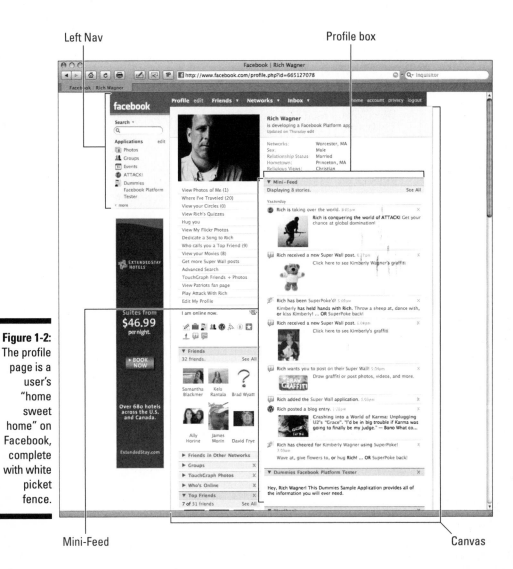

Figure 1-2:
The profile page is a user's "home sweet home" on Facebook, complete with white picket fence.

Mini-Feed

Canvas

The Facebook page contains a variety of elements. Some of the most notable for application developers include the following:

- ✔ **Left Nav:** The Left Nav sidebar (measuring 150 pixels in width) contains an Applications menu in which users can quickly access applications. Users can drag and drop their five favorite apps into the topmost section.

- ✔ **Canvas:** The canvas is the 650-pixel section to the right of the left side menu and below the top navigation menu. Not only is the profile page contained within the canvas, but every Facebook application is included as well.

- ✔ **Mini-Feed:** Mini-Feed contains a snapshot summary of the activities of a user. Notice the difference from the News Feed: Whereas News Feed on Facebook.com displays stories of friends, a profile's Mini-Feed presents stories only related to the user. As a Facebook developer, you can publish a Mini-Feed story using the API.

- ✔ **Profile box:** Profile boxes on a user's profile page consist of built-in Facebook boxes (Mini-Feed, Friends, Education, and Work) and Facebook applications. They can either be wide (400 pixels) and be displayed in the main profile section, or narrow (200 pixels) on the left sidebar. A user can drag and drop profile boxes to various parts of the page and can remove an application's profile box without deleting the application. Figures 1-3 and 1-4 show the My Flickr profile box in wide and narrow views, respectively.

Figure 1-3:
My Flickr application displayed as a wide profile box.

Figure 1-4:
My Flickr
displayed
in the left
sidebar.

✔ **Wall:** You can think of the Wall as a "bulletin board" of sorts that people can use to post notes, comments, or other feedback about a person. As a Facebook developer, you cannot post directly to the Wall inside of your application. However, you can provide a Wall attachment for your users. A Wall attachment provides a way for users of your application to add application-specific content to their Walls.

For example, the iLike application provides an Attachment that makes it easy for users to add music to their Walls. For example, by clicking the Add Music button (see Figure 1-5), a user can select a song to add to his or her Wall to share with friends (see Figure 1-6).

Figure 1-5:
Facebook
developers
can add
Attach-
ments to
the Wall.

The iLike Add Music button

Nearly everything about Facebook is oriented toward social networking with friends. This topic is so key to Facebook that I devote the next section to it. So, as you begin to think about developing an application for Facebook, you should always consider how you can best take advantage of the social, viral nature of the Facebook Platform.

Figure 1-6: Attachments help get your application noticed.

New Wall entry

Discovering the Pulse of Facebook: The Social Graph

The term *social network* has become so popular and familiar during the past couple of years that even non-techie people understand what the term means. Facebook, however, has its own vernacular when it comes to understanding social networking. They call it the *social graph*. The social graph can be defined as the interconnections that exist among family, friends, and acquaintances that every person has.

Take me as an example. I have a wife and three boys, parents who live in Indiana, a sister who lives in Ohio, many friends from my church, acquaintances from my town, coworkers at previous places of employment, and so on. Some of these people have interconnections of their own. My wife knows my sister, and my kids know my parents. Others members of my network do not know each other. My boys, for instance, have never met my former boss, Sal.

Social relationships like these are bound together by some type of interdependency between each other. It can be family, faith, friends, common interests, geography, or line of work. But there is always some sort of tie between each other, however loose.

In daily life, people place great value on their social graph. If I am looking for a job, I probably begin by networking my friends and former coworkers or acquaintances in the high tech world. If I am looking for someone to watch our dog while we are on vacation, I am willing to trust the niece of a close friend to do the job well, even though I barely know the niece personally. Moreover, when I am looking for a dentist, I ask around and get recommendations from people whose opinions I value within my social graph.

Online communities like Facebook and MySpace seek to re-create this natural human phenomenon in the digital world. Within these communities, you establish these links between people based on some sort of interdependency. Through the community services, you are able to get to know what your friends are up to, the music they are listening to, the movies they recommend, and what apps they are using.

However, the practices, behavior, and culture of these various social networking sites impact how well they emulate the real world. On MySpace, for example, I may collect hundreds or even thousands of connections, but only a handful are truly "friends" with any degree of interdependency. In contrast, in an environment like Facebook, which does not promote "friendship collecting" per se, I may currently only have a few dozen friends, but nearly all of those connections are backed by real-world relationships. As a result, I place much more weight on the opinions and activities of my friends on Facebook than I would on a site like MySpace. This value of the social interconnection is significant for the Facebook application developer creating social-enabled apps.

One issue that is curious to many is the use of the word "graph" in the term *social graph*. The term *network* in *social network* is intuitive enough, but the word *graph* conjures up images of something you create in Microsoft Excel for your boss.

Although *graph* may be a synonym for *chart* in everyday usage, Facebook uses mathematical definition of the term. In this context, you can think of a graph as an abstraction for modeling relationships between sets of nodes.

What Is the Facebook Platform?

The Facebook Platform is a standards-based programming framework that enables developers to create applications that interact and integrate with core Facebook services.

Points of integration

When you create an application for the Facebook Platform (see Chapter 2 for how to get started), you can integrate it at several points in the framework. Take, for example, Super Wall, one of the most popular third-party Facebook applications available. Consider the ways in which it is integrated into Facebook itself — so much so it becomes harder and harder to distinguish between apps created by Facebook and those developed by third parties. Here are several points of integration:

- ✔ **Display in the Application directory:** As Figure 1-7 shows, Super Wall is listed in the application directory after the developer adds it to Facebook.

- ✔ **Provide an About page:** An application provides an About page to explain to users what the application is and what it can do for them. Facebook also lets potential users know which of their friends have already added this application. The Super Wall about page (see Figure 1-8) provides an image and brief product description.

The Super Wall app

Figure 1-7: Every Facebook application can be listed in the directory.

Figure 1-8: The Super Wall About page invites users to install the application.

✔ **Give the user a choice:** Users always have the last word on determining the level of integration that your application is permitted to have with their accounts. By default, Facebook encourages users to provide full integration. (See Figure 1-9.)

Figure 1-9:
Users
decide
how much
integration
an
application
can have.

✔ **Invite friends:** With access to the friends data of a user, an application can ask users if they wish to invite their friends to add the application as well. You can easily understand the viral growth nature of this functionality. Figure 1-10 shows the Super Wall friends invitation request.

✔ **Display inside Facebook Canvas Pages:** Facebook applications are displayed within the Facebook canvas. As you can see from Figure 1-11, Super Wall gets the entire Facebook page, except for the top menu and Left Nav. This presentation layer is provided to Facebook either as Facebook Markup Language (FBML, an HTML-like language) or as an `iframe` element.

Figure 1-10:
Application
developers
encourage
users to
invite their
friends.

Figure 1-11:
Facebook
Canvas
Pages allow
third-party
apps to
seamlessly
integrate
into the
Facebook
presentation
environment.

✔ **Appear in the Left Nav:** Applications can have their name and icon displayed in the Left Nav menu on the left side of the page (see Figure 1-12). Applications can be launched by clicking these links. Users can drag and drop applications, placing their top five apps in the topmost section.

✔ **Display a profile box:** Applications can have a profile box that is displayed on the user's profile. Although in this case a user does not run your application inside of the profile box, you can provide updated information useful to the user or actions for launching the application itself (see Figure 1-13).

Super Wall icon

Figure 1-12:
The Left
Nav is the
Facebook
application
launcher.

Figure 1-13:
The Super
Wall
profile box
provides
frequently
requested
actions
for a user.

Super Wall profile box

✔ **Create profile action links:** Also on a user's profile page, an application can add items in the Profile action links list, located just under the user's picture. For example, as Figure 1-14 shows, Super Wall adds an action link for inviting friends.

Super Wall action link

Figure 1-14:
Applications
can add
items to
the profile
links list.

  ✔ **Access and post to News Feed:** Applications can post stories to the user's
    News Feed to communicate with a user's friends. For example, Super Wall
    sends a story out to my friends when I write something new on my wall.
    Each application has a maximum number of stories that can be on a News
    Feed at a time.

  ✔ **Send e-mail alerts:** If a user allows this activity, applications can send
    e-mail alerts and notifications to users.

  ✔ **Generate requests:** Applications can create new requests that require
    a response from a user. Often a request takes the form of an invitation
    from one user to another to add an application or perform an action.

  ✔ **Create message attachments:** As I describe in the "Discovering Facebook"
    section earlier in this chapter, message attachments can be added to
    Facebook message composers, such as the Wall. Using this point of
    integration, applications can provide app-prepared content into the
    composer.

  ✔ **Integrate into Facebook privacy settings:** In the privacy settings of their
    profiles, users can specify who can view their applications' profile
    boxes — everyone, some networks, only friends, only themselves, or
    no one. Application developers can also add additional privacy settings
    inside of their own applications. (See Figure 1-15.)

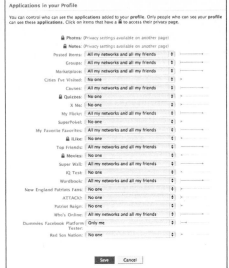

Figure 1-15:
Users can
configure
the level
of privacy
desired for
applications.

Facebook application architecture

Facebook applications are not installed directly onto the Facebook server. Instead, they are placed on the developer's server and then called by Facebook when the application URL is requested.

To interact with applications, Facebook uses a *callback metaphor*. Let me explain. The URL of your application is associated with a registered application in Facebook. When the Facebook application URL (such as www.face book.com/dummies) is requested, Facebook redirects the request to your server. Your application processes the request, communicates with Facebook using the Facebook Application Programming Interface (API) or Facebook Query Language (FQL), and returns Facebook Markup Language (FBML) to Facebook for presentation to the user inside of its canvas.

Figure 1-16 shows the architecture of a typical Web application, whereas Figure 1-17 displays the architecture of a Facebook application.

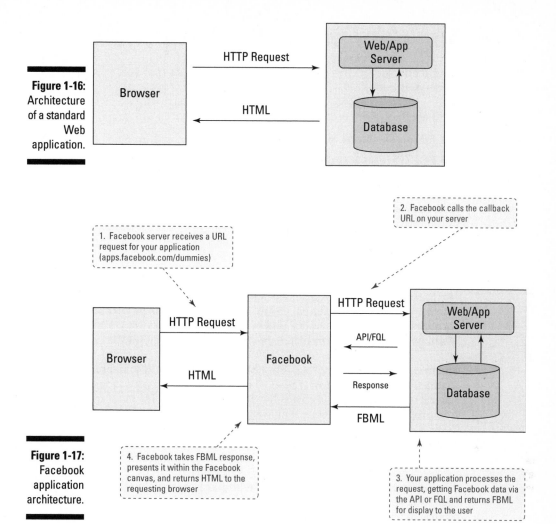

Figure 1-16:
Architecture
of a standard
Web
application.

Figure 1-17:
Facebook
application
architecture.

Exploring the Framework Components

The Facebook Platform consists of four components that you work with inside your code:

- Facebook API
- FBML (Facebook Markup Language)
- FQL (Facebook Query Language)
- Facebook JavaScript

Each of these is described in the following sections.

Facebook API

The Facebook API is a Web services programming interface for accessing core services (profile, friends, group, event, photo) and performing other Facebook-centric functionality (log in, redirect, update view). The API is based on a REST-based architecture (which I explain in Chapter 3).

Facebook officially supports client libraries for PHP (4 and 5) and Java. These can be downloaded at `developers.facebook.com/resources.php`. Several unofficial client libraries have been developed for most every major Web programming language, including ASP.NET, ASP (VBScript), ColdFusion, C++, C#, D, Emacs List, PHP4, Lisp, Perl, Python, Ruby on Rails, VB.NET, and Windows Mobile. To download these unofficial versions, go to `wiki.developers.facebook.com`.

When you use a client library, you use language-specific methods to access Facebook services. For example, here's how you can retrieve the name and picture of a user and then display it on a page:

```
$user_data = array('name', 'pic', 'activities');
$current = $facebook->api_client->users_getInfo($user, $user_data);
echo "<p>Your name is {$current[0]['name']} </p>";
echo "<p>Here is what you look like: <img src='{$current[0]['pic']} /></p>";
```

Don't concern yourself with the details for now. Just notice that the user-specific information is accessed using the `$facebook->api_client->users_getInfo()` call.

Chapter 3 provides the details you need to work with the Facebook API.

Facebook Markup Language

Facebook Markup Language (FBML) is an HTML-like language used to display pages inside of the Facebook canvas. Here are three basic facts about FBML:

- ✔ FBML contains a subset of HTML elements. Such common elements as `p`, `ul`, and `h1` are part of FBML.

- ✔ FBML provides qualified support for `script` and `style` elements. Normal JavaScript is not supported in a `script` element, although Facebook JavaScript (see the "Facebook JavaScript" section below) does permit some scripting capabilities. You cannot use the `style` element to link to external style sheets, but you can use it for internal CSS.

- ✔ FBML also includes several proprietary extensions for Facebook-specific UI elements as well as program flow.

For example, the `fb:name` element displays the name of the user based on the value of the `uid` attribute:

```
<p>Your name is: <fb:name uid="665127078" useyou="false"/></p>
```

Some FBML elements help control the flow of a program. For example, `fb:if-can-see` only displays the content inside of it if the user has permission to see a specified feature (the `what` attribute) for the specified user (the `uid` attribute). Consider the following:

```
<fb:if-can-see uid="665127078" what="profile">
  <p>You are granted access, you lucky one!</p>
  <fb:else>Go somewhere else, you unfortunate one.</fb:else>
</fb:if-can-see>
```

See Chapter 4 for full details on working with FBML.

Facebook Query Language

Facebook Query Language (FQL) is a SQL-based interface into Facebook data. You can access many Facebook database tables, including `user`, `friend`, `group`, `group_member`, `event`, `event_member`, `photo`, `album`, and `photo_tag`.

The language itself is similar to standard SQL, though with a few restrictions:

- ✔ SELECT statements must be performed one table at a time.
- ✔ Join queries are not permitted.
- ✔ A query must be indexable.

You can actually perform most of the same data access routines using either API or FQL. To that point, several of the API calls are nothing more than wrappers for FQL queries. FQL even has some advantages over the standard API interface. It reduces bandwidth and parsing overhead and can help minimize the number of data requests in complex situations.

Here's an example of using FQL to retrieve a list of friends of the current user (where the $user variable is the current user):

```
$friends = $facebook->api_client->fql_query("SELECT uid, name FROM user WHERE
            uid IN (SELECT uid2 FROM friend WHERE uid1=$user)");
```

If you want to discover more about FQL queries, turn to Chapter 5.

Facebook JavaScript

FBML does not support the use of standard JavaScript using the script element. However, Facebook JavaScript (or FBJS, for short) allows for limited scripting functionality inside a Facebook application. Here are some of the differences between FBJS and JavaScript:

- ✔ Instead of using the standard JavaScript DOM, Facebook provides its own alternative DOM implementation.
- ✔ Many FBJS object implementations are the same as standard JavaScript, although there are some differences. For example, instead of accessing a JavaScript property (such as document.href), FBJS uses a pair of get and set methods instead (getHref, setHref).
- ✔ When Facebook processes scripting code inside of script elements, it tacks on the application ID to function and variable names. Facebook does this to create an application-specific scope.

Facebook JavaScript does provide AJAX and Facebook dialog objects for developers to take advantage of.

Chapter 6 provides full details on how to work with Facebook JavaScript.

Three amigos: Developer centers on Facebook.com

You should bookmark these three useful developer links on Facebook.com:

✔ `facebook.com/developers` is the "home base" for Facebook developers. You can set up a new application, access your list of installed applications, and read the latest news and developer discussions.

✔ `developers.facebook.com` is the official documentation center for Facebook Platform developers. You can access all of the Facebook-approved reference material here.

✔ `wiki.developers.facebook.com` is a user-based Facebook developer's Wiki, providing access to documentation, FAQs, sample code, and more.

Chapter 2

The App Walkabout: Building Your First Facebook Application

. . . .

In This Chapter

▶ Registering your app with Facebook

▶ Writing your first code for the Facebook API

▶ Setting default FBML for the Profile box

▶ Adding an icon and About page

. . . .

*L*et's do this! The explorers of old would get a "lay of the lands" before venturing off into the unknown wilderness. In studying the geography, they would grasp the steepness of the mountains, the width of the valleys and plains, and the nature of the rivers or swamps. However, at some point, the explorers would eventually put down their maps and survey instruments and lead their teams into the wild.

Now that you have had a chance to get a solid grasp of the Facebook Platform and its Social Graph, you are probably feeling antsy like those explorers and are ready to *just do this*.

That's what this chapter is all about. I walk you through each step of building your first application for the Facebook Platform. I keep the sample straightforward at this early stage, but you'll be able to see each of the basic tasks you will want to perform, regardless of the complexity of your application.

In this walkthrough, I show you how to build a basic PHP-based app. However, if you are using Java or another programming language, you can also follow along, substituting the PHP-specific commands as needed.

Registering an Application with Facebook

Before coding the application itself, you are going to need to get some application-specific information from Facebook to communicate with the Facebook Platform. Your first step is, therefore, to register the application with Facebook. When you do so, you'll get an API key and secret key that you can plug into your code.

The following steps guide you through this registration process:

1. **Go to** `www.facebook.com/developers`.

   If you are not logged in to Facebook, you will be prompted to log in first.

   Figure 2-1 shows you the main Facebook developer's page.

Set Up New Application button

Figure 2-1: Facebook.com/developers is the place to start for setting up a new application.

2. Click the Set Up New Application button.

The New Application page is displayed, as shown in Figure 2-2.

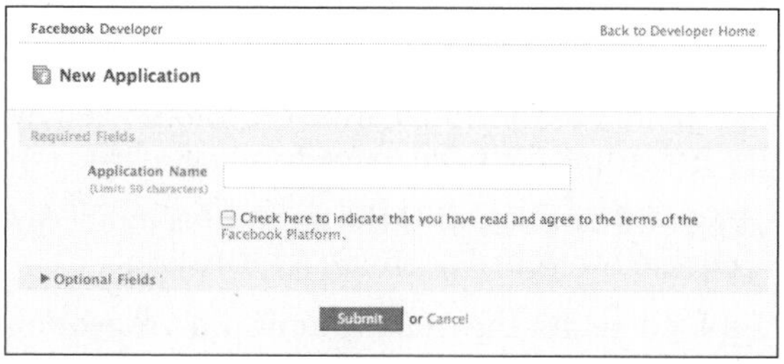

Figure 2-2:
Creating
a new
Facebook
application.

3. Enter the name of your application in the space provided.

Choose it carefully because it will be the one displayed everywhere within Facebook. I am naming my test application `Dummies Facebook Platform Tester`.

4. Select the check box to confirm that you have read and accepted the terms of the Facebook Platform.

Be sure that you fully read the terms before checking the box. Pay special attention to the permissible usage of the terms *Facebook* and *Face*.

5. Click the Optional Fields link to display several more settings, as shown in Figure 2-3.

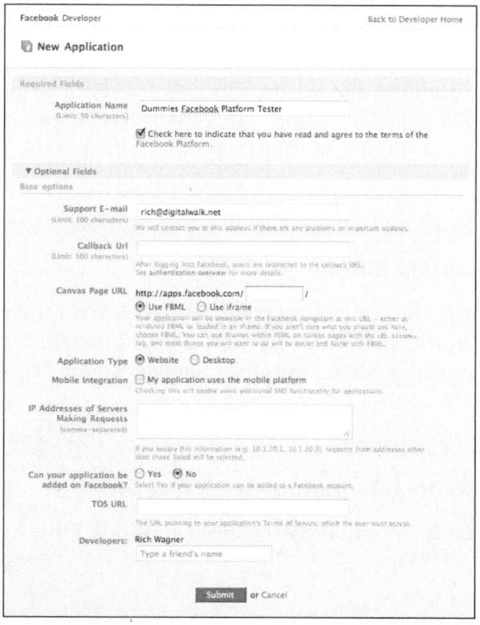

Figure 2-3:
Additional
application
options.

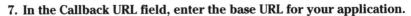

6. **Add an e-mail address that you want to use for technical support issues.**

   Facebook adds your account e-mail address by default, but you can change it as needed.

7. **In the Callback URL field, enter the base URL for your application.**

   The callback URL points to the application on *your* server. Be sure to point to a folder, not a specific page name (`index.php`).

8. **In the Canvas Page URL field, enter the subfolder name that you would like to request for your Facebook application.**

   All Facebook apps are under the `apps.facebook.com` domain, and then each has a unique subfolder name.

   Pick a folder name that's identical or similar to your application name. You can use letters, underscores, or dashes, but numbers are not permitted.

   I highly recommend using all lowercase letters to avoid potential case sensitivity issues.

   When you enter the desired name, Facebook provides immediate feedback on whether it is available.

   For my example, I chose `dummies` because it was available. (Who else would be "dumb" enough to choose that URL?)

   If no validation seems to have occurred, try clicking into the text box again and tabbing to the next box. Occasionally, the validation routine needs to reset itself.

9. **Select the Use FBML option button.**

   You can display your application inside Facebook using FBML (Facebook Markup Language) or an iframe. When you select FBML, your pages are rendered by Facebook servers. When you select iframe, the content is rendered by your host server and displayed in an iframe on a Facebook page.

   Later I show you how to work with iframes, but for now, select FBML.

10. **Select the Website option button.**

    Facebook allows you to define your application as a Web site or Desktop. A Web site app is a traditional Web app that integrates with Facebook. A Desktop app is a desktop-based app that accesses Facebook using the API.

    Use Web site for this example.

11. **Do not select the Mobile Integration check box for now.**

    See Chapter 12 for more on creating mobile Facebook apps.

12. Leave the IP Addresses of Servers Making Requests text box blank.

You can use this option to specify the IP address(es) of your Web server(s). This option is useful if your secret key is stolen, as it would prevent other apps from impersonating your own if they do not originate from your servers.

I recommend ignoring this option at this initial stage but considering it before your real-life application goes live to the world.

13. Select the Yes option button for Can Your Application Be Added on Facebook?

This option is required to add your application to your own account. Don't worry; you can limit other people's access to your application in a moment.

When you select Yes, more installation options are displayed at the end of the page.

14. If you have a terms of service document, specify its URL in the TOS URL field.

Facebook requires users to accept the terms before they can install their terms of service documents.

15. In the Developers field, enter the name of any additional person who developed the Facebook application.

Facebook does a lookup on the name you are typing and searches for a name match in the Facebook database.

If others need to modify or have access to the application in Developer Mode, you can enter their names now. Or, if you prefer, you can always add them later.

Figure 2-4 shows the completed form. You are now ready to continue with the Installation Options section.

16. Select the Users check box for Who Can Add Your Application to Their Facebook Account?

17. Select the All Pages option button.

Facebook pages are specific business- or organization-oriented pages that can also have apps added to them. By choosing All Pages, you open up a wider audience to your application.

18. In the Post-Add URL text box, enter the URL that users are redirected to after installing the application.

This URL is the canvas page URL (the Facebook URL you picked back in Step 8). It should *not* point to the callback URL on your server.

▼ Optional Fields
Base options

Support E-mail (Limit: 100 characters)	rich@digitalwalk.net We will contact you at this address if there are any problems or important updates.
Callback Url (Limit: 100 characters)	http://d9340086.fb.joyent.us After logging into Facebook, users are redirected to the callback URL. See authentication overview for more details.
Canvas Page URL	http://apps.facebook.com/ dummies / Available ⦿ Use FBML ○ Use iframe Your application will be viewable in the Facebook navigation at this URL – either as rendered FBML or loaded in an iframe. If you aren't sure what you should use here, choose FBML. You can use iframes within FBML on canvas pages with the `<fb:iframe>` tag, and most things you will want to do will be easier and faster with FBML.
Application Type	⦿ Website ○ Desktop
Mobile Integration	☐ My application uses the mobile platform Checking this will enable some additional SMS functionality for applications.
IP Addresses of Servers Making Requests (comma-separated)	 If you supply this information (e.g. 10.1.20.1, 10.1.20.3), requests from addresses other than those listed will be rejected.
Can your application be added on Facebook?	⦿ Yes ○ No Select Yes if your application can be added to a Facebook account.
TOS URL	 The URL pointing to your application's Terms of Service, which the user must accept.
Developers:	Rich Wagner Type a friend's name

Figure 2-4:
Completing
the basic
application
form.

19. **Enter a short description of your application in the Application Description text box.**

Be sure to clearly and succinctly describe what your application does for Facebook users. Never force a user to install your application to see what it does.

20. **If you want to specify a URL that you want to redirect users to when they uninstall your application from their Facebook profile, enter one in the Post-Remove URL field.**

I am going to leave this box blank for this basic example.

21. **In the Default FBML field, you can specify some default FBML or plain text that will appear in the canvas on the user's profile page.**

For now, keep it simple. I show you how to do this programmatically later using the setFBML API call.

22. **In the Default Action FBML field, you can specify default FBML to appear as an action item under the user's profile picture.**

23. **For the Default Profile Box Column, select the Wide option button to specify the default column of a user's profile.**

24. **Select the Developer Mode check box to prevent anyone else but you from installing the application.**

Until your application is ready to roll, be sure that this option is enabled (see Figure 2-5).

You have one final section to fill in before you submit the application.

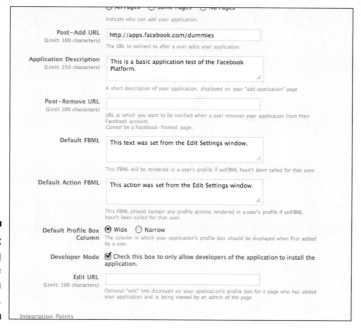

Figure 2-5:
Configuring
the
installation
options.

25. In the Side Nav URL field, enter the canvas page URL of your application.

This option is used when you want to add a link to your application from the left-side navigation menu. It should be a Facebook apps URL (`http://apps.facebook.com/`*yourapp*), not your callback URL.

26. If you have a privacy configuration page, add its URL in the Privacy URL field.

I recommend leaving this option blank for this initial walk-through.

27. Specify Help documentation in the Help URL field.

Again, at this early point, just skip this option.

28. Select the Private Installation check box.

By enabling this option, you prevent adding stories to your News Feed and Mini-Feed concerning the application. Until you are ready to go live, you should probably select this box to keep your testing quiet.

29. Leave the Attachments fields blank.

Applications can create "attachments" that are displayed in a drop-down menu on the message composer. When the user selects the attachment, the content you provide from the attachment callback URL is retrieved and placed inside an attachment box below the text in the message composer. For this initial application, I ignore this functionality. However, turn to Chapter 13 for details on how to work with attachments.

The final options are displayed in Figure 2-6.

Integration Points

Side Nav URL (Limit: 100 characters)	http://apps.facebook.com/dummies URL for your app if you want a link in the side nav. Must be a Facebook canvas page.
Privacy URL (Limit: 100 characters)	 Link to a privacy configuration page for your application.
Help URL (Limit: 100 characters)	 Link to a help page for your application.
Private Installation	☑ Check this box to disable News Feed and Mini-Feed installation stories for your application.
Attachments	**Attachment Action:** The action in a dropdown or button for creating a wall or message attachment. (Limit: 20 characters)
	Callback URL: The URL from which to fetch content for attachments. (Limit: 100 characters)

Submit or Cancel

Figure 2-6:
Specifying
how to
integrate
with
Facebook.

30. Click the Submit button.

When you click the Submit button, you are taken to the My Applications page (see Figure 2-7). Your application is added to Facebook, and an API key is created for it.

If you encounter an error, it may appear as if you have to enter everything over again. However, check your My Applications page to see if the app was added in spite of the error. If so, simply click the Edit Settings link and correct the mistake.

Facebook Developer   Back to Developer Home

🔲 My Applications

API key created.

You have 1 key | Apply for another key

🔲 **Dummies Facebook Platform Tester** | Edit Settings | Feed Templates | Delete App | Stats

About Page	View About Page	Edit About Page
API Key		
Secret		
Support Email	rich@digitalwalk.net	
Callback URL	http://d9349086.fb.joyent.us	

Submit Application »

Once you have completed your application you may submit it to our product directory.

Eager to get started? Check Out Example Code for this application.

Quick Start

Sometimes it's easier to learn by seeing something in action. That is why we've provided you with a sample application you can dive right into. In addition, you can add Big Picture to see how a simple application might work within Facebook.

📄 **Download Sample Application**
This package has all the files that make up Footprints and the PHP 5 Client Library.

More Helpful Links

Platform Documentation	**Download a Client Library**
Anatomy of a Facebook Application	📄
Code Samples	PHP (4 and 5) Client Library	Description of contents
FBML Test Console	Updated November 13, 2007.

Figure 2-7:
My
Applications
page.

The My Applications page displays meta information for all your registered applications. Notice, in particular, the API key and secret key. You'll need these two pieces of information to call Facebook from within your application.

Creating a Simple Facebook Application

When you have an API key and secret key, you are ready to create an application that can communicate with the Facebook Platform. Here's how to do it using PHP:

1. **Download the client library files of your programming language from the My Applications page (**facebook.com/developers/apps.php**).**

   The client library files are your link to Facebook. As I mention in Chapter 1, Facebook officially supports PHP and Java client libraries, though you can find unofficial libraries for several additional languages at the Facebook Developers Wiki (wiki.developers.facebook.com).

2. **Uncompress the downloaded file and copy the client library files via FTP to your Web server.**

   Place these files in the folder you specified as the callback URL for your application.

   If you have problems uncompressing the .tar.gz file, you may wish to check out a compression utility like 7-Zip.

   The PHP client library is contained inside a main folder named facebook-platform. Inside this folder are these three subfolders:

   - client contains the PHP5 client library files: facebook.php, facebook_desktop.php, and facebookapi_php5_restlib. php.

   - footprints is a sample PHP5 application.

   - php4client provides a PHP4 version of the client library.

   For this example, you only need to use the facebook.php and face bookapi_php5_restlib.php files. However, I recommend copying all the files to your server using the existing folder structure so that you can be sure to have all files on hand as needed. In this walk-through, I assume that you'll use this structure.

3. **In your text editor, create a new file and save it as** appinclude.php**.**

   You'll add the Facebook initialization code in this file to connect to the Facebook Platform. This file should be included at the top of every PHP file used in your application.

4. **Enter the following code into the** `appinclude.php` **file, inserting your API key, secret key, and callback URL in the appropriate places.**

   Better yet, to save typing, you can also retrieve the code from this book's companion Web site.

   ```php
   <?php
   require_once '../facebook-platform/client/facebook.php';

   // *** Add your Facebook API Key, Secret Key, and Callback URL here ***
   $appapikey = '[your_api_key]';
   $appsecret = '[your_secret_key]';
   $appcallbackurl = '[your_web_app_url]';

   // Connect to Facebook, retrieve user
   $facebook = new Facebook($appapikey, $appsecret);
   $user = $facebook->require_login();

   // Exception handler for invalid session_keys
   try {
     // If app is not added, then attempt to add
     if (!$facebook->api_client->users_isAppAdded()) {
       $facebook->redirect($facebook->get_add_url());
     }
   } catch (Exception $ex) {
     // Clear out cookies for app and redirect user to a login prompt
           $facebook->set_user(null, null);
           $facebook->redirect($appcallbackurl);
   }
   ?>
   ```

5. **On your Web server, create a new folder for your application.**

   This folder will be used for `appinclude.php` and additional application files.

   The `facebook.php` path in the `require_once` statement of `app include.php` assumes that your app files are located in a separate, parallel folder structure than the Facebook client library files, such as

   `\your_test_app`

   `\facebook-platform`

   Be sure to update the path for `facebook.php` if your folder structure differs.

6. **FTP** `appinclude.php` **to the application folder on your Web server.**

7. **In your text editor, create a new file and save it as** `index.php`.

8. **Add an h1 title, PHP start and end tags, and a** `require_once` **statement to your** `appinclude.php` **file, as follows:**

Avoiding dependencies

If you prefer, you can also use the following procedure to include the `facebook.php` file but avoid potential issues with relative paths:

```
require_once($_SERVER["DOCUMENT_ROOT"] .
    '/facebook-
    platform/client/facebook.php");
```

```
<h1>Dummies Sample Application</h1>
<?php
require_once 'appinclude.php';

?>
```

9. **After the** `require_once` **statement, enter the following two lines of PHP code to display the user's ID and name:**

```
echo "<p>Your User ID is: $user</p>";
echo "<p>Your name is: <fb:name uid=\"$user\" useyou=\"false\"/></p>";
```

The `$user` variable is set inside the `appinclude.php` file to be the ID number of the current Facebook user. This value is printed in the first statement.

The `fb:name` tag in the second statement is an FBML tag that renders the name of the specified user ID. The `$user` variable is used as the value of the `uid` attribute. The `useyou` attribute is set to false to prevent Facebook from substituting "you" with the username when the `uid` value is identical to the logged-on user ID.

10. **Add a bulleted list of Facebook friends by entering the following code:**

```
echo "<p>You have several friends: </p>";
$friends = $facebook->api_client->friends_get();
echo "<ul>";
foreach ($friends as $friend)  {
  echo "<li><fb:name uid=\"$friend\" useyou=\"false\" /></li>";
}
echo "</ul>";
```

In this code, recall that the `$facebook` object was initiated in the `appinclude.php` file. With `$facebook` ready to go, the `$facebook->api_client` object is then used for all Facebook API calls. In this case, the `friends_get()` method is called to return a list of user IDs of the user's friends.

Using a `foreach` construct, each of the friends is displayed as a list item. The `fb:name` tag is used to display the user's name instead of the ID.

11. **Save the file and copy it to the application folder via FTP on your Web server.**

    You are now ready to display your app inside Facebook.

12. **Enter the canvas page URL for your application in your browser.**

    In my case, I access `http://apps.facebook.com/dummies`.

    If you browse to the canvas page URL from outside of Facebook, you will be presented with a Logon screen, with two checkboxes (Allow access to my info and Keep me logged in check boxes). Check these boxes to allow for tighter application integration. If you have never added the app to your Facebook account, then you will be asked whether or not to add it.

    The Facebook Platform redirects the request to your callback URL and then renders the results back inside the Facebook canvas, as shown in Figure 2-8.

Figure 2-8: Displaying the sample application.

Listing 2-1 lists the full source code for the sample application.

Listing 2-1: index.php

```php
<h1>Dummies Sample Application</h1>
<?php
require_once 'appinclude.php';

echo "<p>Your User ID is: $user</p>";
echo "<p>Your name is: <fb:name uid=\"$user\" useyou=\"false\" /></p>";

echo "<p>You have several friends: </p>";
$friends = $facebook->api_client->friends_get();
echo "<ul>";
```

```
foreach ($friends as $friend) {
  echo "<li><fb:name uid=\"$friend\" useyou=\"false\" /></li>";
}
echo "</ul>";
?>
```

Note that if you access the callback URL folder from your browser, the page rendered would not contain the usernames, because non-Facebook application servers do not support FBML.

Adding an Icon to the Application

During the initial submittal process, Facebook does not provide the option of customizing the icon for the application. The icon is displayed alongside the application name in the left-side menu. Here's how to add an image:

1. **Point your Web browser to** www.facebook.com/developers.

2. **Click the See My Apps link in the My Applications box.**

3. **In the My Applications list, click the Edit Settings link for your application.**

4. **In the Base Options section, click the Change Your Icon link (see Figure 2-9).**

The Icon section

Figure 2-9:
Adding an icon to your application.

The Upload an Icon page is displayed, as shown in Figure 2-10.

Figure 2-10:
Most any square image can do the trick.

5. **Click the Choose File button and locate an image on your hard drive that graphically represents your application.**

   You can use any normal Web graphic — JPG, PNG, or GIF. Facebook can convert your image into a 16x16 GIF image.

6. **Select the certification check box to ensure that your image is appropriate for usage on Facebook.**

7. **Click the Upload Image button.**

   After the file is uploaded and converted, you are taken back to the Edit Settings page.

8. **Click the Save button.**

   The icon is now displayed on the left-side menu (see Figure 2-11).

Dummies icon

Figure 2-11:
Icon is
displayed
beside the
application
name.

Setting the Initial Content of the Application's Profile Box

When your application appears as a box on the Profile page, you can set its initial content in two ways:

✓ **Using an interactive form:** If you recall, back in Step 21 of the section "Registering an Application with Facebook," earlier in this chapter, you can supply default FBML during the interactive registration process.

✓ **By code:** You can also use the `profile_setFBML()` method to set the display inside your code.

To add default FBML to your application using `profile_setFBML()`, add the following code to your `index.php` file just after the `require_once 'appinclude.php'` statement:

```
$default_text = "<p>Hey, <fb:name uid=\"$user\" useyou=\"false\" />! This
        Dummies Sample Application provides all of the information you
        will ever need.</p>";
$facebook->api_client->profile_setFBML($default_text);
```

When the application is accessed again, the supplied FBML is displayed in its box on the Profile page (see Figure 2-12).

Figure 2-12: You can supply default FBML for the Profile box.

Adding an About Page

Before you are done, you will want to add an About page for the application that describes the application to Facebook users. For a sample application like you have been building in this chapter, this step is optional. However, when you are developing the real thing, its About page is an important step in successfully marketing it to the Facebook community.

Follow these instructions to create an About page:

1. **Point your Web browser to** www.facebook.com/developers.
2. **Click the See My Apps link in the My Applications box.**

   The My Applications page is displayed.
3. **Click the Edit About Page link in your application box.**
4. **Click the Edit link beside the Application Information box.**

   The Edit About Page page is displayed, as shown in Figure 2-13.

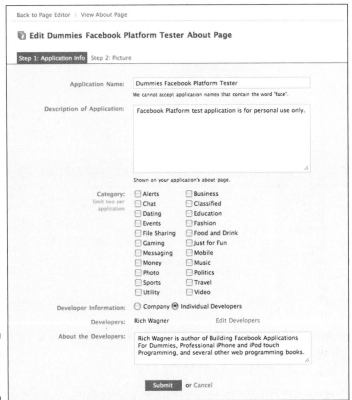

Figure 2-13:
Edit the
About page.

5. If needed, modify the name of your application in the Application Name box.

6. Enter a description of your application in the Description of Application text box.

Fully explain what your application does here.

7. Select the category(ies) that your application fits into.

For a sample application, you can skip this option. But for real applications, be sure to be descriptive.

8. Specify developer information in the fields at the bottom of the page.

9. Click the Submit button.

You will be taken to a page to add a picture (see Figure 2-14). Note that this is a larger image (such as 200 or 300 pixels in width), not the icon image that is used on the left-side menu.

Figure 2-14:
Adding
an image
for your
application.

10. Click the Choose File button and locate the desired Web graphic on your hard drive.

11. Select the terms of use check box to ensure that the image is appropriate for Facebook usage.

12. Click the Upload Picture button.

You are returned to the My Applications page.

13. Click the View About Page link to see the page that you created. (See Figure 2-15.)

Figure 2-15:
Viewing the
description
of your
application.

Part II
Poking the API

The 5th Wave   By Rich Tennant

"Your news feed set up looks fine. I don't know
why you're not receiving any announcements.
Have you explored the possibility that you may
not have any friends?"

In this part . . .

If you spend much time around Facebook, you may find yourself "poking" someone else. The exact interpretation of a "poke" is open to debate. To some, poking is a form of flirting. To others, a poke is merely the digital equivalent of a friendly, "Howdy." In this part, you begin poking the Facebook Platform. You get a chance to flirt with the Facebook API and get to know it far better than just as a casual acquaintance.

Chapter 3

Working with the Facebook API

Want to take a surefire "geek developer" test? Okay, here we go. . . .

On a scale from 1 to 10, when I say "API," what is your level of excitement?

If you said a number higher than 8, I suspect that you're probably geek material. But, if so, don't feel bad. . . . The truth is, whether you get excited about application programming interfaces (APIs) or not, an API is one of the most powerful tools available — enabling a Web programmer to tap into an otherwise impenetrable Web service.

The Facebook API is the gateway to integrating your application with the Facebook Platform. You can retrieve a boatload of user, friend, event, group, and page data through its many methods. In this chapter, I introduce you to these API methods, show you how to call them, and demonstrate what to do with the results.

And, whether you are a geek developer or not, I believe you'll be excited when you see the power that's available through this programming interface.

Calling the Facebook API

You can think of the Facebook API as a folder of specific questions that you can ask Facebook and commands that you can tell it to do. *Can I get a list of friends for the current user? Or, can you send this story to friends of the user?* The API defines those things that Facebook will let you ask or let you tell it to do.

Each programming language — be it PHP, Java, C++, or whatever — that is used to access the Facebook API has a language-specific syntax for calling it. Using PHP, for example, every API call is made by calling a method from the `$facebook->api_client` object. This object is created when you establish a Facebook session and instantiate the `$facebook` object using initialization code, such as the boilerplate code shown in Listing 3-1.

Listing 3-1: appinclude.php

```php
<?php
require_once '../facebook-platform/client/facebook.php';

// *** Add your Facebook API Key, Secret Key, and Callback URL here ***
$appapikey = 'your_api_key';
$appsecret = 'your_secret_key';
$appcallbackurl = 'your_callback_url';

// Connect to Facebook, retrieve user
$facebook = new Facebook($appapikey, $appsecret);
$user = $facebook->require_login();

// Exception handler for invalid session_keys
try {
  // If app is not added, then attempt to add
  if (!$facebook->api_client->users_isAppAdded()) {
    $facebook->redirect($facebook->get_add_url());
  }
} catch (Exception $ex) {
  // Clear out cookies for app and redirect user to a login prompt
            $facebook->set_user(null, null);
            $facebook->redirect($appcallbackurl);
}
?>
```

The official Facebook API documentation lists the API in a standard dot notation syntax, such as `events.get`. However, to use these methods, you have to translate them into the appropriate syntax for each language. The PHP client library, for example, replaces the dot with an underscore. So, for example, `events.get` is actually called with the following:

```
$facebook->api_client->events_get()
```

Tables 3-1 through 3-12 list each of the API methods organized by group. You can find more information on these and other methods in the online documentation located at `http://wiki.developers.facebook.com/index.php/API`.

Table 3-1	Users Methods
Method	*Description*
users.getInfo	Gets user-specific information
users.getLoggedInUser	Gets the current user ID
users.hasAppPermission	Checks whether the logged-in user has opted in to an extended application permission with the current application (unofficial at time of writing)
users.isAppAdded	Checks to see whether the logged-in user has added the calling application
users.setStatus	Updates a user's Facebook status (unofficial at time of writing)

Table 3-2	Friends Methods
Method	*Description*
friends.areFriends	Checks to see whether specified users are friends with each other
friends.get	Gets a list of friends for the current user
friends.getAppUsers	Gets a list of friends of the user who are signed up with the calling application
friends.getLists	Gets the current user's Facebook friend lists

Table 3-3	Events Methods
Method	*Description*
events.get	Returns events that match specified criteria
events.getMembers	Returns members of an event

Table 3-4	Groups Methods
Method	*Description*
groups.get	Gets groups based on specified criteria
groups.getMembers	Gets members of a group

Table 3-5	Photos Methods
Method	**Description**
photos.addTag	Adds a tag to a photo
photos.createAlbum	Creates a new album
photos.get	Gets photos based on supplied criteria
photos.getAlbums	Gets metadata on photo albums
photos.getTags	Gets a set of tags on specified photos
photos.upload	Uploads a photo

Table 3-6	Pages Methods
Method	**Description**
pages.getInfo	Retrieves Facebook pages visible to the user based on the specified criteria
pages.isAdmin	Checks whether current user is the admin for a page
pages.isAppAdded	Checks whether a specified page has added the application
pages.isFan	Checks whether a specified user is a fan of a page

Table 3-7	Feed and Notifications Methods
Method	**Description**
feed.publishStoryToUser	Publishes a News Feed story to the current user
feed.publishActionOfUser	Publishes a Mini-Feed story to current user and publishes News Feed stories to the friends of that user
feed.publishTemplatizedAction	Publishes a Mini-Feed story to a user and News Feed stories to friends/fans, or publishes a Mini-Feed story to the current page

Method	Description
notifications.get	Gets outstanding Facebook notifications for current user
notifications.send	Sends a notification to one or more users
notifications.sendEmail	Sends an e-mail to one or more users of the application

See Chapter 9 for more on publishing stories and notifications.

Table 3-8	Profile Methods
Method	**Description**
profile.setFBML	Sets the FBML for a user's profile for current application, including the content for the profile box, profile actions, and the mobile device profile box
profile.getFBML	Gets the FBML markup that is currently set for a user's profile of current application

Table 3-9	Administrative and Authentication Methods
Method	**Description**
admin.getAppProperties	Returns properties of a Facebook application
admin.setAppProperties	Sets property values of a Facebook application
auth.createToken	Creates a temporary authentication token that is placed in the Facebook session when the user logs in (use with Desktop applications)
auth.getSession	Returns the session key

See Chapter 10 for info on how to use these administrative and authentication methods.

Table 3-10	FBML and FQL Methods
Method	**Description**
`fbml.refreshImgSrc`	Fetches and recaches an image specified by an absolute URL
`fbml.refreshRefUrl`	Fetches and recaches content specified by an absolute URL
`fbml.setRefHandle`	Associates a "handle" with FBML markup content (used with `fb:ref`)
`fql.query`	Evaluates an FQL query

See Chapters 4 and 5 for more on working with these methods.

Table 3-11	Local Cookie Storage Methods
Method	**Description**
`data.getCookies`	Returns cookies for a user and application
`data.setCookies`	Sets a cookie for a user and application

Table 3-12	Marketplace Methods
Method	**Description**
`marketplace.createListing`	Creates or modifies a listing in the Marketplace for the currently logged-in user if the user has granted the app the `create_listing` permission
`marketplace.getCategories`	Gets all Marketplace categories
`marketplace.getListings`	Gets Marketplace listings by specified criteria
`marketplace.getSubCategories`	Gets Marketplace subcategories for a particular category
`marketplace.removeListing`	Removes a listing from Marketplace for the current user
`marketplace.search`	Searches Marketplace for listings filtering by category, subcategory, and a query string

Evaluating What Comes Back from Facebook

When you call a Facebook API method, your results normally come back in either XML (the default) or JSON format. (However, if you are using PHP, hold tight. I'll show you in a moment that you can also work with the results as PHP arrays.)

The native response format is XML. Consider, for example, the `friends.get()` method. When I call this method, an XML response is returned containing the user IDs of the current logged-in user's friends:

```xml
<?xml version="1.0" encoding="UTF-8"?>
<friends_get_response xmlns="http://api.facebook.com/1.0/"
            xmlns:xsi="http://www.w3.org/2001/XMLSchema-instance"
            xsi:schemaLocation="http://api.facebook.com/1.0/
            http://api.facebook.com/1.0/facebook.xsd" list="true">
  <uid>55714303</uid>
  <uid>530377451</uid>
  <uid>530771206</uid>
  <uid>685578792</uid>
  <uid>693048091</uid>
</friends_get_response>
```

Depending on the client library you use, you may need to process the XML document that is returned.

You can also specify JSON as the results format by indicating your preference as a parameter in the API call. For example, the `friends.get()` method would return the user IDs in JSON format:

```
[55714303,530377451,530771206,685578792,693048091]
```

When you access the API using the PHP client library, results come back by default in an array. The call in PHP would be as follows:

```php
echo "<pre>";
print_r($facebook->api_client->friends_get());
echo "</pre>";
```

Get some REST

The Facebook API is a REST (REpresentational State Transfer)-based interface. A typical REST operation involves sending an HTTP request to Facebook and then waiting for an HTTP response. The request contains a request method, a Uniform Resource Identifier (URI), request headers, and optionally, a request body and query string. The response contains a status code, response headers, and sometimes a response body.

The following is output:

```
Array
(
    [0] => 55714303
    [1] => 530377451
    [2] => 530771206
    [3] => 685578792
    [4] => 693048091
)
```

Therefore, to access the Facebook data, you would capture the response in an array:

```
$friends = $facebook->api_client->friends_get();
echo "The first friend is $friends[0].";
```

The output would be

```
The first friend is 55714303.
```

Getting Friendly with Friends

The heart and soul of Facebook is the ability for friends to interact as part of the social graph. Facebook provides three methods for working with friends: `friends.get`, `friends.areFriends`, and `friends.appUsers`. These are explored in the sections that follow.

Getting friends with friends.get

The `friends.get` method returns the user IDs of the friends of the current user. Its PHP syntax is as follows:

```
$facebook->api_client->friends_get()
```

To demonstrate how this method is used, I am going to call it twice. For the first call, I simply print the results I get from Facebook. In the second, I use it in an applied example to demonstrate how you could use it in an application. Here's the PHP code:

```php
<?php
require_once 'appinclude.php';

echo "<h1>friends_get</h1>";
echo "<hr />";

echo "<pre>";
echo "<h2>Scenario 1: Getting all friends of current user</h2>";
echo "<h5>Raw output:</h5>";
print_r($facebook->api_client->friends_get());

echo "<h5>Applied example:</h5>";
echo "<p>Friends of <fb:name uid=\"$user\" useyou=\"false\" />:</p>";
$friends = $facebook->api_client->friends_get();
echo "<ul>";
foreach ($friends as $friend) {
  echo "<li><fb:name uid=\"$friend\" useyou=\"false\" /></li>";
}
echo "</ul>";
echo "</pre>";
?>
```

Remember that for this and all PHP-based examples in the book, your code needs to be inside of a Facebook application you already set up (see Chapter 2) that can interact with the Facebook API.

In the first call to `friends_get()`, the `print_r` command outputs the raw response. In the second call, the resulting array of friends is assigned to the `$friends` variable. The `foreach` control structure is used to iterate through each of these friends. The FBML tag `fb:name` is used to display the name of the friend. (See Chapter 4 for more on FBML.)

The following content is generated:

```
Scenario 1: Getting all friends of current user
Raw output:
Array
(
    [0] => 18601493
    [1] => 20715969
    [2] => 55700210
    [3] => 55713606
    [4] => 55714303
)
Applied example:
Friends of Rich Wagner:

_   Louis Wagner
_   Jason Wagner
_   Justus Worley
_   Andrew Wilson
_   Josh Wyatt
```

Evaluating friends with friends.areFriends

The `friends.areFriends` method is used to determine whether a pair of users are friends. Its syntax is shown here:

```
$facebook->api_client->friends_areFriends($uids1, $uids2)
```

The `$uids1` and `$uids2` variables are a list of user IDs separated by commas. The corresponding IDs in each list are compared with each other — the first ID of `$uids1` is evaluated with the first ID of `$uids2`, the second IDs against each other, and so on. If you only are comparing a single pair of IDs, you don't need to use an array structure.

The result of the evaluation is either a 1 (yes, they are friends) or 0 (no, they are most certainly not).

Check out the following example in which I use `friends.areFriends` in three different instances. The first case compares two users by ID, and the second compares a list of users and prints the raw output. The final case displays a bulleted list that tells the results of the evaluation. Look at the following code:

```php
<?php
require_once 'appinclude.php';

echo "<pre>";
echo "<h1>friends_areFriends</h1>";
echo "<hr />";

echo "<h2>Scenario 1: Determine whether two users are friends or not</h2>";
echo "<h5>Raw output:</h5>";
print_r($facebook->api_client->friends_areFriends(685578792, 531385404 ));

echo "<hr />";
$uids1 = array( 20715969, 55713606, 696951095);
$uids2 = array( 705671487, 55714303, 549572223);
echo "<h2>Scenario 2: Determine whether a set of users are friends or not</h2>";
echo "<h5>Raw output:</h5>";
print_r($facebook->api_client->friends_areFriends($uids1, $uids2));

echo "<h5>Applied example:</h5>";
$uids1 = array( 20715969, 55713606, 696951095);
$uids2 = array( 705671487, 55714303, 549572223);
$friendsMatch = $facebook->api_client->friends_areFriends($uids1, $uids2);
echo "<ul>";
echo "<li>Are <fb:name uid=\"{$friendsMatch[0]['uid1']}\" useyou=\"false\" />
            and <fb:name uid=\"{$friendsMatch[0]['uid2']}\" useyou=\"false\"
            /> friends? {$friendsMatch[0]['are_friends']}</li>";
echo "<li>Are <fb:name uid=\"{$friendsMatch[1]['uid1']}\" useyou=\"false\" />
            and <fb:name uid=\"{$friendsMatch[1]['uid2']}\" useyou=\"false\"
            /> friends? {$friendsMatch[1]['are_friends']}</li>";
echo "<li>Are <fb:name uid=\"{$friendsMatch[2]['uid1']}\" useyou=\"false\" />
            and <fb:name uid=\"{$friendsMatch[2]['uid2']}\" useyou=\"false\"
            /> friends? {$friendsMatch[2]['are_friends']}</li>";
echo "</ul>";
echo "</pre>";
?>
```

As you can see from the following resulting output, the two users were not
friends in the first case. The second comparison uncovered one friendship
among the three tests. The final case uncovered one more friendship:

```
friends_areFriends

Scenario 1: Determine whether two users are friends or not
Raw output:
Array
(
    [0] => Array
        (
            [uid1] => 685578792
            [uid2] => 531385404
```

```
                    [are_friends] => 0
            )

    )
Scenario 2: Determine whether a set of users are friends or not
Raw output:
Array
(
    [0] => Array
        (
            [uid1] => 20715969
            [uid2] => 705671487
            [are_friends] => 0
        )

    [1] => Array
        (
            [uid1] => 55713606
            [uid2] => 55714303
            [are_friends] => 1
        )

    [2] => Array
        (
            [uid1] => 696951095
            [uid2] => 549572223
            [are_friends] => 0
        )

)
Applied example:
_   Are Ann Stephens and Chris Nope friends? 0
_   Are Sam Blackmere and Josh Wattly friends? 1
_   Are Alex Stephens and Phillip Burr friends? 0
```

Getting friends who are app users with friends.appUsers

The friends.appUsers method is used to determine which friends of the user have added the application to their Facebook profiles. The method can be called in PHP using the following code:

```
$facebook->api_client->friends_getAppUsers()
```

The method has no parameters.

The following code makes this API call twice:

```php
<?php
require_once 'appinclude.php';

echo "<pre>";
echo "<h1>friends_getAppUsers</h1>";
echo "<hr />";

echo "<h2>Scenario 1: Getting all friends of current user who are users of this
        app</h2>";
echo "<h5>Raw output:</h5>";
print_r($facebook->api_client->friends_getAppUsers());

echo "<h5>Applied example:</h5>";
echo "<p>App friends of <fb:name uid=\"$user\" useyou=\"false\" />:</p>";
$friends = $facebook->api_client->friends_getAppUsers();
echo "<ul>";
if($friends){
            foreach ($friends as $friend)  {
                echo "<li><fb:name uid=\"$friend\" useyou=\"false\" /></li>";
            }
}else{
            echo "<li>None of your friends are using this app.</li>";
}
echo "</ul>";
echo "</pre>";
?>
```

Here is the output generated:

```
friends_getAppUsers
Scenario 1: Getting all friends of current user who are users of this app
Raw output:
Array
(
    [0] => 18601493
    [1] => 20715969
    [2] => 55700210
    [3] => 55713606
    [4] => 55714303
)

Applied example:
App friends of Rich Wagner:
_   Jason Verede
_   Ronald Smithers
_   Dooley Wilson
_   Carl Manhammer
_   Lefty Mulligan
```

Accessing Events

The Facebook API offers two functions that you can use to access calendar-based events of a user — `events.get` and `events.getMembers`.

Each Facebook event has a specified list of properties that are helpful to know when looking for a specific piece of information. These include: `eid`, `name`, `tagline`, `nid`, `pic`, `pic_big`, `pic_small`, `host`, `description`, `event_type`, `event_subtype`, `start_time`, `end_time`, `creator`, `update_time`, `location`, and `venue` (`street`, `city`, `state`, `country`, `latitude`, and `longitude`). Note that subarrays are shown in parentheses.

Getting the events of a user

You can retrieve the events of a user with the `events.get` method. To call it in PHP, you use the following syntax:

```
$facebook->api_client->events_get($uid, $eids, $start_time, $end_time,
            $rsvp_status)
```

You can use the parameters to filter the events you want to retrieve, as follows:

- ✔ The `$uid` parameter allows you to specify a user ID. If `null`, the current user is used.

- ✔ `$eids` is a comma-separated list of event IDs.

- ✔ The `$start_time` and `$end_time` parameters are for filtering based on the UTC date/time value. (The time-zone-dependent times specified by the event creator are converted to UTC and then into a UNIX time-stamp, like is created with the PHP `time()` function, when stored in the Facebook database.)

- ✔ The `$rsvp_status` is one of four values: `attending`, `unsure`, `declined`, or `not_replied`.

The following example uses `events.get` to get all events for the current user, all events for a specified user, and specific events by event ID. Here's the code:

```
<?php

require_once 'appinclude.php';

echo "<pre>";
```

```php
echo "<h1>events_get</h1>";
echo "<hr />";

echo "<h2>Scenario 1: Getting all events for current user</h2>";
echo "<h5>Raw output:</h5>";
print_r($facebook->api_client->events_get(null, null, null, null, null));

echo "<h5>Applied example:</h5>";
echo "<p>Active events for <fb:name uid=\"$user\" useyou=\"false\" />:</p>";
$events = $facebook->api_client->events_get(null, null, null, null, null);
echo "<ul>";
if($events){
    foreach ($events as $event)  {
      echo "<li>{$event['name']} - {$event['location']} </li>";
    }
}else{
    echo "<li>No events for this user</li>";
}
echo "</ul>";
echo "<hr />";

echo "<h2>Scenario 2: Getting all events for a specified user</h2>";
echo "<h5>Raw output:</h5>";
print_r($facebook->api_client->events_get(55714303, null, null, null, null));

echo "<h5>Applied example:</h5>";
echo "<p>Active events for <fb:name uid=\"55714303\" useyou=\"false\" />:</p>";
$events = $facebook->api_client->events_get(55714303, null, null, null, null);
echo "<ul>";
if($events){
    foreach ($events as $event)  {
      echo "<li>{$event['name']} - {$event['location']} </li>";
    }
}else{
    echo "<li>No events for this user</li>";
}
echo "</ul>";
echo "<hr />";

echo "<h2>Scenario 3: Getting an event by id</h2>";
echo "<h5>Raw output:</h5>";
print_r($facebook->api_client->events_get(null, array(6589513372, 8182230950),
              null, null, null));

?>
```

In the first scenario, the calls to events_get uses null as the value for each
parameter to get all events for the logged-in user. In the second case, a user
ID is provided to get that person's events other than the current user. Finally,
the third scenario uses an array of event IDs to retrieve details for these specific events.

The events returned contain 23 properties that can be accessed from a results array. The output is as follows:

```
events_get

Scenario 1: Getting all events for current user
Raw output:
Array
(
    [0] => Array
        (
            [eid] => 6770688818
            [name] => Justy's Birthday
            [tagline] => The Big Fourteen
            [nid] => 0
            [pic] =>
                http://profile.ak.facebook.com/object2/1209/121/s6770688818_7452.
                jpg
            [pic_big] =>
                http://profile.ak.facebook.com/object2/1209/121/n6770688818_7452.
                jpg
            [pic_small] =>
                http://profile.ak.facebook.com/object2/1209/121/t6770688818_7452.
                jpg
            [host] => Rich Wagner
            [description] => Yeah for Justy
            [event_type] => Party
            [event_subtype] => Birthday Party
            [start_time] => 1201921200
            [end_time] => 1201928400
            [creator] => 665127078
            [update_time] => 1199553869
            [location] => Our house
            [venue] => Array
                (
                    [street] =>
                    [city] => Princeton
                    [state] => Massachusetts
                    [country] => United States
                    [latitude] => 42.4486
                    [longitude] => -71.8778
                )

        )

    [1] => Array
        (
```

```
              [eid] => 8182230950
              [name] => The Expeditionary Man Bike Tour
              [tagline] => ad atla simul
              [nid] => 0
              [pic] =>
                 http://profile.ak.facebook.com/object2/396/26/s8182230950_78.jpg
              [pic_big] =>
                 http://profile.ak.facebook.com/object2/396/26/n8182230950_78.jpg
              [pic_small] =>
                 http://profile.ak.facebook.com/object2/396/26/t8182230950_78.jpg
              [host] => Rich Wagner
              [description] =>
              [event_type] => Trips
              [event_subtype] => Roadtrip
              [start_time] => 1214661600
              [end_time] => 1217026800
              [creator] => 665127078
              [update_time] => 1199553396
              [location] => San Diego
              [venue] => Array
                 (
                     [street] =>
                     [city] => San Diego
                     [state] => California
                     [country] => United States
                     [latitude] => 32.7153
                     [longitude] => -117.156
                 )


       )


)
Applied example:
Active events for Rich Wagner:

Justy's Birthday - Our house
The Expeditionary Man Bike Tour - San Diego


Scenario 2: Getting all events for a specified user
Raw output:
Array
(
    [0] => Array
        (
            [eid] => 6589513372
            [name] => High School Ski Trip '08
            [tagline] => Notoriously one of the best events of the year . . .
            [nid] => 0
            [pic] =>
                http://profile.ak.facebook.com/object2/935/61/s6589513372_8557.jpg
```

```
            [pic_big] => http://profile.ak.facebook.com/object2/935/61/
                n6589513372_8557.jpg
            [pic_small] => http://profile.ak.facebook.com/object2/935/61/
                t6589513372_8557.jpg
            [host] => The Commons
            [description] => 3 Days @ Mount Sunapee, New Hampshire complete with
                skiing/snowboarding/snowblading, spiritual growth, hanging with
                friends, making new ones, and invading the game room
                (pool/darts/ping-pong/cards/foosball/air-hockey, etc.)!

//Grab an info packet @ The Commons.
//Registration & Deposit Deadline: Nov. 25th
            [event_type] => Trips
            [event_subtype] => Group Trip
            [start_time] => 1200094200
            [end_time] => 1200283200
            [creator] => 55714303
            [update_time] => 1192647498
            [location] => Mt. Sunapee : : : Dexter's Inn
            [venue] => Array
                (
                    [street] =>
                    [city] => Sunapee
                    [state] => New Hampshire
                    [country] => United States
                    [latitude] => 43.3875
                    [longitude] => -72.0883
                )

        )

    [1] => Array
        (
            [eid] => 2233964858
            [name] => wedding
            [tagline] => my wedding
            [nid] => 0
            [pic] => http://profile.ak.facebook.com/object/963/28/s2233964858_
                30773.jpg
            [pic_big] => http://profile.ak.facebook.com/object/963/28/
                n2233964858_30773.jpg
            [pic_small] => http://profile.ak.facebook.com/object/963/28/
                t2233964858_30773.jpg
            [host] => me and sara
            [description] => ryan and saras wedding day
            [event_type] => Other
            [event_subtype] => Festival
            [start_time] => 1192302000
            [end_time] => 1192327200
```

```
            [creator] => 513119649
            [update_time] => 1170982520
            [location] => my church
            [venue] => Array
                (
                    [street] =>
                    [city] =>
                    [state] =>
                    [country] =>
                )

        )

    [2] => Array
        (
            [eid] => 4706509087
            [name] => International Talk Like a Pirate Day
            [tagline] => Arrrr, matey
            [nid] => 0
            [pic] => http://profile.ak.facebook.com/object2/1197/22/s4706509087_
                7843.jpg
            [pic_big] => http://profile.ak.facebook.com/object2/1197/22/
                n4706509087_7843.jpg
            [pic_small] => http://profile.ak.facebook.com/object2/1197/22/
                t4706509087_7843.jpg
            [host] => Everyone
            [description] => Very self descriptive... talk like a pirate... All
                day. Tell everyone you know about it.
            [event_type] => Causes
            [event_subtype] => Rally
            [start_time] => 1190185200
            [end_time] => 1190271600
            [creator] => 35907261
            [update_time] => 1188968989
            [location] => Everywhere
            [venue] => Array
                (
                    [street] =>
                    [city] =>
                    [state] =>
                    [country] =>
                )

        )

Scenario 3: Getting an event by id
Raw output:
```

```
Array
(
    [0] => Array
        (
            [eid] => 6589513372
            [name] => High School Ski Trip '08
            [tagline] => Notoriously one of the best events of the year . . .
            [nid] => 0
            [pic] => http://profile.ak.facebook.com/object2/935/61/s6589513372_
                8557.jpg
            [pic_big] => http://profile.ak.facebook.com/object2/935/61/
                n6589513372_8557.jpg
            [pic_small] => http://profile.ak.facebook.com/object2/935/61/
                t6589513372_8557.jpg
            [host] => The Commons
            [description] => 3 Days @ Mount Sunapee, New Hampshire complete with
                skiing/snowboarding/snowblading, spiritual growth, hanging with
                friends, making new ones, and invading the game room
                (pool/darts/ping-pong/cards/foosball/air-hockey, etc.)!

//Grab an info packet @ The Commons.
//Registration & Deposit Deadline: Nov. 25th
            [event_type] => Trips
            [event_subtype] => Group Trip
            [start_time] => 1200094200
            [end_time] => 1200283200
            [creator] => 55714303
            [update_time] => 1192647498
            [location] => Mt. Sunapee : : : Dexter's Inn
            [venue] => Array
                (
                    [street] =>
                    [city] => Sunapee
                    [state] => New Hampshire
                    [country] => United States
                    [latitude] => 43.3875
                    [longitude] => -72.0883
                )

        )

    [1] => Array
        (
            [eid] => 8182230950
            [name] => The Expeditionary Man Bike Tour
            [tagline] => ad atla simul
            [nid] => 0
            [pic] =>
                http://profile.ak.facebook.com/object2/396/26/s8182230950_78.jpg
            [pic_big] =>
                http://profile.ak.facebook.com/object2/396/26/n8182230950_78.jpg
```

```
            [pic_small] =>
               http://profile.ak.facebook.com/object2/396/26/t8182230950_78.jpg
            [host] => Rich Wagner
            [description] =>
            [event_type] => Trips
            [event_subtype] => Roadtrip
            [start_time] => 1214661600
            [end_time] => 1217026800
            [creator] => 665127078
            [update_time] => 1199553396
            [location] => San Diego
            [venue] => Array
               (
                   [street] =>
                   [city] => San Diego
                   [state] => California
                   [country] => United States
                   [latitude] => 32.7153
                   [longitude] => -117.156
               )


       )


)
```

Getting the members of an event

The `events.getMembers` method is used to retrieve the members of an
event based on the event ID. Here's the PHP syntax:

```
$facebook->api_client->events_getMembers($eid)
```

In the following example, I get all the members of an event and simply output
the array results:

```php
<?php
require_once 'appinclude.php';

echo "<h1>events_getMembers</h1>";
echo "<hr />";

echo "<h2>Scenario 1: Getting all members of an event (grouped by status)</h2>";
echo "<h5>Raw output:</h5>";
echo "<pre>";
print_r($facebook->api_client->events_getMembers(6589513372));
echo "</pre>";
?>
```

The results are shown here:

```
events_getMembers
Scenario 1: Getting all members of an event (grouped by status)
Raw output:
Array
(
    [attending] => Array
        (
            [0] => 729427552
            [1] => 787340441
            [2] => 644453917
            [3] => 530987125
            [4] => 561260764
            [5] => 588343354
        )

    [unsure] => Array
        (
            [0] => 577940038
            [1] => 685578792
        )

    [declined] => Array
        (
            [0] => 501777965
            [1] => 215200237
            [2] => 719441622
            [3] => 530377451
            [4] => 705671487
        )

    [not_replied] =>
)
```

The results are provided in PHP in an associative array whose elements are grouped by the rsvp_status of the members.

Consider a second example in which I work with the resulting array that is returned. Check out the code:

```php
<?php
require_once 'appinclude.php';

echo "<pre>";
echo "<h2>Scenario 1: Getting all members of an event (grouped by status)</h2>";
echo "<h5>Applied example:</h5>";
$events = $facebook->api_client->events_get(null, 6589513372, null, null, null);
echo "<p>Members for {$events[0]['name']}</p>";

$members = $facebook->api_client->events_getMembers(6589513372);

echo "<p>Attending:</p>";
```

```php
echo "<ul>";
if ($members['attending'][0]) {
  foreach ($members['attending'] as $member)  {
    echo "<li><fb:name uid=\"$member\" useyou=\"false\" /></li>";
  }
} else {
  echo "None";
}
echo "</ul>";

echo "<p>Maybe, maybe not:</p>";
echo "<ul>";
if ($members['unsure'][0]) {
  foreach ($members['unsure'] as $member)  {
    echo "<li><fb:name uid=\"$member\" useyou=\"false\" /></li>";
  }
} else {
  echo "None";
}
echo "</ul>";

echo "<p>Not attending:</p>";
echo "<ul>";
if ($members['declined'][0]) {
  foreach ($members['declined'] as $member)  {
    echo "<li><fb:name uid=\"$member\" useyou=\"false\" /></li>";
  }
} else {
  echo "None";
}
echo "</ul>";

echo "<p>Unsure:</p>";
echo "<ul>";
if ($members['not_replied'][0]) {
  foreach ($members['not_replied'] as $member)  {
    echo "<li><fb:name uid=\"$member\" useyou=\"false\" /></li>";
  }
} else {
  echo "None";
}
echo "</ul>";
echo "</pre>";
?>
```

The events_get method is used to retrieve the event details. I then use this info to display the event name using $events[0]['name']. I then use events_getMembers to retrieve the members of the event in the $members array. The first foreach looping structure iterates through the $members['attending'] elements (the members whose rsvp_status is attending). The member's name is output as a bulleted list item. The next three foreach loops create similar lists for these other elements.

Be sure to notice the test I conduct on the associative arrays before using the `foreach` looping. Because Facebook can return an empty list for each of these membership status values, you would get a PHP error if you try to perform a `foreach` loop on an empty list. To make life even more interesting for developers, you cannot simply check `count($members['attending'])`. An empty subarray still returns a count of 1, making it impossible to distinguish between a status list of 1 and 0 members using `count()`. Instead, I am using an `if...else` block to evaluate the first element of each subarray to ensure that it is not blank.

The output is as follows:

```
Applied example:
Members for High School Ski Trip '08

Attending:

Jan Brythe
Ashley Rolands
Em Martellin
Ty Prancer
Emelie MacTigue
Elizabeth Lewis

Maybe, maybe not:

Jared Wagner
Ashley Marie Martell

Not attending:

Amanda Prancer
Jal Hutchinson
Steve Apple
Jordan Wagner
Betty Noel

Unsure:
```

Getting Cozy with Groups

Facebook *groups* are networks of Facebook users who join together for a particular common interest. You can work with groups much like you work with events (see the section "Accessing Events," earlier in this chapter). You have two methods for accessing Facebook group-related information — getting groups of a user with `groups.get` and getting members of a particular group with `groups.getMembers`.

These two functions are discussed in the following sections.

Each Facebook group has several data properties that you may wish to retrieve including, `gid`, `name`, `nid`, `description`, `group_type`, `group_subtype`, `recent_news`, `pic`, `pic_big`, `pic_small`, `creator`, `update_time`, `office`, `website`, and `venue` (`street`, `city`, `state`, `country`).

Getting groups with groups.get

You can retrieve groups with the `groups.get` method. In PHP, you call it by using the following syntax:

```
$facebook->api_client->groups_get($uid, $gids)
```

The `$uid` parameter allows you to retrieve groups based on a user ID. The `$gids` parameter optionally enables you to retrieve based on an array of group IDs.

The following example shows four different scenarios of using `groups_get()`: getting all groups for the current user, all groups for a specific user, info for a specific group, and info about several groups. Note how the different results are achieved through the parameters used. Here's the code:

```php
<?php
require_once 'appinclude.php';

echo "<h1>groups_get</h1>";
echo "<hr />";

/* Scenario 1 */
echo "<h2>Scenario 1: Getting all groups for current user</h2>";

$uid = null;
$gid = null;
$groups = $facebook->api_client->groups_get($uid,$gid);

echo "<h5>Raw output:</h5>";

echo "<pre>";
print_r($groups);
echo "</pre>";

echo "<h5>Applied example:</h5>";
echo "<p>Active events for <fb:name uid=\"$user\" useyou=\"false\" />:</p>";

echo "<ul>";
```

```php
if($groups){
  foreach ($groups as $group)  {
    echo "<li>{$group['name']}</li>";
  }
}else{
  echo "<li>User is not a member of any groups</li>";
}
echo "</ul>";
echo "<hr />";

/* Scenario 2 */
echo "<h2>Scenario 2: Getting all groups for a specific user</h2>";

$uid = 585166905;
$gid = null;
$groups = $facebook->api_client->groups_get($uid,$gid);

echo "<h5>Raw output:</h5>";
echo "<pre>";
print_r($groups);
echo "</pre>";
echo "<hr />";

/* Scenario 3 */
echo "<h2>Scenario 3: Getting info for a specific group</h2>";

$uid = 585166905;
$gid = 17342247576;
$groups = $facebook->api_client->groups_get($uid,$gid);

echo "<h5>Raw output:</h5>";
echo "<pre>";
print_r($groups);
echo "</pre>";
echo "<hr />";

/* Scenario 4 */
echo "<h2>Scenario 4: Getting info about several groups</h2>";

$uid = null;
$gid = array(2208108698,2210253039,17342247576);
$groups = $facebook->api_client->groups_get($uid,$gid);

echo "<h5>Raw output:</h5>";
echo "<pre>";
print_r($groups);
echo "</pre>";

?>
```

The results are as follows:

```
groups_get

Scenario 1: Getting all groups for current user
Raw output:
Array
(
    [0] => Array
        (
            [gid] => 2208108698
            [name] => HECK YES I QUOTE MOVIES
            [nid] => 0
            [description] => None
            [group_type] => Entertainment & Arts
            [group_subtype] => Movies
            [recent_news] =>
            [pic] => http://profile.ak.facebook.com/object/1961/40/s2208108698_
                37065.jpg
            [pic_big] => http://profile.ak.facebook.com/object/1961/40/
                n2208108698_37065.jpg
            [pic_small] => http://profile.ak.facebook.com/object/1961/40/
                t2208108698_37065.jpg
            [creator] =>
            [update_time] => 1173885432
            [office] =>
            [website] =>
            [venue] => Array
                (
                    [street] =>
                    [city] =>
                    [state] =>
                    [country] =>
                )

        )

    [1] => Array
        (
            [gid] => 8900080125
            [name] => Six Degrees Of Separation - The Experiment
            [nid] => 0
            [description] => You are invited to take part in the most ambitious
                facebook experiment ever...

Using the Six Degrees of Separation theory, I want to see if it's possible to
                contact every single person on facebook. The theory states that
                everybody on this planet is separated by only six other people.
                (it could be argued that we're all only six degrees from the
                entire Indian Cricket team!).
```

```
            [group_type] => Just for Fun
            [group_subtype] => Facebook Classics
            [recent_news] => Jan 10 (19:40)
            [pic] => http://profile.ak.facebook.com/object2/1538/101/
               s8900080125_4899.jpg
            [pic_big] => http://profile.ak.facebook.com/object2/1538/101/
               n8900080125_4899.jpg
            [pic_small] => http://profile.ak.facebook.com/object2/1538/101/
               t8900080125_4899.jpg
            [creator] =>
            [update_time] => 1199994165
            [office] =>
            [website] => www.steve-jackson.net
            [venue] => Array
               (
                    [street] =>
                    [city] =>
                    [state] =>
                    [country] =>
               )


     )

[2] => Array
     (
          [gid] => 8298576990
          [name] => Sheep Among Wolves
          [nid] => 0
          [description] =>A Christian Rock band
          [group_type] => Music
          [group_subtype] => Rock
          [recent_news] =>
          [pic] => http://profile.ak.facebook.com/object2/1105/5/s8298576990_
             8816.jpg
          [pic_big] => http://profile.ak.facebook.com/object2/1105/5/
             n8298576990_8816.jpg
          [pic_small] => http://profile.ak.facebook.com/object2/1105/5/
             t8298576990_8816.jpg
          [creator] => 713210144
          [update_time] => 1197033084
          [office] => Wagner's House
          [website] => http://hs.facebook.com/profile.php?id=6653134479
          [venue] => Array
               (
                    [street] =>
                    [city] => Princeton
```

```
                        [state] => Massachusetts
                        [country] => United States
                        [latitude] => 42.4486
                        [longitude] => -71.8778
                )


        )


Applied example:
Active events for Rich Wagner:

HECK YES I QUOTE MOVIES
Six Degrees Of Separation - The Experiment
Sheep Among Wolves


Scenario 2: Getting all groups for a specific user
Raw output:
Array
(
    [0] => Array
        (
            [gid] => 17342247576
            [name] => Telecom Council of Silicon Valley
            [nid] => 0
            [description] =>
            [group_type] => Organizations
            [group_subtype] => Professional Organizations
            [recent_news] => The Council is taking Founding Members, filling its
                Board, and looking for connected and energetic people in the
                local telecom industry to fill key leadership positions.  Drop us
                a line of you are interested.
            [pic] => http://profile.ak.facebook.com/object2/1428/65/
                s17342247576_3165.jpg
            [pic_big] => http://profile.ak.facebook.com/object2/1428/65/
                n17342247576_3165.jpg
            [pic_small] => http://profile.ak.facebook.com/object2/1428/65/
                t17342247576_3165.jpg
            [creator] => 718570130
            [update_time] => 1199227600
            [office] =>
            [website] => http://www.telecomcouncil.com
            [venue] => Array
                (
                    [street] =>
                    [city] =>
                    [state] => CA
```

```
                    [country] => United States
            )


    )

Scenario 3: Getting info for a specific group
Raw output:
Array
(
    [0] => Array
        (
            [gid] => 17342247576
            [name] => Telecom Council of Silicon Valley
            [nid] => 0
            [description] =>
            [group_type] => Organizations
            [group_subtype] => Professional Organizations
            [recent_news] => The Council is taking Founding Members, filling its
                Board, and looking for connected and energetic people in the
                local telecom industry to fill key leadership positions.  Drop us
                a line of you are interested.
            [pic] => http://profile.ak.facebook.com/object2/1428/65/
                s17342247576_3165.jpg
            [pic_big] => http://profile.ak.facebook.com/object2/1428/65/
                n17342247576_3165.jpg
            [pic_small] => http://profile.ak.facebook.com/object2/1428/65/
                t17342247576_3165.jpg
            [creator] => 718570130
            [update_time] => 1199227600
            [office] =>
            [website] => http://www.telecomcouncil.com
            [venue] => Array
                (
                    [street] =>
                    [city] =>
                    [state] => CA
                    [country] => United States
                )

        )

)

Scenario 4: Getting info about several groups
Raw output:
Array
```

```
(
    [0] => Array
        (
            [gid] => 2208108698
            [name] => HECK YES I QUOTE MOVIES
            [nid] => 0
            [description] =>
            [group_type] => Entertainment & Arts
            [group_subtype] => Movies
            [recent_news] =>
            [pic] => http://profile.ak.facebook.com/object/1961/40/s2208108698_
                37065.jpg
            [pic_big] => http://profile.ak.facebook.com/object/1961/40/
                n2208108698_37065.jpg
            [pic_small] => http://profile.ak.facebook.com/object/1961/40/
                t2208108698_37065.jpg
            [creator] =>
            [update_time] => 1173885432
            [office] =>
            [website] =>
            [venue] => Array
                (
                    [street] =>
                    [city] =>
                    [state] =>
                    [country] =>
                )

        )

    [1] => Array
        (
            [gid] => 2210253039
            [name] => All I ever needed to know in life, I learned by reading
                Dr. Seuss.
            [nid] => 0
            [description] => To all of us who have gained perspective of the
                world by stepping into the wondrous world of Dr Seuss when we
                were young.
            [group_type] => Just for Fun
            [group_subtype] => Totally Random
            [recent_news] => None
            [pic] =>
                http://profile.ak.facebook.com/object/1345/125/s2210253039_22864.
                jpg
```

```
       [pic_big] =>
          http://profile.ak.facebook.com/object/1345/125/n2210253039_22864.
          jpg
       [pic_small] =>
          http://profile.ak.facebook.com/object/1345/125/t2210253039_22864.
          jpg
       [creator] => 512826063
       [update_time] => 1165737138
       [office] => Whoville
       [website] =>
       [venue] => Array
          (
                [street] =>
                [city] =>
                [state] =>
                [country] =>
          )


    )

)
```

Retrieving member info with groups.getMembers

The `groups.getMembers` call is used to gather membership information from one or more groups. It contains a single parameter indicating the group ID (`$gid`) as shown in the PHP call:

```
$facebook->api_client->groups_getMembers($gid)
```

The call returns an associative array of user IDs, grouped by their membership status: `members`, `admins`, `officers`, and `not_replied`.

Consider the following example. In the first case, it prints the raw results of the call using `print_r`. In the second case, the results are organized into separate bulleted lists by performing a `foreach` loop for each of the four membership status values: `$members['members']`, `$members['admins']`, `$members['officers']`, and `$members['no_replies']` to print the list items. Here's the code:

```php
<?php
require_once 'appinclude.php';

echo "<h1>groups_getMembers</h1>";
```

```
echo "<hr />";

echo "<h2>Scenario 1: Getting all members of a group (grouped by type)</h2>";

$gid = 8298576990;
$uid = null;
$members = $facebook->api_client->groups_getMembers($gid);
$groups = $facebook->api_client->groups_get($uid, $gid);

echo "<h5>Raw output:</h5>";
echo "<pre>";
print_r($members);
echo "</pre>";

echo "<h5>Applied example:</h5>";
echo "<p>Members for {$groups[0]['name']}</p>";

echo "<p>Regular members:</p>";
echo "<ul>";
if ($members['members'][0]) {
  foreach ($members['members'] as $member){
    echo "<li><fb:name uid=\"$member\" useyou=\"false\" /></li>";
  }
} else {
  echo "<li>None</li>";
}
echo "</ul>";

echo "<p>Administrators:</p>";
echo "<ul>";
if ($members['admins'][0]) {
  foreach ($members['admins'] as $member)  {
    echo "<li><fb:name uid=\"$member\" useyou=\"false\" /></li>";
  }
} else {
  echo "<li>None</li>";
}
echo "</ul>";

echo "<p>Officers:</p>";
echo "<ul>";
if ($members['officers'][0]) {
  foreach ($members['officers'] as $member){
    echo "<li><fb:name uid=\"$member\" useyou=\"false\" /></li>";
  }
} else {
  echo "<li>None</li>";
}
```

```
echo "</ul>";

echo "<p>No replies:</p>";
echo "<ul>";
if ($members['not_replied'][0]){
    foreach ($members['not_replied'] as $member){
        echo "<li><fb:name uid=\"$member\" useyou=\"false\" /></li>";
    }
} else {
    echo "<li>None</li>";
}

echo "</ul>";
?>
```

As I indicate earlier in the chapter, pay special attention to the test performed on the associative array before using `foreach`. The results can return an empty list for each of these membership status values. If you perform a `foreach` loop on one of these empty lists, you'll get an error. To further complicate matters, you cannot simply check `count($members['officers'])` because the empty subarray still returns a count of 1, making it impossible to distinguish between a status list of 1 and 0 members using `count()`. Therefore, I am using an `if...else` block to evaluate the first element of each subarray to ensure that it is not blank.

The results are shown here:

```
groups_getMembers

Scenario 1: Getting all members of a group (grouped by type)
Raw output:
Array
(
    [members] => Array
        (
            [0] => 532605112
            [1] => 809149455
            [2] => 537552695
            [3] => 801079753
        )

    [admins] => Array
        (
            [0] => 713210144
        )

    [officers] =>
    [not_replied] => Array
```

```
        (
            [0] => 810334061
            [1] => 55706757
        )

    )

Applied example:

Members for Sheep Among Wolves

Regular members:

_   Dave Lazlo
_   Larry More
_   Rob Larice
_   Tuck Laughon

Administrators:

_   Kels Rollings

Officers:

_   None

No replies:

_   Steve Mistry
_   Syndal Dylan
```

Facebook Pages

Facebook pages provide a business, band, or artist a way to establish a presence with their customers or fans. Facebook users can become fans of pages, and applications can be added to a Facebook page. As a developer, you can work with Facebook pages using the pages.getInfo, pages.isAppAdded, pages.isAdmin, and pages.isFan methods.

Each Facebook page has many data properties associated with it that you may wish to retrieve in your queries. These properties correspond to the values that the admin of the page fills in interactively through the online forms. These include page_id, name, pic_small, pic_square, pic_big, pic, pic_large, type, website, locationlocation (street, city, state, country, zip), hours, hours (mon_1_open, mon_1_close, tue_1_open, tue_1_close, wed_1_open, wed_1_close, thu_1_open, thu_1_close, fri_1_open, fri_1_close, sat_1_open, sat_1_close, sun_1_open, sun_1_close, mon_2_open, mon_2_close, tue_2_open, tue_2_close, wed_2_open, wed_2_close, thu_2_open, thu_2_close, fri_2_open, fri_2_close, sat_2_open, sat_2_close, sun_2_open, sun_2_close), band_members, bio, hometown, genre, genre (dance, party, relax, talk, think, workout, sing, intimate, raunchy, headphones), record_label, influences, has_added_app, founded, company_overview, mission, products, release_date, starring, written_by, directed_by, produced_by, studio, awards, plot_outline, network, season, schedule. Note that inclusive list contains many elements that are specific to particular page types. For example, a band page would have a band_members value but would leave a field like hours blank.

Getting page information with pages.getInfo

The pages.getInfo method is used to retrieve one or more pages based on the criteria you use in the parameters. Here's the syntax in PHP:

```
$facebook->api_client->pages_getInfo($pids, $fields, $uid, $type)
```

The parameters are as follows:

- ✔ The $pids parameter is an array of page IDs.
- ✔ The $fields parameter is an array of fields you want to return.
- ✔ The $uid parameter is the user ID if you want to retrieve pages of a particular user.
- ✔ The $type parameter allows you to specify results based on the page type.

The following example walks you through three scenarios of retrieving pages. The first scenario gets all the pages that the current user is a fan of, while the second example specifies a particular user ID. The final call specifies a list of page IDs to retrieve. In each case, a list of fields is specified in the $fields parameter. Check out the code:

```
<?php
require_once 'appinclude.php';

echo('<pre>');
echo "<h1>pages_getInfo</h1>";
```

```
echo "<hr />";

echo "<h2>Scenario 1: Get all pages in which current user is a fan</h2>";
echo "<h5>Raw output:</h5>";
print_r($facebook->api_client->pages_getInfo( null, array('page_id', 'name',
            'pic_small', 'type'), $user, null));

echo('<hr />');
echo "<h2>Scenario 2: Get all pages in which specified user is a fan</h2>";
echo "<h5>Raw output:</h5>";

$uid = '705396409';
print_r($facebook->api_client->pages_getInfo( null, array('page_id', 'name',
            'pic_small', 'type'), $uid, null));

echo('<hr />');
echo "<h2>Scenario 3: Get info on pages specified by page_id</h2>";
echo "<h5>Raw output:</h5>";
print_r($facebook->api_client->pages_getInfo( array(6829493713, 6233046685),
            array('page_id', 'name', 'pic_small', 'type'), null, null));
echo('</pre>');
?>
```

The results of these three method calls are as follows:

```
Scenario 1: Get all pages in which current user is a fan
Raw output:
Array
(
    [0] => Array
        (
            [page_id] => 6829493713
            [name] => (RED)
            [pic_small] => http://profile.ak.facebook.com/object2/432/64/
                t6829493713_3248.jpg
            [type] => CONSUMER_PRODUCTS
        )

)
Scenario 2: Get all pages in which specified user is a fan
Raw output:
Array
(
    [0] => Array
        (
            [page_id] => 6829493222
            [name] => Charleston Bikes
            [pic_small] => http://profile.ak.facebook.com/object2/432/64/
                t6829493713_3248.jpg
```

```
                  [type] => CONSUMER_PRODUCTS
         )

)

Scenario 3: Get info on pages specified by page_id
Raw output:
Array
(
    [0] => Array
        (
            [page_id] => 6829493713
            [name] => (RED)
            [pic_small] => http://profile.ak.facebook.com/object2/432/64/
                t6829493713_3248.jpg
            [type] => CONSUMER_PRODUCTS
        )

    [1] => Array
        (
            [page_id] => 6233046685
            [name] => Ron Paul
            [pic_small] => http://profile.ak.facebook.com/object2/512/17/
                t6233046685_4045.jpg
            [type] => POLITICIANS
        )

)
```

Scoping out with pages.isAppAdded

You can check to see whether your application is added to a page using pages.isAppAdded. Here's the code:

```
$facebook->api_client->pages_isAppAdded($pid)
```

The $pid parameter specifies a specific page ID. The call returns a 1 (true) or 0 (false).

For example:

```php
<?php
require_once 'appinclude.php';
echo('<pre>');
echo "<h1>pages_isAppAdded</h1>";
echo "<hr />";
echo "<h2>Scenario 1: Checks whether a page has added the application</h2>";
echo "<h5>Raw output:</h5>";
print_r($facebook->api_client->pages_isAppAdded('6829493713'));
echo('</pre>');
?>
```

Getting current user info with pages.isAdmin and pages.isFan

The `pages.isAdmin` and `pages.isFan` methods are used to determine whether the current user is an admin or a fan of the specified page. You can call these two methods in a similar manner:

```
$facebook->api_client->pages_isFan($pid)
$facebook->api_client->pages_isAdmin($pid)
```

The `$pid` parameter is a page ID of a single page. Both of these methods return a 1 (true) or 0 (false) response.

Pulling User Data

Facebook provides extended access to user data from inside your application. To access this data, you have four methods: `users.getLoggedInUser`, `users.getInfo`, `users.isAppAdded`, and `users.hasAppPermission`.

Getting the current user with users.getLoggedInUser

The `users.getLoggedInUser` method is used to return the user ID of the currently logged-in user. It is usually called at the beginning of a session and stored in a variety of ways to avoid calling this method multiple times. The syntax using PHP is as follows:

```
$facebook->api_client->users_getLoggedInUser()
```

It takes no parameters.

The following example shows this method in action:

```
$user = $facebook->api_client->users_getLoggedInUser();
echo "The user that is currently logged in is {$user}";
```

The result is the user's ID:

```
The user that is currently logged in is 665127078
```

Getting info with users.getInfo

The `users.getInfo` call enables you to retrieve user profile information based on the view of the current user. The PHP syntax is as follows:

```
$facebook->api_client->users_getInfo($uids, $fields)
```

The `$uids` parameter indicates an array of user IDs.

The `$fields` parameter is an array of fields that you want to return about the user. These properties correspond to the pieces of information that a user enters online about himself or herself in the Edit Profile pages. See Table 3-13 for a complete list of these fields.

Table 3-13	User Elements	
Element	**Description**	**Child Elements**
uid	The user ID corresponding to the user info returned (always returned, even if unspecified)	
about_me	Corresponds with About Me profile field	
activities	Corresponds with user entered Activities profile field	
affiliations	Network affiliations of user, starting with the user's primary network	year, type ['college", "high school", "work", "region"], status, name, and nid
birthday	User's Birthday	
books	User's Favorite books	
current_location	Current location	city, state, country, and zip
education_history	List of education_info elements	education_info children: name, year, and concentration
first_name	Generated from name in profile	

Element	Description	Child Elements
has_added_ app	Specifies whether user has added the calling app (0 or 1)	
hometown_ location	Hometown profile fields	city, state, country, and zip
hs_info	High school information	hs1_name, hs2_name, grad_year, hs1_key, and hs2_key
interests	Corresponds with Interests profile field	
is_app_user	Specifies whether the user has ever used the calling app (0 or 1)	
last_name	Generated from name in profile	
meeting_for	List of desired relationships (blank, Friendship, A Relationship, Dating, Random Play, Whatever I can get)	
meeting_sex	List of desired genders corresponding to the Interested In profile element	
movies	Favorite movies	
music	Favorite music	
name	Name of user	
notes_count	Total number of notes written by user	
pic	URL of user profile picture (max. 100x300 px)	
pic_big	URL of user profile picture (max. 200x600 px)	
pic_small	URL of user profile picture (max. 50x150 px)	
pic_square	URL of square picture (max. 50x50 px)	

(continued)

Table 3-13 *(continued)*

Element	Description	Child Elements
`political`	Political view (blank, Very Liberal, Liberal, Moderate, Conservative, Very Conservative, Apathetic, Libertarian, Other)	
`profile_ update_time`	Time (in seconds since epoch) that the user's profile was last updated. `0` is returned if no recent updates have occurred.	
`quotes`	Favorite quotes	
`relationship_ status`	Relationship status (blank, Single, In a Relationship, In an Open Relationship, Engaged, Married, It's Complicated)	
`religion`	Religious views	
`sex`	Sex	
`significant_ other_id`	User ID of the person the user is in a relationship with	
`status`	Status message	`message`, `time`
`timezone`	Offset from GMT	
`tv`	Favorite TV shows	
`wall_count`	Total number of posts to the user's wall	
`work_history`	List of `work_info` elements	`location`, `company_ name`, `position`, `description`, `start_ date`, and `end_date`

In the following example, I use `users_getInfo` to retrieve basic details of the currently logged-in user and output them using `print_r`. I then apply that same logic to a more in-depth example by assigning the results to the

`$user_details` array. The data elements are then accessed from the array and output using `echo`. Here's the code:

```php
<?php
require_once 'appinclude.php';

echo "<h1>users_getInfo</h1>";
echo "<hr />";

echo "<h2>Scenario 1: Get info on current user</h2>";

$uid = $facebook->api_client->users_getLoggedInUser();
$desired_details = array('first_name', 'last_name', 'birthday', 'movies', 'pic',
            'status');
$user_details = $facebook->api_client->users_getInfo($uid, $desired_details);

echo "<h5>Raw output:</h5>";
echo "<pre>";
print_r($user_details);
echo "</pre>";

echo "<h5>Applied example:</h5>";
$status = $user_details[0]['status']['message'];
$first_name = $user_details[0]['first_name'];
$last_name = $user_details[0]['last_name'];

echo "<p>$first_name $last_name $status</p>";
?>
```

The results are shown here:

```
users_getInfo
Scenario 1: Get info on current user
Raw output:
Array
(
    [0] => Array
        (
            [uid] => 665127078
            [first_name] => Rich
            [last_name] => Wagner
            [birthday] =>
            [movies] => Casablanca, The Shawshank Redemption, It's A Wonderful
                Life, Babette's Feast, Field of Dreams, Pride & Prejudice (A&E
                Version), The Band of Brothers (HBO), Chariots of Fire, Amélie
                (Le Fabuleux destin d'Amélie Poulain), Groundhog Day, Braveheart,
                Princess Bride, Les Miserables (1998 version), Signs, The Lord of
                the Rings trilogy, Benny & Joon, Vertigo, Sense & Sensibility,
                The Count of Monte Cristo, A Little Princess, Double Indemnity,
                Forrest Gump, The Incredibles, The African Queen, Henry V (1989
                version), The Truman Show
```

```
            [pic] => http://profile.ak.facebook.com/profile6/1237/103/
              s665127078_3837.jpg
      )


)
Applied example:
Rich Wagner says "bring on the Colts"
```

A second example shows how to combine API calls to retrieve Facebook information. It shows how to use `friends_get()` and `users_getInfo()` to gather basic information on all the friends of the current user. The name and status message are displayed in a bulleted list. The code is as follows:

```php
<?php
require_once 'appinclude.php';

echo "<h2>Scenario 2: Get status of all friends of current user</h2>";
echo "<h5>Applied example:</h5>";

$friends = $facebook->api_client->friends_get();
$desired_details = array('last_name','first_name', 'status');
$friends_details = $facebook->api_client->users_getInfo($friends,
              $desired_details);

echo "<ul>";
if($friends_details){
  foreach ($friends_details as $user_details) {
    $status = $user_details['status']['message'];
    $first_name = $user_details['first_name'];
    $last_name = $user_details['last_name'];

    echo "<li>$first_name $last_name $status</li>";
  }
} else {
  echo "<li>This user has no friends :(</li>";
}
echo "</ul>";
?>
```

And it displays as this:

```
Scenario 2: Get status of all friends of current user
Applied example:

Jared Wagner has a very tiny brain
Justus Wagner solved immigration but then he forget how
Jordan Wagner is chanting snow snow go away, come back on tuesday
```

Checking whether a user has your app with users.isAppAdded

The `users.isAppAdded` determines whether the currently logged-in user has added the calling application. The syntax is as follows when using PHP:

```
$facebook->api_client->users_isAppAdded()
```

The method returns a 1 (true) or 0 (false).

Checking permissions with users.hasAppPermissions

Facebook requires that users grant special permission to an application to access certain parts of the API. The specific cases are setting a user's status, uploading images to an album, and creating a listing.

To allow users to opt in to these extended abilities, direct users to the following URL:

```
www.facebook.com/authorize.php?api_key=YOUR_API_KEY&v=1.0&ext_perm=PERMISSION_
            NAME
```

The `PERMISSION_NAME` parameter can be `status_update`, `photo_upload`, or `create_listing`.

Before performing one of these actions, you can check the extended permissions of a user using `users.hasAppPermissions`. Here is the syntax:

```
$facebook->api_client->users_hasAppPermission($ext_perm)
```

The `$ext_perm` parameter can be `status_update`, `photo_upload`, or `create_listing`.

The result is a 1 (true) or 0 (false).

Chapter 4

Writing Facebook Markup Language (FBML)

*A*lthough the Facebook API (see Chapter 3) is primarily used for retrieving Facebook data, Facebook Markup Language (FBML) is the tool that allows you to fully embed your app within the Facebook environment. FBML allows you to render content onto the Facebook canvas, conditionally display info to different users depending on their permissions, and tap into several Facebook staples, such as Wall, Board, and profile box. In short, FBML is the developer's primary tool for building applications that deeply integrate into the Facebook Platform.

In this chapter, I walk you through using FBML productively as you develop your Facebook application.

Exploring FBML

FBML is a combination of Facebook-specific elements (tags) and a subset of HTML elements that are appropriate for use in the Facebook environment. When the Facebook server processes FBML (which can be sent as a parameter from many of the Facebook API calls), it processes the markup and displays the output in HTML for rendering in a browser.

You can divide FBML into six main types of elements:

✔ **Facebook field placeholders:** Several elements are used as placeholders to display Facebook-related data. For example, the fb:name tag is used to output the name of the specified user:

```
<fb:name uid="loggedinuser" useyou="false" capitalize="true"/>
```

✔ **Conditional programming elements:** FBML contains several elements used for adding conditional logic to your code. Consider, for example, the fb:if-can-see element. It allows you to tailor the content based on the permission level of the logged-in user. Here's how you could display different content depending on the user's ability to see another user's Wall:

```
<fb:if-can-see uid="585166905" what="wall">
    <p>Would you like to write on the Wall?</p>
  <fb:else>
    <p>What do you want to do?</p>
  </fb:else>
</fb:if-can-see>
```

✔ **Presentation elements:** A third group of elements is used for presenting text and media content. The fb:photo element, for example, displays a Facebook photo based on its photo ID:

```
<fb:if-can-see-photo pid="2856699047694594570">
  <fb:photo pid="2856699047694594570" />
</fb:if-can-see-photo>
```

✔ **Facebook widgets:** A fourth group of elements is used to insert a familiar Facebook UI element, such as a Wall, a Board, or the Dashboard. Using these elements, you can take advantage of these Facebook UI elements without having to code and format them yourself. For instance, if you want to display a Wall in your app, you could use the fb:wall element:

```
<fb:wall>
  <fb:wallpost uid="loggedinuser">Congrats on your prom queen
        award.</fb:wallpost>
</fb:wall>
```

✔ **General markup elements:** The fifth group of tags exposes a wide variety of general functionality in the Facebook Platform that is needed for developing robust applications. The fb:error tag, for example, is used to display a Facebook error message:

```
<fb:error>
      <fb:message>Application Error</fb:message>
      <p>Something weird just happened to our app. We have no idea how this
        happened.</p>
  </fb:error>
```

✔ **HTML subset of elements:** Lest we forget HTML, FBML also includes a subset of HTML elements that you can work with inside of the environment. As Table 4-1 shows, you can work with the vast majority of body-level elements. However, because you are working within the Facebook environment, the top- and head-level elements are not available.

Table 4-1	Supported and Unsupported HTML Elements	
Group	*Supported Elements*	*Unsupported Elements*
Block-level elements	`address, blockquote, center, del, div, h1, h2, h3, h4, h5, h6, hr, ins, p, pre`	`noscript`
List elements	`dl, dt, dd, li, ol, ul`	`dir, menu`
Table elements	`table, caption, tbody, td, tfoot, th, thead, tr`	`colgroup, col`
Form elements	`form, fieldset, legend, input, label, optgroup, option, select, textarea`	`button`
Special inline elements	`a, bdo, br, font, img, q, span, script, style, sub, sup`	`applet, basefont, iframe, map, area, object, param`
Phrase elements	`abbr, acronym, cite, code, dfn, em, kbd, samp, strong, var`	
Text style	`b, big, i, s, small, strike, tt, u`	
Top-level, head, and frame elements		`html, head, body,` and `frameset, base, isindex, link, meta, style, title`

Table 4-2 provides a listing of all the FBML elements, organized by their group.

Table 4-2	FBML Tags	
Groups	*FBML Elements*	*Description*
Users and groups	`fb:name`	Outputs the name of the specified user
	`fb:grouplink`	Outputs the name of the specified group

(continued)

Table 4-2 *(continued)*

Groups	FBML Elements	Description
	`fb:user`	Specifies that the contained content is owned by the specified user
	`fb:pronoun`	Outputs a pronoun for the specified user
	`fb:profile-pic`	Displays the specified user's profile picture
Conditional content displays	`fb:is-in-network`	Displays content if the user is inside a specified network
	`fb:if-can-see`	Displays the contained content if the current user passes a privacy check for a specific condition
	`fb:if-can-see-photo`	Displays enclosed content only if the current user has permission to see the specified photo
	`fb:if-is-app-user`	Displays contained content only if the specified user has accepted the terms of service of the application
	`fb:if-is-friends-with-viewer`	Displays the contained content only if the specified user is friends with the current user
	`fb:if-is-group-member`	Displays the contained content only if the specified user is a member of the specified group
	`fb:if-is-user`	Displays contained content only if the current user is one of the specified users
	`fb:if-user-has-added-app`	Displays the contained content only if the specified user has added the app to his or her profile
	`fb:if`	Displays content if the condition evaluates to `true`
	`fb:else`	Takes care of the else case inside any of the `fb:if*` or `fb:is-in-network` tags
	`fb:switch`	Evaluates every contained FBML tag and outputs the first one that evaluates to a nonblank string

Groups	FBML Elements	Description
	`fb:default`	Used inside of an `fb:switch` element, it outputs content if all other FBML tags before it are blank
Profiles	`fb:wide`	Displays contained content only when profile box is in the wide column of the user's profile
	`fb:narrow`	Displays contained content only when profile box is in the narrow column of the user's profile
	`fb:profile-action`	Displays a link on the user's profile underneath his or her photo
	`fb:user-table`	Displays a user table displaying the name and thumbnail picture of the user. This tag only works in a profile box.
	`fb:user-item`	Specifies a user to be displayed inside of a `fb:user-table`
	`fb:subtitle`	Specifies the subtitle for the profile box
	`fb:action`	Displays an action link on the right side of a profile box or Dashboard
Media	`fb:iframe`	Adds an `iframe` element to the page
	`fb:photo`	Displays a Facebook photo
	`fb:mp3`	Displays a Flash audio player
	`fb:swf`	Displays a Shockwave Flash object
	`fb:flv`	Displays a Flash FLV player for video/audio streaming
	`fb:silverlight`	Displays a Microsoft Silverlight control
Status messages	`fb:error`	Displays a standard error message
	`fb:explanation`	Outputs a standard explanation message
	`fb:success`	Displays a standard success message
	`fb:message`	Displays the heading for a message (used inside an error, explanation, or success message)

(continued)

Table 4-2 *(continued)*

Groups	FBML Elements	Description
Dialog boxes	fb:dialog	Displays a standard pop-up dialog box
	fb:dialog-title	Displays the title to the dialog box
	fb:dialog-content	FBML contents of the dialog box
	fb:dialog-button	Displays a button in the dialog box
Editor displays	fb:editor	Creates a two-column form
	fb:editor-button	Outputs a Submit button inside an editor form
	fb:editor-buttonset	Container for editor buttons
	fb:editor-cancel	Outputs a cancel button inside an editor form
	fb:editor-custom	Enables you to display any valid FBML content in the editor form
	fb:editor-date	Creates a date selector
	fb:editor-divider	Displays a horizontal line spacer
	fb:editor-month	Displays a month selector
	fb:editor-text	Outputs a text box for an editor form
	fb:editor-textarea	Displays a text area for an editor form
	fb:editor-time	Displays a time selector
Request forms	fb:request-form	Defines a request form
	fb:multi-friend-input	Renders a tabular display of friends in a request form (or, if condensed="true", displays a condensed list)
	fb:request-form-submit	Displays a Submit button for condensed request forms

Groups	FBML Elements	Description
	fb:req-choice	Defines a button at the bottom of a user's request page
Page navigation	fb:dashboard	Renders a top Dashboard
	fb:action	Displays an action link in a Dashboard
	fb:create-button	Adds a Create button to the Dashboard
	fb:help	Adds a Help link to the Dashboard
	fb:header	Displays a Facebook title header
	fb:mediaheader	Displays a media-oriented header
	fb:header-title	Provides a title for a media header
	fb:owner-action	Specifies an action link inside a media header
	fb:tabs	Defines a tab set for page navigation
	fb:tab-item	Defines a tab link
Facebook widgets and UI elements	fb:wall	Renders a Wall on the page
	fb:wallpost	Displays a post on a Wall
	fb:wallpost-action	Outputs an action link at the bottom of a wallpost
	fb:board	Renders a discussion board (Facebook handles all the board duties)
	fb:comments	Renders a Wall for comments (Facebook handles all the Wall duties)
	fb:friend-selector	Displays a box for selecting friends
	fb:typeahead-input	Displays a customized type-ahead box
	fb:typeahead-option	Specifies custom settings for the type-ahead input box

(continued)

Table 4-2 *(continued)*

Groups	FBML Elements	Description
	`fb:random`	Picks an item inside the tag based on weights specified in the `fb:random-option` items
	`fb:random-option`	Displays content to be rendered when selected in an `fb:random` tag
	`fb:share-button`	Outputs a standard Share button
	`fb:submit`	Transforms an image or text link into a Submit button
Attachments	`fb:attachment-preview`	Displays a link in a Wall or message attachment that inserts new content when clicked
Miscellaneous	`fb:fbml`	Specifies that the FBML code it contains is specific to a particular version of FBML
	`fb:fbmlversion`	Outputs the current version of FBML (for debugging use only)
	`fb:title`	Sets the page title or, when contained by `fb:comments` or `fb:board`, sets the title for these widgets
	`fb:js-string`	Renders a block of FBML into an FBML block JavaScript variable
	`fb:redirect`	Redirects to the specified URL inside the Facebook canvas page
	`fb:ref`	Outputs FBML content from a given source
	`fb:time`	Outputs the date/time based on the current user's time zone
	`fb:page-admin-edit-header`	Adds a standard edit header for quick access to a page's app configuration (only for apps that can be added to Facebook pages)
	`fb:user-agent`	Displays contained content to a specific user-agent (browser)

Groups	FBML Elements	Description
	`fb:google-analytics`	Adds Google Analytics code to page
	`fb:mobile`	Displays the contained content only when accessed from the Facebook mobile Web site

Working with Users and Groups

FBML has several tags that enable you to output information about a user. Perhaps the most basic is the `fb:name` element, which displays the name of the user based on the criteria supplied in the attributes. For example, to render a person's Facebook name, I supply the user ID through the `uid` parameter:

```
My friend's name is <fb:name uid="530377451"/>
```

Facebook renders the text as shown in Figure 4-1. The name is displayed and hyperlinked to the profile page of the user.

Figure 4-1: Displaying a name using `fb:name`.

If you want to display the name of the logged-in user, a variety of options are available to do so, such as the following:

✔ You can specify the reserved phrase `loggedinuser` as the value for the `uid`.

```
<fb:name uid="loggedinuser"/>
```

✔ You can supply the user ID from a variable. For example, in PHP, I could write the following (where `$user` is the variable for the logged in user):

```
echo "<fb:name uid='$user'/>"
```

✔ You could hardcode the ID value:

```
<fb:name uid="665127078"/>
```

However, the uid parameter alone is usually not enough when dealing with the current user. You need to specify exactly how you want to refer to the person. By default, Facebook refers to the current user as you when it renders a name. Therefore, the following code

```
Hello <fb:name uid="665127078"/>
```

would display as

```
Hello you
```

If you would like to display a user's actual name instead of you, add useyou as an attribute:

```
Hello <fb:name uid="665127078" useyou="false"/>
```

This tag displays the following when I am the current user:

```
Hello Rich Wagner
```

The fb:name tag has several additional attributes (see Table 4-3) that enable you to specify how a user's name is presented.

Table 4-3	fb:name Attributes
Attribute	*Description*
uid	Specifies the desired user ID (or page ID) (can also use loggedinuser or profileowner). (Required)
firstnameonly	Displays the first name of the user only. (Defaults to false)
linked	Specifies whether to link the user's name to his or her profile. (Defaults to true)
lastnameonly	Displays the last name of the user only. (Defaults to false)
possessive	Displays the name as possessive (usually adding 's). (Defaults to false)
reflexive	Output yourself if the useyou attribute is true. (Defaults to false)
shownetwork	Displays the primary network of user. (Defaults to false)

Attribute	Description
useyou	Replaces user name with you if uid is the current logged-in user. (Defaults to true)
ifcantsee	Outputs alternate text if the current user cannot access the user specified in uid.
capitalize	Capitalizes the text if useyou is true and uid is the current user.
subjected	Specifies the ID of the subject in a sentence where this name is the object of the verb. Reflexive is used when it makes sense.

Here are some common ways to use the fb:name attributes:

✔ To display the first name only, use firstnameonly:

```
Hello <fb:name uid="665127078" firstnameonly="true" useyou="false"/>
```

✔ To display the last name only, use lastnameonly:

```
Hello <fb:name uid="665127078" lastnameonly="true" useyou="false"/>
```

✔ To capitalize the name if useyou="true" and uid="loggedinuser" are set, use capitalize="true":

```
<fb:name uid="665127078" capitalize="true" useyou="false"/> is capitalized.
```

✔ To make the name possessive, use possessive="true":

```
<fb:name uid="665127078" possessive="true" firstnameonly="true"
         useyou="false"/> calendar is ready for viewing.
```

This displays as

```
Rich's calendar is ready for viewing.
```

✔ If you don't want to link the user's name to his or her profile, set the linked attribute accordingly:

```
It does not make sense to link to <fb:name uid="loggedinuser"
         possessive="true" useyou="false" linked="false"/> profile.
```

In addition to fb:name, you can also use the fb:pronoun tag to output the appropriate pronoun for a particular user. Table 4-4 lists the various attributes.

Table 4-4	fb:pronoun Attributes
Attribute	*Description*
uid	User ID. (Required)
useyou	Use "you" if current user is the iud. Default is true.
possessive	Use his, her, your, or their. Default is false.
reflexive	Use himself, herself, yourself, or themselves. Default is false.
objective	Use him, her, you, or them. Default is false.
usethey	Use "they" if no gender is specified. Default is true.
capitalize	Capitalize the pronoun. Default is false.

To display the profile picture of a user (or Facebook page), you can use the fb:profile-pic element. Its size attribute enables you to specify one of four image sizes: thumb (50px wide), small (100px wide), normal (200px wide), or square (50wx50h). Consider the following code using both fb:pronoun and fb:profile-pic:

```
<p><fb:name uid='685578792'/> recently updated <fb:pronoun possessive="true"
        uid='685578792' /> profile picture to: </p>
<fb:profile-pic uid="685578792" size="normal" linked="true" />
```

Displaying Content Conditionally

One of the key building blocks of Facebook is the ability of a user to specify who gets to see his or her information and content. Typically, friends get to see most everything, a few friends get to see a limited profile, and the public gets to see basic friends lists. Therefore, as application developers for the Facebook Platform, you have to be aware of the visibility of any user data you want to display. FBML provides several elements that enable you to display content conditionally — depending on the view of the current user.

However, the context in which you can use these tags is very specific. The elements starting with fb:if, for example, are available on a canvas page, but not in a profile box. The fb:visible elements are designed for testing inside the profile box only (see Chapter 1 for more on the canvas pages and profile boxes).

Testing on canvas pages

The following elements are available on a Facebook canvas page, but not in a profile box:

- ✔ fb:if-can-see
- ✔ fb:if-can-see-photo
- ✔ fb:if-is-app-user
- ✔ fb:if-is-friends-with-viewer
- ✔ fb:if-is-group-member
- ✔ fb:if-is-user
- ✔ fb:if-user-has-added-app
- ✔ fb:is-in-network

Each of these works like an if statement that you are probably used to in another programming language. If the tag evaluates to true, the content contained inside of it is displayed. Each of these also supports the use of the fb:else tag to display content when the tag evaluates to false.

Testing with fb:if-can-see

The fb:if-can-see tag displays the content it contains depending whether the current user has privileges to see the area specified by its what parameter. For example, the following code tests to see whether the current user can see the profile for user 685578792:

```
<fb:if-can-see uid="685578792" what="profile">
  <fb:name uid="685578792" /> is excited to hear from you.
  <fb:else><fb:name uid="685578792" /> is unavailable for comment.</fb:else>
</fb:if-can-see>
```

Because I am friends with this user, when I am signed in, I get the following output:

```
Jared Wagner is excited to hear from you.
```

However, for nonfriends, the fb:else content is displayed:

```
Jared Wagner is unavailable for comment.
```

The what attribute can be any of the following values: search (default), profile, friends, not_limited, online, statusupdates, wall, groups, courses, photosofme, notes, feed, contact, email, aim, cell, phone, mailbox, address, basic, education, professional, personal, and seasonal.

Displaying photos with fb:if-can-see-photo

Similarly, the `fb:if-can-see-photo` tag is used when you are trying to determine whether you can display a photo using `fb:photo`, which can be used to reference any photo on Facebook. For example:

```
<fb:if-can-see-photo pid="2856699047694594570">
<p><fb:name uid="685578792" /> recently snapped the following picture:</p>
  <fb:photo pid="2856699047694594570" />
</fb:if-can-see-photo>
```

The `pid` attribute specifies the ID of the photo you can check on. The `pid` is something you can obtain using the `photos.get` API method. Alternatively, you can specify a `pid` that you obtain from a Facebook photo URL if you also supply the optional `uid` attribute. For example, suppose I have a photo I want to render that is at the following URL:

```
http://www.facebook.com/photo.php?pid=570575&id=530377451&ref=nf
```

By identifying the `pid` and `uid` values from the URL, I can use them in my FBML call:

```
<fb:if-can-see-photo pid="570575" uid="530377451">
<p><fb:name uid="530377451" /> recently snapped the following picture:</p>
  <fb:photo pid="570575" uid="530377451" />
<fb:else>
<p>Who said a picture is worth a 1,000 words? I am sure it wasn't that good of
            picture anyway.</p>
</fb:if-can-see-photo>
```

Notice that `fb:else` can be used with `fb:if-can-see-photo`, as well as with any of the other conditional FBML tags.

Testing for app users

You can use the `fb:if-is-app-user` and `fb:if-user-has-added-app` elements when you want to conditionally display content based on whether the specified user (not necessarily the current user) is a user of your app. These two elements are quite similar, but the difference is as follows:

- ✔ `fb:if-is-app-user` displays content if the specified user has accepted the terms of service of the application.
- ✔ `fb:if-user-has-added-app` outputs contained content if the specified user has added the app to his or her account.

For example:

```
<fb:if-is-app-user uid="530377451">
  <p>The user you requested is already a user of DétenteFussion.</p>
  <fb:else>
<p>Would you like to send an invitation to <fb:name uid="530377451" />
now to sign up for DétenteFussion?</p></fb:else>
</fb:if-is-app-user>
```

Checking for specific users

You may want to display content only when the specified user is friends with
the currently logged-in user. To do so, use `fb:if-is-friends-with-`
`viewer`. Here's a sample:

```
<fb:if-is-friends-with-viewer uid="530377451">
  <p>You are already friends with <fb:name uid="530377451"/></p>
  <fb:else><p>Would you like to send a request to <fb:name uid="530377451"/>
            become your friend?</p></fb:else>
</fb:if-is-friends-with-viewer>
```

The `fb:if-is-friends-with-viewer` has an optional `includeself`
attribute to return `true` if the viewer is the same as the `uid`.

You can also display content conditionally using `fb:if-is-user` only if
the user shows up in a comma-separated list of user IDs. If the ID of the current user is inside the list, content is displayed. Otherwise, the user is out of
luck. Here's a sample:

```
<fb:if-is-user uid="530377451,533317452,431343451">
<p>Hey, you are among the finalists to receive a free iPod Nano.</p>
<fb:else><p>Better luck next time!</p></fb:else>
</fb:if-is-user>
```

Finally, you can also perform a couple more conditional checks using `fb:is-`
`in-network` (if user is in the specified network) and `fb:if-is-group-`
`member` (if user is in the specified group).

Showing and hiding content in profile boxes

Because of the potential for abuse, the `fb:if*` elements are no longer allowed
to be used within profile boxes starting with FBML 1.1. Instead, you can use the
following `fb:visible-to*` tags:

- `fb:visible-to-owner`
- `fb:visible-to-user`

- ✔ fb:visible-to-friends
- ✔ fb:visible-to-app-users
- ✔ fb:visible-to-added-app-users
- ✔ fb:visible-to-connection

These tags enable you to customize the content of the profile box depending on the viewer. However, while the fb:if* tags preprocess the content that is output based on the conditional logic, these fb:visible-to* elements simply show or hide already-processed content depending on the viewer. For example, the following FBML code displays various content in the profile box depending on the user:

```php
<?php
require_once 'appinclude.php';

$profileOnlyContent = <<<HERE

<fb:visible-to-owner>
  <p>Hello <fb:name uid="loggedinuser" useyou="false" firstnameonly="true" />,
            this is your very own box.</p>
</fb:visible-to-owner>
<fb:visible-to-user uid="530377451">
  <p>Hello Jordan. You alone get to see this message.</p>
</fb:visible-to-user>
<fb:visible-to-friends>
  <p>Hello friends of <fb:name uid="loggedinuser" useyou="false"
            firstnameonly="true"/>. If your friend liked this app, we bet you
            will too!</p>
</fb:visible-to-friends>
<fb:visible-to-app-users>
  <p>Awesome dude- you use this app like <fb:name uid="loggedinuser"
            useyou="false" firstnameonly="true"/> does.</p>
</fb:visible-to-app-users>
<fb:visible-to-added-app-users>
  <p>Super! You already have this added to your profile. You are cool too!</p>
</fb:visible-to-added-app-users>
<fb:visible-to-connection>
  <p>For Facebook pages, this content is only displayed if use is a fan of the
            Facebook page.</p>
</fb:visible-to-connection>
HERE;

$facebook->api_client->profile_setFBML($profileOnlyContent);

?>
```

The fb:visible-to-user tag renders for the owner. Therefore, all of the text rendered by the code shown above will be visible to the owner.

When using any of the `fb:visible-to*` elements, be sure not to display private or personal information inside the content. Although the content inside the blocks is not visible to the people outside the intended viewer, it is actually still in the page's source code. Therefore, if your diet-monitoring app contained the following code:

```
<fb:visible-to-owner bgcolor="#666666">
<p>Congrats. You have lost another pound. You are now just 184 pounds.</p>
</fb:visible-to-owner>
```

anyone coming to the user's profile who viewed the page source code could see this rather sensitive info.

Each of these tags contains a `bgcolor` attribute that enables you to specify the color of the profile box if the user is not allowed to see the visible content. Therefore, in the following snippet, the content is visible to the profile owner, but everyone else sees a gray box:

```
<fb:visible-to-owner bgcolor="#666666">
<p>Hello <fb:name uid="loggedinuser" useyou="false" firstnameonly="true"/>, this
            is your very own box.</p>
</fb:visible-to-owner>
```

See Chapter 10 for more details on working with the profile box.

Using fb:if and fb:switch

The `fb:if-*` elements (described in the previous section) use conditional logic to display content based on the permissions of the current user. You can also use two additional FBML tags to control the output of your application:

- `fb:if`
- `fb:switch`

The `fb:if` tag displays the content if the value attribute evaluates to `true`. You can use it in conjunction with `fb:else` to create a typical if...else conditional block. Here's an example from PHP:

```
$page_id = 6829493713;
$check = $facebook->api_client->pages_isAdmin($page_id);
echo "<fb:if value='$check'>Would you like to edit the page?";
echo "<fb:else>Not Authorized!</fb:else>";
echo "</fb:if>"
```

The `fb:switch` element evaluates each of the FBML tags inside of it and renders the first one that evaluates to a non-empty string. You can use the `fb:default` tag to display content if no other tags are rendered. Note that I use the `fb:swf` element to render a Shockwave/Flash object in my page:

```
<fb:switch>
<fb:swf swfsrc="http://apps.facebook.com/dummies//i.swf"
  imgsrc='http://apps.facebook.com/dummies//i.jpg'
  width="300" height="250"/>
<fb:photo pid="3839129212" />
<p>This is the first thing that evaluates to a non-empty string...</p>
<fb:default>Well, at least you have this nice text to look at.</fb:default>
</fb:switch>
```

Adding Facebook UI Elements and Widgets

One of the most powerful aspects of FBML is that it allows you to instantly add Facebook core UI elements and "widgets" into your application with just a few lines of markup code. The benefits are twofold:

- ✔ It eliminates the need for you to reinvent the wheel and write your own custom solution.
- ✔ It enables your application to easily take on the look and feel of Facebook itself.

You can add several core UI elements to your canvas page, including the following:

- ✔ Dashboard page header (`fb:dashboard`)
- ✔ Dashboard navigational link (`fb:action`)
- ✔ Dashboard Create button (`fb:create-button`)
- ✔ Dashboard help link (`fb:help`)
- ✔ Title header (`fb:header`)
- ✔ Media header (`fb:mediaheader`)
- ✔ Navigation tabs (`fb:tabs`, `fb:tab-item`)

These core elements are used as basic interface building blocks for constructing the navigation of most any application. I discuss how to work with these FBML tags in Chapter 8.

You also find several general-purpose Facebook widgets with built-in functionality that you can drop onto your canvas page, including the following:

✔ Discussion board (fb:board)

✔ Comments Wall (fb:comments)

✔ Do-it-yourself Wall "constructor kit" (fb:wall, fb:wallpost, fb:wallpost-action)

✔ Friend selector box (fb:friend-selector)

✔ Type-ahead text box (fb:typeahead-input, fb:typeahead-option)

The following sections discuss these tags in further detail.

Discussing it on the board

To add a discussion board to your app, use the fb:board element and customize its setting through the attributes:

```
<fb:board xid="dummies_board" canpost="true" candelete="true"
  canmark="false" cancreatetopic="true" numtopics="5"
  returnurl="http://apps.facebook.com/dummies//discuss.php">
  <fb:title>Discuss this Dummies app</fb:title>
</fb:board>
```

The xid is the only required parameter. Each board you create should have a unique ID. The ID can only contain alphanumeric characters, underscores, and hyphens. The canpost, candelete, canmark (as relevant or irrelevant), and cancreatetopic attributes all enable you to specify how much users can do on the discussion board. The numtopics parameter determines the number of topics to display on a page. The returnurl determines what URL should be displayed when a back link is clicked (default is the current page).

You can use the fb:title tag inside of an fb:board (or fb:comments) to set the title for the board. The results are displayed in Figure 4-2.

Figure 4-2:
fb:board
creates a
discussion
board.

Discuss this Dummies app

There are no discussions. Start the first topic.

Content can now be added to your board without writing any additional code. When a user adds content or browses through it (see Figure 4-3), the user leaves the canvas page of your application and goes to a page devoted to the board. The user can click the Back link to return to your application (see Figure 4-4).

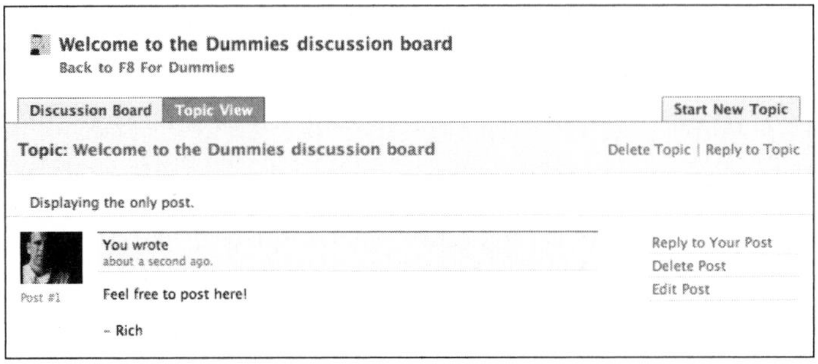

Figure 4-3:
User leaves
app page
to enter
the board.

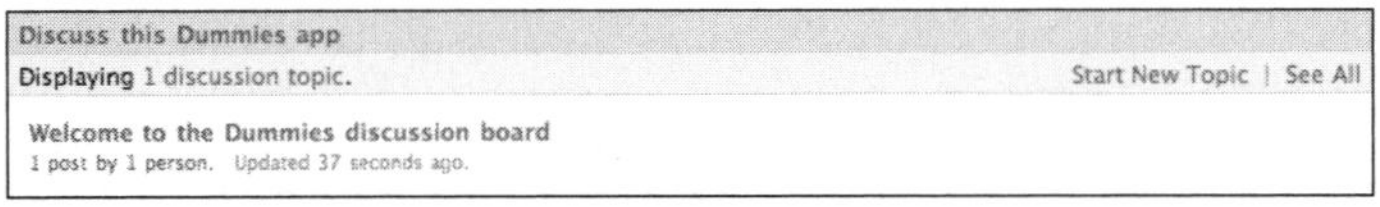

Figure 4-4:
Returning
to the app
after the
board.

Although you don't have full access to the data of these widgets, Facebook handles all the application and data-management responsibilities for you.

Another comment on the Wall

The `fb:comments` tag is used to create a fully functional Wall in much the same way as `fb:board` creates a discussion board. It has many of the same attributes as `fb:board` as well. Here's a sample:

```
<fb:comments xid="dummies_wall" canpost="true" candelete="true"
  numposts="5" showform="true"
            returnurl="http://apps.facebook.com/dummies//discuss.php">
  <fb:title>Write on the Dummies Wall</fb:title>
</fb:board>
```

The `returnurl` provides the URL to return to when the user clicks the Back link. Also, notice the `showform` attribute. When set to `true`, the entry form is displayed inside your page. If `false`, the user needs to click the Write Something link (see Figure 4-5) to add text.

Figure 4-5:
Dropping a
Wall onto
your page
is as easy
as using
an fb:
comments
tag.

Building a Wall post by post

Although the fb:comments element allows you to add a Wall to your page, Facebook handles all the post-entry and other interaction with users through its Wall interface. However, at some point, you may want to have greater control over your Wall and construct the entries yourself. To do so, you can use the fb:wall, fb:wallpost, and fb:wallpost-action elements.

The fb:wall element serves as the Wall container; fb:wallpost, which should be placed inside an fb:wall, outputs a Wall post. Placed inside an fb:wallpost, the fb:wallpost-action tag places an action link at the end of the post. Note that, unlike fb:comments, the fb:title element does not work with fb:wall.

The following code renders a Wall with three posts:

```
<h1>Facebook Wall For Dummies</h1>
<fb:wall>
 <fb:wallpost uid="loggedinuser">Glad you could come today!
   <fb:wallpost-action href="http://apps.facebook.com/dummies/reply.php">Reply
            to <fb:name useyou="false" firstnameonly="true" uid="loggedinuser"
            /></fb:wallpost-action>
 </fb:wallpost>
 <fb:wallpost uid="530377451">Great app. I am telling all my friends.
   <fb:wallpost-action href="http://apps.facebook.com/dummies/reply.php">Reply
            to <fb:name useyou="false" firstnameonly="true" uid="530377451"
            /></fb:wallpost-action>
 </fb:wallpost>
<fb:wallpost uid="685578792">Cool!
   <fb:wallpost-action href="http://apps.facebook.com/dummies/reply.php">Reply
            to <fb:name useyou="false" firstnameonly="true" uid="685578792"
            /></fb:wallpost-action>
 </fb:wallpost>
</fb:wall>
```

Figure 4-6 shows how this Wall is displayed.

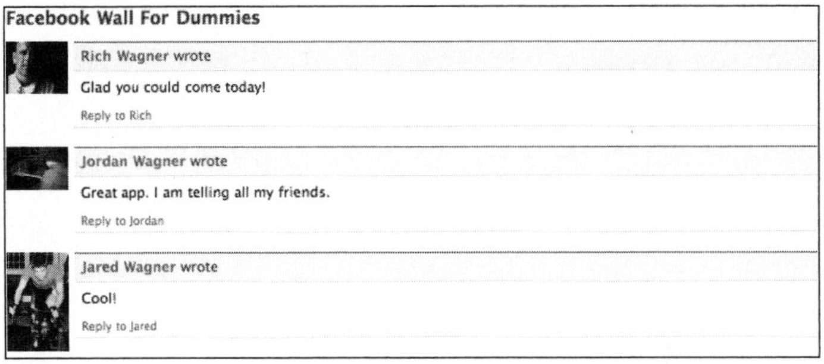

Facebook Wall For Dummies

Rich Wagner wrote

Glad you could come today!

Reply to Rich

Jordan Wagner wrote

Great app. I am telling all my friends.

Reply to Jordan

Jared Wagner wrote

Cool!

Reply to Jared

Figure 4-6:
Create
your own
Wall with
`fb:wall`.

Creating Requests and Invitations

The `fb:request-form` tag is used to display the ubiquitous Facebook request form for sending requests to the friends that the current user specifies. Most everything is packaged up from a UI standpoint, freeing you from re-creating the form and its controls.

Note that users can only invite a total of 20 users per day for a given application using `fb:request-form`.

Building a standard-sized request form

The typical scenario is to use an `fb:request-form` in conjunction with the `fb:multi-friend-selector`, which displays a tabular arrangement of users for users to select from. Consider the following code:

```
<fb:request-form type="invite" content="Would you like to use F8 For Dummies?"
            action="index.php" method="POST" invite="true" >
  <fb:multi-friend-selector showborder="false" actiontext="Invite your friends
            to use F8 For Dummies.">
</fb:request-form>
```

Both the `type` and `content` attributes are required. The `type` attribute contains the type of request you are generating, while `content` is used to define the contents of the request itself. The `content` value is FBML code that contains plain text, links, or the `fb:req-choice` tag.

The `fb:req-choice` element is used to define a button at the bottom of a request on the user's Requests page. It contains two attributes: `label` (the display text on the button) and `url` (an absolute URL that the user will be taken to). When you are working with this attribute value, be sure to encode it. For example, in PHP, you would use the `htmlentities` function:

```
content="Please join today. Don't delay, sign up today.<?php echo
        htmlentities("<fb:req-choice
        url=\"http://apps.facebook.com/dummies//signup.php" label=\"Add F8
        For Dummies\" />"); ?>">
```

Getting back to the `fb:request-form`, the `invite` attribute specifies whether the message is an invitation or a request. The `action` attribute determines the location that the user goes to when he or she is done with the process or has clicked the Skip This Step button.

As I mentioned already, `fb:multi-friend-selector` displays an arranged table of users and profile pictures that the user uses to select the friends for the request. It has several attributes of note:

- ✔ `actiontext` displays the instructional caption at the top of the control. (Required)

- ✔ `showborder` draws a border around the outside of the control.

- ✔ `rows` indicates the number of rows to display at once. (Default is 5.)

- ✔ `max` specifies the maximum number of users that can be selected.

- ✔ `exclude_ids` is an array of user IDs to exclude from the user list.

- ✔ `bypass` specifies the type of the Bypass button — `step` (Skip This Step), `cancel` (Cancel), or `skip` (Skip). (Default is `skip`.)

The POST variables that are returned are an array of user IDs that the user selected.

Consider an example of an application invite. The first step is to gather a list of friends of the current user and then compile these lists of user IDs into an exclusion list. (You never want to send an invitation to someone who already has the app installed!) I use the `friends.getAppUsers` API method for this task:

```
$app_users=$facebook->api_client->friends_getAppUsers();
if ($app_users) {
  for ($i=0;$i<count($app_users); $i++ ) {
    if ($i != 0){
      $exclude_list .= ",";
    }
    $exclude_list .= $app_users[$i]["uid"];
  }
}
```

The remaining code shown here builds a comma-delimited string of user IDs and assigns it to the `$exclude_list` variable.

Next, the FBML content for the invitation needs to be put together. The following code adds basic text as well as the `fb:req-choice` button. All the FBML code is assigned to the `$invite_text` variable:

```
$ref_user = urlencode("&refuid=".$user);
$invite_text = <<<FBML
You've been invited to sign up with the grandest app in FacebookLand: F8 For
            Dummies!
<fb:name uid="$user" firstnameonly="true"/> selfishly wants you to add F8 For
            Dummies! so that <fb:pronoun uid="$user"/> can get credit for it.
<fb:req-choice
            url="http://www.facebook.com/add.php?api_key=$appapikey&next=$ref_
            user" label="Sign up and become a Dummy!" />
FBML;
```

Finally, these variables are then inserted into the `fb:request-form` and `fb:multi-friend-selector` tags:

```
<fb:request-form action="http://apps.facebook.com/dummies//index.php?c=skipped"
            method="POST" invite="true" type="Dummies"
            content="<?=htmlentities($invite_text)?>">
    <fb:multi-friend-selector showborder="false" actiontext="Invite your friends
            to use F8 For Dummies." exclude_ids="<?=$exclude_list?>" />
</fb:request-form>
```

Here's the full source code for the example:

```php
<?php
require_once 'appinclude.php';

// Get a list of friends who are existing users of the app
$app_users=$facebook->api_client->friends_getAppUsers();
if ($app_users) {
  for ($i=0;$i<count($app_users); $i++ ) {
    if ($i != 0){
      $exclude_list .= ",";
    }
    $exclude_list .= $app_users[$i]["uid"];
  }
}

$ref_user = urlencode("&refuid=".$user);
$invite_text = <<<FBML
You've been invited to sign up with the grandest app in FacebookLand: F8 For
            Dummies!
<fb:name uid="$user" firstnameonly="true"/> selfishly wants you to add F8 For
            Dummies! so that <fb:pronoun uid="$user"/> can get credit for it.
```

```
<fb:req-choice
            url="http://www.facebook.com/add.php?api_key=$appapikey&next=$ref_
            user" label="Sign up and become a Dummy!" />
FBML;

?>

<fb:request-form action="http://apps.facebook.com/dummies//index.php?c=skipped"
            method="POST" invite="true" type="Dummies"
            content="<?=htmlentities($invite_text)?>">
    <fb:multi-friend-selector showborder="false" actiontext="Invite your friends
            to use F8 For Dummies." exclude_ids="<?=$exclude_list?>" />
</fb:request-form>
```

Figure 4-7 shows the request form, while Figure 4-8 displays the request message to be sent to the selected users.

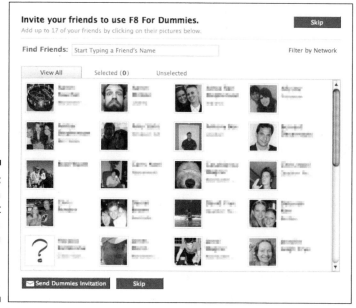

Figure 4-7:
Building a
request
form is a
snap with
`fb:`
`request-`
`form.`

Figure 4-8:
Displaying
the request
message.

Building a condensed request form

You can also use a condensed version (see Figure 4-9) of the `fb:multi-friend-selector` tag by adding a `condensed="true"` attribute value to the `fb:multi-friend-selector` tag. If you use this option, I recommend specifying the width by adding a `style` attribute. For example:

```
<fb:request-form action="http://apps.facebook.com/dummies//index.php?c=skipped"
          method="POST" invite="true" type="Dummies"
          content="<?=htmlentities($invite_text)?>">
  <fb:multi-friend-selector condensed="true" style="width:220px;"
          showborder="false" actiontext="Invite your friends to use F8 For
          Dummies." exclude_ids="<?=$exclude_list?>" />
  <fb:request-form-submit />
</fb:request-form>
```

Figure 4-9:
Displaying
a smaller
version of
the request
form.

Chapter 5

Exploring FQL: Facebook Query Language

Some Web developers love APIs, although others would much prefer to do everything via database queries. API folks like working in their normal language, although query-hounds prefer the efficiency of SQL, the *lingua franca* of the relational database world. If you read Chapter 3, you already know that you can use Facebook API calls to access Facebook data. However, the Facebook Platform also enables you to access the same databases using a query language as well.

In this chapter, you explore Facebook Query Language (FQL) and walk through steps you can take to access Facebook social data in your applications. Along the way, I point out certain technical advantages that FQL has over the API.

Discovering Why SQL + Facebook API = FQL

FQL gives Facebook developers traditional SQL-like access to Facebook databases. SQL stands for Structured Query Language, which is the tried-and-true standard query language for relational database systems. Therefore, if you are used to SQL keywords like SELECT, WHERE, and IN, you will find yourself right at home querying Facebook data with FQL.

Database terminology

If you are new to the world of databases, here's a quick primer to the terminology used. A *database* consists of one or more tables of data.

Much like a spreadsheet, a *table* contains *fields* (columns) that capture different types of info and *records* (rows) of actual data.

Comparing FQL and API access

The data-gathering capabilities of FQL are identical to many of the API calls. (*Psstt,* here's a secret — the API calls are actually wrappers around lower-level FQL calls!) However, before dismissing FQL as redundant, it is important to recognize that FQL does have some notable advantages over API access to Facebook, including the following:

✔ **FQL is more efficient.** When you retrieve data using the API, you bring back all of the field data for a given record. However, with effective use of the SELECT clause in an FQL statement, you can specify only those specific fields you want to have included in the result set. In fact, FQL does not even support selecting all records in a table with SELECT * statements.

✔ **FQL can reduce the number of server requests for complex requests.** When you are retrieving data, you often find yourself making an initial request, working with the results, and then making a second request for more specific information. I show that practice in Chapter 3. For example, suppose I need to get the name and status of all members attending an event. Using the API, I would call events.getMembers to get all members attending a specific event. Next, I would take that array of members and use users.getInfo to get the name and status for each of them. In contrast, with FQL, these two requests can be done inside a single complex query (using the IN clause for a subquery).

✔ **FQL is Web-language neutral.** The Facebook API has several versions, each of which is written for a particular programming language, such as PHP, Java, or Ruby on Rails. Therefore, if you work in multiple programming environments, your Facebook code must be specific to each one. In contrast, because FQL is programming-language independent, you can use the same FQL statements anywhere.

In the end, even if you prefer to spend most of your time working with the API, you may find specific occasions in which you want to take advantage of the efficiency of FQL.

It's a matter of pronunciation

SQL is usually pronounced *ess-que-ell,* though some prefer to call it *sequel.* However, I don't think the same carries over too well in the

Facebook Platform. You should pronounce FQL like *eff-que-ell,* which sounds much more tasteful than the alternative *fequel.*

Making an FQL statement

To make an FQL query, use the `fql.query` API method. Its syntax in PHP looks like this:

```
$result_set = $facebook->api_client->fql_query("SELECT name FROM user WHERE
            uid=665127078");
```

The `fql_query` method sends the FQL query string to Facebook for processing. The results are returned to the PHP client as an array. Note that you can also return results in XML and JSON format as well for other clients. The array result set you'd get back in PHP would be:

```
(
  [0] => Array
    (
      [name] => Rich Wagner
    )
)
```

You can then work with the result set just like you would with an array obtained from a Facebook API call. (See Chapter 3 for complete details on working with result sets.)

Note that because Facebook manages the database connections for you, you do not need to open and close databases as part of your application.

Differences between SQL and FQL

Although FQL is based on SQL syntax, the two are not the same. SQL is designed to be a flexible query language in a variety of contexts. FQL, on the other hand, is a query language for a specific, very targeted data set. Therefore, FQL has some limitations compared to SQL that you need to be aware of, particularly if you already know SQL. These include the following:

✔ SELECT * is not allowed. You need to specify all the fields by name in which you want to include in the result set.

✔ The FROM clause can only include a single table.

✔ At least one field in the WHERE clause must be classified as indexable.

✔ JOIN is not supported (though IN subqueries are).

✔ The GROUPBY, ORDER BY, COUNT, and LIMIT keywords are not supported.

✔ The BETWEEN and LIKE operators are not supported.

✔ Because you have read-only access, you obviously cannot use keywords like UPDATE, DELETE, INSERT INTO, or CREATE TABLE.

Writing a Basic Query

An FQL query has at least three parts to it:

```
SELECT [fields] FROM [table] WHERE [conditions]
```

Take a look at each of the parts:

✔ The SELECT clause lists the fields that you want to include in the result set.

✔ The FROM clause identifies the table in which you want to search. (Table 5-1 lists each of the 16 tables available.)

✔ The WHERE clause specifies the conditions that need to be met to create a match.

As with all FQL keywords, you don't have to capitalize SELECT, FROM, or WHERE. The FQL constructs are case insensitive. However, it is common practice to capitalize keywords to make the query itself more readable.

Table 5-1	Facebook Tables
Table	*Contains Info About*
album	Photo albums
cookies	Cookies
event	Events

Table	Contains Info About
event_member	Invited members of an event
friend	Friends of a user
friend_request	Requests to be friends with current user
friendlist	Friend lists for current user
friendlist_member	Members of a friend list of current user
group	Groups
group_member	Members of a group
listing	Facebook Marketplace listing
page	Facebook pages
page_fan	Fans of a Facebook page
photo	Photos
photo_tag	Photo tags
user	Users

To demonstrate, if you want to return the name of a user whose user ID is 665127078, here's the query:

```
SELECT name FROM user WHERE uid=665127078
```

Using `fql.query`, the results are returned to the calling application in one of three formats. As shown earlier, if you are using PHP, then you'll receive the results as an array. However, if you working with other languages, you can specify the result format as a parameter in the API call (see Chapter 2).

Plain XML displays the following:

```
<?xml version="1.0" encoding="UTF-8"?>
<fql_query_response xmlns="http://api.facebook.com/1.0/"
              xmlns:xsi="http://www.w3.org/2001/XMLSchema-instance"
              list="true">
  <user>
    <name>Rich Wagner</name>
  </user>
</fql_query_response>
```

If you use JSON format, it outputs as

```
[{"name":"Rich Wagner"}]
```

Finally, as I show earlier in the chapter, the array-based output for PHP is

```
Array
(
    [0] => Array
        (
            [name] => Rich Wagner
        )
)
```

Every FQL query must contain at least one field in the WHERE clause that can be classified as indexable. If you specify anything else, you get an error. (I mention this earlier in the section "Differences between SQL and FQL," but let me go into greater detail.) The indexable fields are typically the unique IDs of the table (such as uid or pid). Table 5-2 lists each of the indexable fields for the tables.

Table 5-2	Indexable Fields
Table	**Indexable Fields**
album	aid, cover_pid, owner
cookies	uid
event	eid
event_member	uid, eid
friend	uid1, uid2
friend_request	uid_to
friendlist	owner
friendlist_member	flid
group	gid
group_member	uid, gid
listing	listing_id, poster
page	page_id, name
page_fan	uid
photo	pid, aid
photo_tag	pid, subject
user	uid, name

The reason behind the indexable field requirement is simple. This requirement means that people cannot simply harvest random data (such as all the users with the first name of Reggie) from the Facebook database. You need to have some specific data points (such as a particular user or event) to fetch information.

You can add multiple fields in the SELECT clause simply by separating them with a comma. For example:

```
SELECT name, movies FROM user WHERE uid=665127078
```

This query returns the name and list of favorite movies of the user 665127078.

Changing the field order in the result set

Because you usually reference a piece of data by its field name instead of its field index, the order in which the fields are returned is often less important within the Facebook Platform context. However, using FQL, you can alter the order of the fields based on the order in which you list the fields in your query. For example, the following query returns the name and favorite movie list of a movie fan:

```
SELECT movies, name FROM user WHERE uid=665127078
```

If you are using PHP, the fuller example would look like:

```
$uid = "665127078";
$FQL = "SELECT movies, name FROM user WHERE uid=$uid";

$result_set = $facebook->api_client->fql_query($FQL);

echo "<pre>";
print_r($result_set);
echo "</pre>";
```

Although movies normally appears below the name in the actual user table, the result set switches the order. Here are the XML results:

```
<?xml version="1.0" encoding="UTF-8"?>
<fql_query_response xmlns="http://api.facebook.com/1.0/"
            xmlns:xsi="http://www.w3.org/2001/XMLSchema-instance"
            list="true">
  <user>
    <movies>Casablanca, The Shawshank Redemption, It's A Wonderful Life,
            Babette's Feast, Field of Dreams, Band of Brothers, Chariots of
            Fire, Amélie (Le Fabuleux destin d'Amélie Poulain), Henry V (1989
            version), The Truman Show</movies>
    <name>Rich Wagner</name>
  </user>
</fql_query_response>
```

Or, results using PHP would be as follows:

```
(
    [0] => Array
        (
            [movies] => Casablanca, The Shawshank Redemption, It's A Wonderful
                Life, Babette's Feast, Field of Dreams, Pride & Prejudice (A&E
                Version), Band of Brothers (HBO), Chariots of Fire, Amélie (Le
                Fabuleux destin d'Amélie Poulain), Groundhog Day, Braveheart,
                Princess Bride, Les Miserables (1998 version), Signs, The Lord of
                the Rings trilogy, Benny & Joon, Vertigo, Sense & Sensibility,
                The Count of Monte Cristo, A Little Princess, Double Indemnity,
                Forrest Gump, The Incredibles, The African Queen, Henry V (1989
                version), The Truman Show
            [name] => Rich Wagner
        )

)
```

Dealing with array-type fields

As I discuss in Chapter 2, some of the fields are containers (or arrays) of data. For example, the `event` table has a `venue` field that actually contains six pieces of site-related data, including `city`, `state`, `country`, `latitude`, and `longitude`. You can retrieve the entire venue array with the following statement:

```
SELECT eid, venue FROM event WHERE eid=101022926233
```

However, if you want to retrieve just a single venue-related field, you can use dot notation to reference the *subfield*. For example, if you wanted to just retrieve the city, you could modify the statement as follows:

```
SELECT eid, venue.city FROM event WHERE eid=101022926233
```

Using operators in the WHERE clause

In the examples I have shown so far, the `WHERE` conditions have always used the equal sign to specify the matches, such as this:

```
WHERE pid=12920201292
```

However, FQL allows you to use several other operators to add power to your queries. Consider a scenario in which you want to retrieve all the events of a user 664567292 that have an `eid` of less than or equal to 7630890908. Here's the query:

```
SELECT eid FROM event_member WHERE uid=664567292 AND eid<= 7630890908
```

The `<=` operator is used to retrieve all the `eid`s that are less than or equal to 7630890908. This query also uses the `AND` operator to add a Boolean condition to the statement — ensuring that both conditions are met. Table 5-3 lists all the available operators.

Table 5-3	WHERE Operators
Operator	*Description*
=	Equal to
<>	Not equal to
>	Greater than
>=	Greater than or equal to
<	Less than
<=	Less than or equal to
AND, OR, NOT	Boolean operators
IN	Used to create a subquery when an exact value is known for one of indexable fields

Writing More Complex Queries with the IN Operator

Shakespeare's *Hamlet* may have featured a "play within a play," but that's old school now. Facebook's FQL can top that with its support for "a query within a query." You connect queries with the `IN` clause.

For example, suppose you wanted to retrieve the name and location of all the events attached to a particular Facebook page (8645672921). The problem is that because the `event` table has only `eid` as an indexable field, you cannot use the page ID in a query on the `event` table.

However, the `event_member` table provides the link you are looking for. I can use the following query to retrieve the `eids` that are linked with the page ID:

```
SELECT eid FROM event_member WHERE uid= 8645672921
```

In PHP, the fuller example would be:

```
$uid = "8645672921";
$FQL = "SELECT eid FROM event_member WHERE uid=$uid";

$result_set = $facebook->api_client->fql_query($FQL);

echo "<pre>";
print_r($result_set);
echo "</pre>";
```

Here's the XML output:

```
<event_member>
    <eid>7688563787</eid>
  </event_member>
  <event_member>
    <eid>9542531788</eid>
  </event_member>
  <event_member>
    <eid>9610357779</eid>
  </event_member>
  <event_member>
    <eid>7714358414</eid>
  </event_member>
  <event_member>
    <eid>20803947584</eid>
  </event_member>
  <event_member>
    <eid>9405416779</eid>
  </event_member>
  <event_member>
    <eid>11573937673</eid>
  </event_member>
  <event_member>
    <eid>9374611460</eid>
  </event_member>
  <event_member>
    <eid>7630890908</eid>
  </event_member>
</fql_query_response>
```

The PHP result set would look like:

```
Array
(
    [0] => Array
        (
            [eid] => 7352524755
        )

    [1] => Array
        (
            [eid] => 11501651899
        )

    [2] => Array
        (
            [eid] => 7902052238
        )

    [3] => Array
        (
            [eid] => 8181301283
        )

    [4] => Array
        (
            [eid] => 8071913190
        )

    [5] => Array
        (
            [eid] => 9536366299
        )

    [6] => Array
        (
            [eid] => 8169259038
        )

    [7] => Array
        (
            [eid] => 20951632704
        )

    [8] => Array
        (
            [eid] => 7552445899
        )

    [9] => Array
```

```
            (
                [eid] => 20424183216
            )

        [10] => Array
            (
                [eid] => 7688563787
            )

        [11] => Array
            (
                [eid] => 9542531788
            )

        [12] => Array
            (
                [eid] => 9610357779
            )

        [13] => Array
            (
                [eid] => 7714358414
            )

        [14] => Array
            (
                [eid] => 20803947584
            )

        [15] => Array
            (
                [eid] => 9405416779
            )

        [16] => Array
            (
                [eid] => 11573937673
            )

        [17] => Array
            (
                [eid] => 9374611460
            )

        [18] => Array
            (
                [eid] => 7630890908
            )

        [19] => Array
```

```
            (
                [eid] => 8082232798
            )

    [20] => Array
            (
                [eid] => 9630616527
            )

    [21] => Array
            (
                [eid] => 19725430231
            )

    [22] => Array
            (
                [eid] => 7166054484
            )

    [23] => Array
            (
                [eid] => 7562862350
            )

    [24] => Array
            (
                [eid] => 8068494785
            )

    [25] => Array
            (
                [eid] => 7179584756
            )

    [26] => Array
            (
                [eid] => 8325821164
            )

)
```

Now that you have the eids you need, you must feed each of them back into a query of the event table to retrieve its name and location. Fortunately, this is very easily done using the IN operator, which essentially creates a query within a query.

Continuing with the event example: Here's how you should construct its query using the IN operator:

```
SELECT name, location FROM event WHERE eid IN (SELECT eid FROM event_member
        WHERE uid= 8645672921)
```

Using PHP, the full example code is:

```php
$uid = "8645672921";
$FQL = "SELECT name, location " .
            "FROM event " .
            "WHERE eid " .
        "IN (" .
                "SELECT eid " .
                "FROM event_member " .
                "WHERE uid=$uid" .
            ")";

$result_set = $facebook->api_client->fql_query($FQL);

echo "<pre>";
print_r($result_set);
echo "</pre>";
```

When Facebook evaluates the query, the subquery (the query inside the IN parentheses) is performed first. Next, the outer query is then performed using all the eids returned from the subquery as eid values in the WHERE clause.

When executed, the desired results are now returned:

```xml
<?xml version="1.0" encoding="UTF-8"?>
<fql_query_response xmlns="http://api.facebook.com/1.0/"
            xmlns:xsi="http://www.w3.org/2001/XMLSchema-instance"
            list="true">
  <event>
    <name>Stage 24: Walterboro, SC to Charleston, SC</name>
    <location>Charleston, SC</location>
  </event>
  <event>
    <name>Stage 23: Waynesboro, GA to Walterboro, SC </name>
    <location>Passing through the South</location>
  </event>
  <event>
    <name>Stage 22: Monroe, GA to Waynesboro, GA</name>
    <location>Georgia</location>
  </event>
  <event>
    <name>Stage 21: Chattanooga, TN to Atlanta, GA</name>
    <location>Georgia</location>
  </event>
  <event>
    <name>Stage 20: Murfreesboro, TN to Chattanooga, TN</name>
    <location>Tennessee</location>
  </event>
  <event>
```

```
    <name>Rest Day in Nashville</name>
    <location>Nashville</location>
  </event>
  <event>
    <name>Stage 19: Huntingdon, TN to Nashville, TN</name>
    <location>Tennessee</location>
  </event>
  <event>
    <name>Stage 18: Malden, MO to Huntingdon, TN</name>
    <location>Crossing the Mississippi</location>
  </event>
  <event>
    <name>Stage 17: West Plains, MO to Poplar Bluff, MO</name>
    <location>Missouri</location>
  </event>
</fql_query_response>
```

In PHP, the results are:

```
Array
(
    [0] => Array
        (
            [name] => Stage 24: Walterboro, SC to Charleston, SC
            [location] => Charleston, SC
        )

    [1] => Array
        (
            [name] => Stage 23: Waynesboro, GA to Walterboro, SC
            [location] => Passing through the South
        )

    [2] => Array
        (
            [name] => Stage 22: Monroe, GA to Waynesboro, GA
            [location] => Georgia
        )

    [3] => Array
        (
            [name] => Stage 21: Birmingham, AL to Atlanta, GA
            [location] => Georgia
        )

    [4] => Array
        (
            [name] => Stage 20: Amory, MS to Birmingham, AL
            [location] => Mississippi
```

```
            )

        [5] => Array
            (
                [name] => Rest Day in Little Rock, AR
                [location] => Little Rock, AR
            )

        [6] => Array
            (
                [name] => Stage 19: Helena, AR to Tupelo, MS
                [location] => Mississippi
            )

        [7] => Array
            (
                [name] => Stage 18:  Little Rock, AR to Helena, AR
                [location] => Arkansas
            )

        [8] => Array
            (
                [name] => Stage 17: Fort Smith, AR vicinity to Little Rock, AR
                [location] => Arkansas
            )

        [9] => Array
            (
                [name] => Stage 16: McAlester, OK to Fort Smith, AR
                [location] => Arkansas
            )

        [10] => Array
            (
                [name] => Stage 15: Oklahoma City, OK to McAlester, OK
                [location] => Oklahoma
            )

        [11] => Array
            (
                [name] => Stage 14: Woodward, OK to Oklahoma City, OK
                [location] => Oklahoma
            )

        [12] => Array
            (
                [name] => Stage 13: Guymon, OK to Woodward, OK
                [location] => Oklahoma
            )

        [13] => Array
```

```
        (
            [name] => Stage 12: Clayton, NM to Guymon, OK
            [location] => Oklahoma
        )

[14] => Array
    (
        [name] => Stage 11: Raton, NM to Clayton, NM
        [location] => New Mexico
    )

[15] => Array
    (
        [name] => Rest Day in Denver/Colorado Springs
        [location] => Denver/Colorado Springs
    )

[16] => Array
    (
        [name] => Stage 10: Mount Evans Summit
        [location] => Mountain Springs Church
    )

[17] => Array
    (
        [name] => Stage 9: Buena Vista, CO to Colorado Springs, CO
        [location] => Colorado Springs
    )

[18] => Array
    (
        [name] => Stage 8: Gunnison, CO to Buena Vista, CO
        [location] => Continental Divide
    )

[19] => Array
    (
        [name] => Stage 7: Durango, CO to Ouray, CO
        [location] => Million Dollar Highway
    )

[20] => Array
    (
        [name] => Stage 6: Kayenta, AZ to Four Corners, CO
        [location] => Monument Valley and Arizona
    )

[21] => Array
    (
        [name] => Stage 5: Flagstaff, AZ to Tuba City, AZ
```

```
                        [location] => Arizona
         )

    [22] => Array
         (
             [name] => Rest Day in Prescott, AZ
             [location] => Prescott, AZ
         )

    [23] => Array
         (
             [name] => Stage 4: Prescott, AZ to Flagstaff, AZ
             [location] => Arizona
         )

    [24] => Array
         (
             [name] => Stage 3: Quartzsite, AZ to Prescott, AZ
             [location] => Arizona
         )

    [25] => Array
         (
             [name] => Stage 2: Brawley, CA to Blythe, CA
             [location] => Brawley, CA to Blythe, CA
         )

    [26] => Array
         (
             [name] => Stage 1: Escondido, CA to Brawley, CA
             [location] => Escondido, CA to Brawley, CA
         )

)
```

Take a second example. If you want to get all the first names of friends who have the current application installed, you could use the following statement:

```
SELECT first_name FROM user WHERE has_added_app=1 AND uid IN (SELECT uid2 FROM
             friend WHERE uid1=665127078)
```

In this example, the subquery selects the total list of friends of user 665127078. This array of records is then drawn upon in the first query. All the users pulled from the subquery are checked to see whether they have the current application installed. For all the matches, their first names are output in the result set.

Finally, if you want to get a list of all the pages that a particular user is a fan of, you could use the following query:

```
SELECT name, pic_small, type FROM page WHERE page_id IN (SELECT page_id FROM
             page_fan WHERE uid= 665127078)
```

Once again, the subquery looks for all the page IDs that are associated with the specified user ID. These IDs are then used in the first query to get the page information for each of these matches.

Using Special Functions

FQL supports several in-query functions that you can call to manipulate your result set. These are listed in Table 5-4. You can insert these in the SELECT and WHERE clauses as you list your fields.

Table 5-4	FQL Functions
Function	*Description*
now()	Outputs the current time
rand()	Produces a random number
strlen(str)	Returns the string length
concat(str1, str2,...)	Concatenates the enclosed strings
substr(str, startPosition, length)	Returns a substring of the string
strpos(str, searchStr)	Returns the position of searchStr in str (–1 if not found)
lower(str)	Converts the string to lowercase
upper(str)	Converts the string to uppercase

For example, suppose you want to combine two user fields in the result set into one field:

```
SELECT concat( first_name, ' loves the following movies: ', movies) FROM user
             WHERE uid= 665127078
```

Using this query in a full PHP example, here's the code:

```php
$uid = "665127078";
$FQL = "SELECT concat(first_name, ' loves the following movies: ', movies) " .
         "FROM user " .
         "WHERE uid = $uid";

$result_set = $facebook->api_client->fql_query($FQL);

echo "<pre>";
print_r($result_set);
echo "</pre>";
```

Using the `concat()` function, the `first_name` field is combined with a text string and the `movies` field. The XML results are as follows:

```xml
<?xml version="1.0" encoding="UTF-8"?>
<fql_query_response xmlns="http://api.facebook.com/1.0/"
            xmlns:xsi="http://www.w3.org/2001/XMLSchema-instance"
            list="true">
  <user>
    <anon>Rich loves the following movies: Casablanca, The Shawshank Redemption,
        It's A Wonderful Life, Babette's Feast, Field of Dreams, Pride
        &amp; Prejudice (A&amp;E Version), Band of Brothers (HBO),
        Chariots of Fire, Amélie (Le Fabuleux destin d'Amélie Poulain),
        Groundhog Day, Braveheart, Princess Bride, Les Miserables (1998
        version), Signs, The Lord of the Rings trilogy, Benny &amp; Joon,
        Vertigo, Sense &amp; Sensibility, The Count of Monte Cristo, A
        Little Princess, Double Indemnity, Forrest Gump, The Incredibles,
        The African Queen, Henry V (1989 version), The Truman Show</anon>
  </user>
</fql_query_response>
```

The PHP output is shown below:

```
(
    [0] => Array
        (
            [anon] => Rich loves the following movies: Casablanca, The Shawshank
                Redemption, It's A Wonderful Life, Babette's Feast, Field of
                Dreams, Pride & Prejudice (A&E Version), Band of Brothers (HBO),
                Chariots of Fire, Amélie (Le Fabuleux destin d'Amélie Poulain),
                Groundhog Day, Braveheart, Princess Bride, Les Miserables (1998
                version), Signs, The Lord of the Rings trilogy, Benny & Joon,
                Vertigo, Sense & Sensibility, The Count of Monte Cristo, A Little
                Princess, Double Indemnity, Forrest Gump, The Incredibles, The
                African Queen, Henry V (1989 version), The Truman Show
        )

)
```

JSON derides those attributes

A *derived attribute* is a field in the result set that does not map directly to a single field in the table being queried. Although FQL supports the use of derived attributes through FQL functions, be aware of a major limitation if you are working with JSON format in the output: JSON supports only one derived attribute per query. For example, consider the following dummy query:

```
SELECT "anon1", "anon2", "anon3", name FROM user WHERE uid=665127078
```

When XML is the output format, Facebook delivers the derived attributes, each packaged in an anon element:

```
<?xml version="1.0" encoding="UTF-8"?>
<fql_query_response xmlns="http://api.facebook.com/1.0/"
        xmlns:xsi="http://www.w3.org/2001/XMLSchema-instance" list="true">
  <user>
    <anon>anon1</anon>
    <anon>anon2</anon>
    <anon>anon3</anon>
    <name>Rich Wagner</name>
  </user>
</fql_query_response>
```

In contrast, the following is output using JSON:

```
[{"name":"Rich Wagner","anon":"anon3"}]
```

As you can see, only the last derived attribute is retained.

As you can see, when you use an FQL function in the SELECT clause, you are creating a derived attribute. FQL returns the field content into a field called anon. (See the nearby sidebar "JSON derides those attributes" if you plan to use derived attributes with JSON.)

You can also use functions in the WHERE clause as well. In the following query, I am retrieving all the events of a Facebook page (8645672921) that have the string "Rest Day" in their name fields:

```
SELECT name, location FROM event WHERE strpos(name, "Rest Day") >=0 AND eid IN
        (SELECT eid FROM event_member WHERE uid= 8645672921)
```

Here's an example using PHP:

```
$uid = "8645672921";
$FQL = "SELECT name, location " .
        "FROM event " .
        "WHERE strpos(name, \"Rest Day\") >= 0 " .
            "AND eid IN (" .
                "SELECT eid " .
```

```
                        "FROM event_member " .
                        "WHERE uid = $uid" .
                ")";

$result_set = $facebook->api_client->fql_query($FQL);

echo "<pre>";
print_r($result_set);
echo "</pre>";
```

The result set includes just 3 of the 22 events:

```
<?xml version="1.0" encoding="UTF-8"?>
<fql_query_response xmlns="http://api.facebook.com/1.0/"
                xmlns:xsi="http://www.w3.org/2001/XMLSchema-instance"
                list="true">
  <event>
    <name>Rest Day in Nashville</name>
    <location>Nashville</location>
  </event>
  <event>
    <name>Rest Day in Denver/Colorado Springs</name>
    <location>Denver/Colorado Springs</location>
  </event>
  <event>
    <name>Rest Day in Prescott, AZ</name>
    <location>Prescott, AZ</location>
  </event>
</fql_query_response>
```

In PHP, the result set is:

```
Array
(
    [0] => Array
        (
            [name] => Rest Day in Little Rock, AR
            [location] => Little Rock, AR
        )

    [1] => Array
        (
            [name] => Rest Day in Denver/Colorado Springs
            [location] => Denver/Colorado Springs
        )

    [2] => Array
        (
            [name] => Rest Day in Prescott, AZ
            [location] => Prescott, AZ
        )

)
```

Chapter 6

Scripting with Facebook JavaScript

Not all technology names or acronyms are created equal. Some are legendary — Java and Windows quickly come to mind. Other names, on the other hand, glide from your tongue as awkwardly as a 16-year-old's words on prom night. I would suggest that Facebook's scripting language — FBJS (Facebook JavaScript) fits into that latter category. Both FBML and FQL sound much like their respective counterparts, HTML and SQL. In contrast, not only does FBJS not rhyme with JavaScript, but it is just plain hard to say — *eff-bee-jay-ess.*

Fortunately, you can come up to speed working with FBJS about as quickly as it takes to pronounce the acronym. In this chapter, you explore the basics of FBJS and identify how it differs from standard JavaScript. You also explore FBJS Animation and AJAX to deliver interactive interfaces for your Facebook apps.

Understanding the Facebook Platform Scripting Approach

Although you can use standard JavaScript and AJAX in sandboxed iframe pages to your heart's content, the Facebook Platform places restrictions over the amount of scripting capabilities you can add to the more tightly integrated FBML pages.

When you place scripting code in your pages, Facebook first needs to ensure that your code safely interacts inside the Facebook environment and does not cause any scoping issues (scope is the context in which a JavaScript script executes). As a result, before the FBML page is rendered, Facebook pre-processes the script by parsing through the code and prepending your application ID to the names of your functions and variables to create a private "scripting sandbox" for your app to have fun in. For example, consider the following JavaScript pseudo-code:

```
var counter = 0;
function showHide(activeItem)  {
  if(activeItem) {
    activeItem.className = 'inactiveItem';
    var myId = activeItem.id.replace(/[^\d]/g,'');
  }
  activeItem = this;
  this.className = 'activeItem';
  var myId = this.id.replace(/[^\d]/g,'');
}
```

When it's embedded in an FBML page, Facebook transforms it to

```
var 4f83a8adc579bb26ae5b4630dc9eefb8_counter = 0;
function 4f83a8adc579bb26ae5b4630dc9eefb8_
            showHide(4f83a8adc579bb26ae5b4630dc9eefb8_activeItem)  {
  if(4f83a8adc579bb26ae5b4630dc9eefb8_activeItem) {
    4f83a8adc579bb26ae5b4630dc9eefb8_activeItem.className = 'inactiveItem';
    var 4f83a8adc579bb26ae5b4630dc9eefb8_myId =
            4f83a8adc579bb26ae5b4630dc9eefb8_activeItem.id.replace(/[^\d]/g,''
            );
  }
  4f83a8adc579bb26ae5b4630dc9eefb8_activeItem = this;
  this.className = 'activeItem';
  var 4f83a8adc579bb26ae5b4630dc9eefb8_myId = this.id.replace(/[^\d]/g,'');
}
```

You don't do any of the name transformation yourself. Facebook does it all behind the scenes for you. The advantage to this "scripting sandbox" approach is that it frees you from the need to be careful about breaking Facebook shell functionality as you script away inside your canvas page or profile box.

Accessing the DOM

Although FBJS provides most of the same Document Object Model (DOM)-related methods that you are used to in JavaScript, Facebook's scripting model fundamentally changes the way in which you can access DOM properties.

Instead of accessing properties directly through dot notation, FBJS requires you to call a `get/set` method instead. Therefore, although JavaScript allows

```
custForm=document.getElementById('cust_form');
custForm.action='http://www.richwagnerwords.com/facebook/process.php';
```

in FBJS, you would need to use the `setAction` method instead, like this:

```
custForm=document.getElementById('cust_form');
custForm.setAction('http://www.richwagnerwords.com/facebook/process.php');
```

Table 6-1 lists all the `get/set` methods for accessing DOM properties.

Table 6-1   Get/Set Methods for Accessing DOM Properties

DOM Property	Get	Set
accessKey	getAccessKey	setAccessKey
action	getAction	setAction
checked	getChecked	setChecked
childNodes	getChildNodes	
className	getClassName	setClassName
clientHeight	getClientHeight	
clientWidth	getClientWidth	
cols	getCols	setCols
dir	getDir	setDir
disabled	getDisabled	setDisabled
firstChild	getFirstChild	
form	getForm	
href	getHref	setHref
id	getId	setId
innerFBML		setInnerFBML
innerHTML		setInnerXHTML
innerText/ textContent		setTextValue
lastChild	getLastChild	

(continued)

Table 6-1 *(continued)*

DOM Property	Get	Set
location		setLocation
name	getName	setName
nextSibling	getNextSibling	
offsetHeight	getOffsetHeight	
offsetWidth	getOffsetWidth	
parentNode	getParentNode	
previousSibling	getPreviousSibling	
readOnly	getReadOnly	setReadOnly
rows	getRows	setRows
scrollHeight	getScrollHeight	
scrollLeft	getScrollLeft	setScrollLeft
scrollTop	getScrollTop	setScrollTop
scrollWidth	getScrollWidth	
selected	getSelected	setSelected
selectedIndex	getSelectedIndex	setSelectedIndex
src	getSrc	setSrc
style	getStyle	setStyle
tabIndex	getTabIndex	setTabIndex
tagName	getTagName	
target	getTarget	setTarget
title	getTitle	setTitle
type	getType	setType
value	getValue	setValue
(None)	getAbsoluteTop	
(None)	getAbsoluteLeft	
(None)	getRootElement	

Setting the Content of DOM Elements

For security reasons, FBJS does not permit full access to setting the innerHTML property of a DOM element. However, there are three alternatives that you can use: setInnerXHTML(), setInnerFBML(), and setInnerText().

The next few sections elaborate on these alternatives.

setInnerXHTML ( )

The setInnerXHTML() method is the FBJS equivalent to setting innerHTML. The difference is that the string is preprocessed by Facebook before it renders it. For example, in the following code, an HTML tale is created using the setInnerXHTML method:

```
var friend_div = document.getElementById('friends');
friend_div.setInnerXHTML("<table><tr><th>Name</th><th>Network</th></tr></table>"
            );
```

Facebook makes sure that the content inside of the markup string is safe and then displays the results inside of the friends div element.

setInnerFBML ( )

You can also use the setInnerFBML() method to insert HTML or FBML content into a DOM object. However, this method requires the parameter to be an fb:js-string object, not an ordinary JavaScript string literal or object variable. Here's an example, which renders the name of the profile owner inside of a div:

```
<fb:js-string var="str1"><fb:name uid="profileowner" useyou="true"
            possessive="true" reflexive="true" /></fb:js-string>
<script>
var = friend_div = document.getElementById('friends');
friend_div.setInnerFBML(str1);
</script>
<div id="friends">
</div>
```

The fb:name content is assigned to the str1 variable, which is used in the setInnerFBML call.

setInnerText ( )

If you only need to assign ordinary text and no HTML or FBML markup to your DOM object, you can use the `setInnerText()` method:

```
var friend_div = document.getElementById('friends');
friend_div.setInnerText("We are glad that you have 1,202 friends. But how do you
            keep in touch with all of them?");
<div id="friends">
</div>
```

Note that calling `setInnerText()` deletes any child nodes that were associated with the object.

Setting Styles through FBJS

FBJS allows you to programmatically set the styles of elements using the `setStyle()` method. To define a single style, you can use the following syntax:

```
setStyle(property, value)
```

For example, to set the `margin` property of the `friendDiv` object, you would use

```
friendDiv.setStyle('margin', '0');
```

To define multiple styles, you can use property-value pairs:

```
setStyle( {property1: value1, property2: value2, ...})
```

For example,

```
friendDiv.setStyle({margin: '0', width', '320px'});
```

However, there are caveats to `setStyle()`. First, you need to transform hyphenated style property names into lower camel case — in other words, this sort of syntax — *lowerCamelCase*. To illustrate:

- ✔ `text-align` becomes `textAlign`
- ✔ `font-size` becomes `fontSize`
- ✔ `margin-right` becomes `marginRight`

Second, when setting values, be sure that you always append the unit of measurement to the value. For example:

```
friendDiv.setStyle('lineHeight', '1.7');   //   <-- Bad :(
friendDiv.setStyle('lineHeight', '1.7em'); // <-- Good :)
friendDiv.setStyle('lineHeight', '14px');  // <-- Good :)
```

FBJS allows you to programmatically work with class styles that you have already defined in your code. For example, if you have a `.redTable` class defined in an embedded style sheet, you can associate a DOM element with it by adding an existing a class style:

```
this.addClassName('redTable');
```

Or, to remove a style:

```
this.removeClassName('redTable');
```

To check to see whether a class is assigned to an element, use `hasClassName()`:

```
if (this.hasClassName('redTable')) {
  this.addClassName('shinyRedTable');
}
```

Including External JavaScript Files on Canvas Pages

In addition to inline scripts, you can also include external .js files on canvas pages (although at the time of this book's publication, you could not include them on profile boxes). Using external script files offers two significant benefits. First, using them makes your code easier to manage and maintain in separating the script's "logic layer" from your presentation markup. Second, Facebook caches external script files, minimizing the response time for your application.

You can reference an external .js file just like you do with a normal Web page — via the `script` tag's `src` attribute. For example:

```
<script src="http://www.richwagnerwords.com/facebook/corelib.js"></script>
```

Because it caches the external file content, Facebook puts two reasonable limitations on their usage:

✔ Your limit to the total number of external script files you can include across all of your apps is 1,000. (I know, it will be hard to keep within that limitation, but do your best.)

✔ Though not a likely scenario, do not reference a common script file by using a unique URL for each user. If you do, Facebook ends up caching duplicate instances of the same script.

Helpful Tips When Using FBJS

The following are tips and techniques that you should keep in mind when you work with FBJS:

✔ FBJS events are not processed inside of your app's profile box when the profile itself loads. Instead, your profile box script needs to wait until a user "activates" the box itself — typically by clicking the box and triggering an `onclick` or `onfocus` event.

✔ FBJS supports the `addEventListener` and `removeEventListener` methods for attaching and detaching events. However, the `useCapture` parameter of the `addEventListener` is not supported.

✔ You can create the FBML element `fb:swf` programmatically through the `document.createElement` method. For example:

```
var shockMe = document.createElement('fb:swf');
```

At the time of writing, the `createElement` method can only be used for the Flash/Shockwave element and nothing else.

✔ You can `get`/`set` text selection in form textboxes using `getSelection()` and `setSelection(start, end)`.

✔ Like `setInnerText()`, `setTextValue()` requires a string passed as a parameter and does not perform markup or type conversions.

Using the FBJS Animation Library

As part of its scripting support, Facebook provides application developers an easy way to add animation to their application user interfaces through its FBJS Animation library. You can do several types of animation, including

✔ Tweening CSS attributes of an object

✔ Hide and show block-level elements

✔ Shrink and expand block-level elements

A scripting object called `Animation` is used to perform all of the animations. Animations are achieved by "chaining" together a series of changes that you want to occur within a given animation.

All of the animations for a given call to Animation occur on the same DOM element.

The Animation uses the methods shown in Table 6-2.

Table 6-2	FBJS Animation Methods
Method	*Description*
`to(property, value)`	Defines a stopping point in the animation. You can chain together multiple `to()` methods within a given animation sequence to transform multiple properties of an object.
`go()`	Closes the animation chain and tells the Animation object to begin the animation.
`from(property, value)`	Optionally used to define an initial starting point of the animation. If no `from()` methods are specified, the current property settings are considered the point of origin.
`by(increment)`	Increments a CSS property value by the specified amount.
`duration(timeLength)`	Specifies the amount of time (in milliseconds) in which to perform the animation. (If you do not specify a duration time, the animation lasts for 1,000 ms.)
`ease(easeFunction)`	Changes the ease rate of the animation. Built-in ease functions include `Animation.ease.begin` (slows beginning), `Animation.ease.end` (slows end), `Animation.ease.both` (slows both).
`show()`	Makes a hidden element (`display:none`) visible at the start of an animation.

(continued)

Table 6-2 *(continued)*

Method	Description
`hide()`	Sets the element's style to `display: none` when animation is completed.
`blind()`	Prevents unwanted text wrapping from occurring during an animation of a text container. Use only when the block element starts or ends hidden.
`checkpoint()`	Creates a checkpoint inside of an animation. All steps in the animation chain before the `checkpoint()` call are executed before continuing to the next set of steps. You can add multiple `checkpoints()` in a given animation.

The next few sections explore the different ways in which the FBJS Animation library can be used.

Tweening animation

Tweening is an animation term that refers to the gradual change that takes place between a starting point and ending point of an object. Tweening can refer either to the motion or a state change of an object. A few examples help explain the concept of tweening and how you can achieve it in FBJS.

Suppose you want to increase the font size of an `a` link when it is clicked. Here's the markup code I use:

```
<div id="div1" style="margin: 20px 0 20px 20px; width:400px; height: 300px;
            border: 1px #666666 solid;">

<a href="#" style="margin: 10px 10px 0 10px;"
            onclick="Animation(this).to('fontSize', '34px').go(); return
            false;">Watch me grow with a single click!</a>

</div>
```

The `a` link's `onclick` handler calls the `Animation` object and passes itself (`this`) as the parameter. The `Animation` object knows that all animation operations will be performed on the `a` link. The tweening animation begins with the called object's current CSS attributes. The `to()` method specifies the value of the CSS property at the end of the animation. It uses a property name and value pair as its two parameters:

```
Animation.to(property, value)
```

Got animation?

The FBJS Animation library has made available an open source version that you can use in non-Facebook apps. You can download this version at `developers.facebook.com/` `animation`. Note that the open-source version requires that you run in standards-compliant mode rather than quirks mode.

In the example, the `to()` specifies a stopping point for the animation after the `font-size` property grows to `34px`. The `go()` is added onto the end to tell the `Animation` object that the animation chain is closed. Figures 6-1 and 6-2 show the start and end points of the animation.

Figure 6-1:
Starting
point of
tweening
animation.

Figure 6-2:
Ending point
of tweening.

You can chain together multiple property changes during the same animation by chaining together `to()` methods. In the code that follows, the background color is changed to gray at the same time that the font size grows:

```
<a href="#" style="margin: 10px 10px 0 10px;"
            onclick="Animation(this).to('fontSize',
            '34px').to('backgroundColor', '#333333').go(); return
            false;">Watch me grow and change my background with a single
            click!</a>
```

Figure 6-3 shows the end result of the animation. (The starting point is just like it was back in Figure 6-1.)

Figure 6-3:
Background
and font size
are both
changed
during the
tween
animation.

If I add in a `from()` method to the chain, the animation starts with the property state defined with it and then goes to the ending states of the `to()` methods. For example, in the code below, the link `background-color` initially turns red before the tweening goes to dark gray:

```
<a href="#" style="margin: 10px 10px 0 10px;"
            onclick="Animation(this).to('fontSize',
            '34px').to('backgroundColor', '#333333').from('backgroundColor',
            '#ff0000').go(); return false;">Watch me grow and change my
            background with a single click!</a>
```

When the `from()` method immediately follows a `to()` that references the same CSS property, you can drop the property declaration as a parameter in the `from()` call. Given that, the following two lines are equivalent:

```
// Full declaration
Animation(this).to('backgroundColor', '#333333').from('backgroundColor',
            '#ff0000').go();
```

```
// Shortcut declaration
Animation(this).to('backgroundColor', '#333333').from('#ff0000').go();
```

You can add multiple `from()` methods to the chain to set multiple property states. For example:

```
<a href="#" style="margin: 10px 10px 0 10px;"
           onclick="Animation(this).to('fontSize',
           '34px').from('100px').to('backgroundColor',
           '#333333').from('#ff0000').go(); return false;">Watch me grow and
           change my background with a single click!</a>
```

You can also give the appearance of motion animation by adjusting the positioning of an element. For example, the following example moves the `div` container of the link by adjusting its left and top margin:

```
<div id="div1" style="margin: 20px 0 20px 20px; width:400px; height: 300px;
           border: 1px #666666 solid">

<a href="#" style="margin: 10px 10px 0 10px;"
           onclick="Animation(document.getElementById('div1')).to('marginLeft
           ', '100px').to('marginTop', '200px').go(); return false;">Tween
           me</a>

</div>
```

The animation begins in the same position as that shown in Figure 6-1, but ends one second later in the new position shown in Figure 6-4.

Figure 6-4:
FBJS
Animation
enables you
to move
objects on-
screen.

Adjusting the speed and ease of the animation

You can add the `duration()` method onto the chain if you would like to change the running time of the animation. The following code changes the motion tweening to take place over the course of three seconds:

```
Animation(document.getElementById('div1')).to('marginLeft',
         '100px').to('marginTop', '200px').duration(3000).go();
```

Animations normally transpire at the same rate from start to finish. However, the `ease()` method enables you to speed up or slow down an animation at points within it. The built-in ease functions are as follows:

- ✔ `Animation.ease.begin` starts the animation slowly and ends it quickly.

- ✔ `Animation.ease.end` starts quickly and ends more slowly.

- ✔ `Animation.ease.both` slows down the animation at the beginning and end, but speeds it up during the middle.

The following animation, for example, starts slow and ends at a turbo level:

```
Animation(document.getElementById('div1')).to('marginLeft',
         '100px').to('marginTop', '200px').ease(Animation.ease.begin).go();
```

Adjusting the size and visibility of block-level events

You can use the FBJS Animation library to animate changes to the sizing and visibility of block-level events. To illustrate, say that I have a headline and start of a news story that I display on a canvas page. However, the full text of the story is hidden unless the user clicks a link to show the whole thing. I can animate this process by using a combination of chained methods of the FBJS Animation library.

I begin by setting up the news story text, consisting of h3, p, and div elements:

```
<h3>Captain Amazing Saves the Day</h3>
<p>An amazing boy who refers to himself as "Captain Amazing" singlehandedly
           rescued a dozen firemen when they were trapped in a glue
           factory.</p>
<div id="news" style="display: none">
```

```
<p>Ut sit amet libero. Sed facilisis, tortor vitae aliquam tincidunt, purus nisi
         suscipit dolor, nec egestas elit mi vel augue. Maecenas eget
         nulla. In hac habitasse platea dictumst. Mauris at quam non odio
         nonummy aliquet. Donec sodales fermentum sem. In non magna at
         turpis feugiat tincidunt. Pellentesque habitant morbi tristique
         senectus et netus et malesuada fames ac turpis egestas. Etiam
         rhoncus adipiscing dui. Curabitur fermentum leo in nisi. Praesent
         vulputate, orci sed ultrices venenatis, dolor turpis ultrices
         dolor, vel bibendum dui magna ultricies libero. Suspendisse
         rhoncus dignissim orci. Quisque rutrum.</p>
</div>
```

Notice that the `div` is hidden at the start because its `display` CSS property
is set to `none`.

I can then add an `a` link to the end of the top paragraph that triggers the animation in its `onclick` handler:

```
Animation(document.getElementById('news')).to('height', 'auto').from('height',
         '0px').to('width', 'auto').from('width', '0px').to('opacity',
         1).from('opacity', 0).blind().show().duration(600).go(); return
         false;
```

This animation simultaneously tweens the appearance of the `div` element's
`height`, `width`, and `opacity`. The `height` and `width` properties go from
`0px` to `auto`, enabling it to expand as needed based on its contents. The
`opacity` starts at `0` and then ends at the full value of `1`.

Because the `div` is hidden at the start, I use `blind()` to ensure that the text
wrapping of the `div`'s content is handled automatically by the Animation
object during the animation. Also, I need to use `show()` to toggle the visibility of the hidden `div`.

Here is the full source of the example:

```
<h3>Captain Amazing Saves the Day</h3>
<p>An amazing boy who refers to himself as "Captain Amazing" singlehandedly
         rescued a dozen firemen when they were trapped in a glue factory.
         <a href="#"
         onclick="Animation(document.getElementById('news')).to('height',
         'auto').from('height', '0px').to('width', 'auto').from('width',
         '0px').to('opacity', 1).from('opacity',
         0).blind().show().duration(600).go(); return false;">Read full
         story >></a></p>
<div id="news" style="display: none">
```

```
<p>Ut sit amet libero. Sed facilisis, tortor vitae aliquam tincidunt, purus nisi
          suscipit dolor, nec egestas elit mi vel augue. Maecenas eget
          nulla. In hac habitasse platea dictumst. Mauris at quam non odio
          nonummy aliquet. Donec sodales fermentum sem. In non magna at
          turpis feugiat tincidunt. Pellentesque habitant morbi tristique
          senectus et netus et malesuada fames ac turpis egestas. Etiam
          rhoncus adipiscing dui. Curabitur fermentum leo in nisi. Praesent
          vulputate, orci sed ultrices venenatis, dolor turpis ultrices
          dolor, vel bibendum dui magna ultricies libero. Suspendisse
          rhoncus dignissim orci. Quisque rutrum.</p>
</div>
```

You can also animate hiding a block-level element on your page. Suppose, for example, you decide to add an advertisement to your Facebook application, but in an act of unimaginable compassion to your users, you allow them to hide the ad. But instead of just making it disappear, you would like the ad to disappear on one last blaze of animated glory. Here's the basic `div`-based ad (shown in Figure 6-5):

```
<div id="ad" style="border: 1px #999999 solid; width: 160px; margin: 30px;" >
<a href="http://freeringtoneswethink.com"><h3>Hail to Your Cell Phone</h3></a>
<img src="http://www.richwagnerwords.com/facebook/phone.jpg" /><br />
<p>Download your free, 12-minute long ring tone of <em>Hail to the Chief</em>,
          one of the most super amazing deals you have ever encountered on
          the web. With each new call, you too can feel as important and
          powerful as the President.</p>
<a href="#">Hide this ad</a>
</div>
```

Figure 6-5:
Basic ad
before
animation.

An `onclick` event handler for the link is, once again, used to trigger the animation:

```
<a href="#" onclick="Animation(document.getElementById('ad')).to('height',
        '0px').to('width', '0px').to('opacity',
        0).blind().hide().duration(3000).go(); return false;">Hide this
        ad</a>
```

The animation begins at the default state of the `div` and then gradually (over a three-second time span) tweens the `height`, `width`, and `opacity` properties (see Figure 6-6). The `hide()` method is used to set the `display` CSS property to `none` at the end of the animation (see Figure 6-7).

Figure 6-6:
Disappearing ad in the middle of animation.

Figure 6-7:
Now you see it, now you don't.

Working with AJAX in FBJS

AJAX, which stands for Asynchronous JavaScript and XML, is the capability of including content in a Web page in a way in which JavaScript obtains data from the server and displays it without refreshing the entire page. FBJS provides an AJAX object that enables you to add AJAX capabilities to your Facebook applications.

Table 6-3 displays the members of the FBJS implementation of the AJAX object.

Table 6-3	FBJS AJAX Object Members	
Member	*Type*	*Description*
requireLogin	Property	Specifies whether the user needs to be logged into your app before an AJAX call is made.
responseType	Property	Indicates the response type (Ajax.RAW, Ajax.JSON, or Ajax.FBML).
useLocalProxy	Property	Specifies whether to use fb:local-proxy to call your server. (Valid for RAW and JSON response types.) (In beta at the time of writing.)
Ajax.RAW	Property	Server response in its native unprocessed state.
Ajax.JSON	Property	Server response converted into a JSON object.
Ajax.FBML	Property	Server response returned as FBML content.
post(url, query)	Method	Initiates an AJAX post.
abort()	Method	Halts an AJAX post.
ondone(data)	Event	Event handler that is triggered when the AJAX call returns. The format of data depends on the responseType property.
onerror	Event	Event handler that is called if a problem occurs in the middle of an AJAX operation.

Consider the following PHP-based example, which demonstrates how you can use the FBJS version of AJAX in your Facebook apps. The purpose of this example is to provide dynamic feedback to the users based on the link that they click on in the canvas page.

To begin, I start with basic FBML content for the page:

```
<div style="margin:10px;">

<h1>Your Customer Survey Is Now Complete</h1>
```

```
<p>Thanks for taking our free customer survey! Your input will help us make a
          better application and sell more ads to bombard you with. Your
          survey was completed in only 3hr. 47min, which is 7% less time
          than the average time most high schoolers take to finish their
          SAT tests.</p>

<p><fb:name uid="<?=$user?>" firstname="true" useyou="false"/>, as a token of
          appreciation for taking our brief survey, which of the following
          complimentary gifts would you like to receive today?</p>

<ul>
<li>I want a <a href="#">free mobile phone</a>.</li>
<li>I want a <a href="#">brand new 2008 SUV</a>.</li>
<li>I want a <a href="#">free unleaded pencil</a>.</li>
</ul>

<div id="userchoice" style="border:1px #666666 solid; padding: 5px; margin:
          30px;">Make your selection please before continuing.</div><br/>

</div>
```

When the user clicks on one of the three list items, I use AJAX to fill in a
response in the `userchoice div`.

The next step is to define the FBJS function that performs the AJAX functionality. Here's the code:

```
<script type="text/javascript">
function updateUi(elem, value) {

  // Create ajax object and set initial properties
  var ajax = new Ajax();
  ajax.responseType = Ajax.FBML;
  ajax.requireLogin = 1;

  // Event handler is triggered when a response is received from $callbackurl
  ajax.ondone = function(response) {
      document.getElementById(elem).setInnerFBML(response);
  }

  // params value to be passed to $callbackurl
  var params={"action": 'userchoice', "option": value};

  // Call server with the supplied params
  ajax.post('<?=$callbackurl?>', params);
}

</script>
```

After defining the `ajax` object and assigning properties, the `ondone` handler
is set. This function, called when the server responds to the AJAX request,

updates the FBML content of the specified DOM element. The `ajax.post()` method makes a request to the specified URL, passing along parameters that I now connect to an a element that the user clicks. To do so, I add event `onclick` handlers to these links, each of which calls the `updateUi()` function:

```
<li>I want a <a href="#" onclick="updateUi('userchoice','mobile phone');return
        false;">free mobile phone</a>.</li>
<li>I want a <a href="#" onclick="updateUi('userchoice','gas guzzler');return
        false;">brand new 2008 SUV</a>.</li>
<li>I want a <a href="#" onclick="updateUi('userchoice','pencil');return
        false;">free unleaded pencil</a>.</li>
```

Finally, I need to add a PHP-based handler for the AJAX request at the start of my `callback.php` file:

```
$callbackurl='http://www.richwagnerwords.com/facebook/ajaxexample.php';

if (isset($_REQUEST['action'])) {

 if ($_REQUEST['option'] != 'pencil' ) {
   echo "Why in the world did you select a ".$_REQUEST['option']."? Try again.";
 }
 else {
   echo "Wise choice. You may <a
       href='http://www.richwagnerwords.com/facebook//prize.php'>continue.</a>";
 }
 exit;
}
```

Listing 6-1 shows the full source for this sample.

Listing 6-1: ajaxexample.php.

```
<?php

$callbackurl='http://www.richwagnerwords.com/facebook/ajaxexample.php';


// ********* Start of AJAX Response Handler *********
// Gets called when $callbackurl is requested
if (isset($_REQUEST['action'])) {

 if ($_REQUEST['option'] != 'pencil' ) {
   echo "Why in the world did you select a ".$_REQUEST['option']."? Try again.";
 }
 else {
```

```
    echo "Wise choice. You may <a
            href='http://www.richwagnerwords.com/facebook/prize.php'>continue.
            </a>";
 }
 exit;
}
// ********* End of AJAX Response Handler **********

// If placed after the AJAX request, then login is required
require_once('appinclude.php');
?>

<div style="margin:10px;">

<h1>Your Customer Survey Is Now Complete</h1>

<p>Thanks for taking our free customer survey! Your input will help us make a
            better application and sell more ads to bombard you with. Your
            survey was completed in only 3hr. 47min, which is 7% less time
            than the average time most high schoolers take to finish their
            SAT tests.</p>

<p><fb:name uid="<?=$user?>" firstname="true" useyou="false"/>, as a token of
            appreciation for taking our brief survey, which of the following
            complimentary gifts would you like to receive today?</p>

<ul>
<li>I want a <a href="#" onclick="updateUi('userchoice','mobile phone');return
            false;">free mobile phone</a>.</li>
<li>I want a <a href="#" onclick="updateUi('userchoice','gas guzzler');return
            false;">brand new 2008 SUV</a>.</li>
<li>I want a <a href="#" onclick="updateUi('userchoice','pencil');return
            false;">free unleaded pencil</a>.</li>
</ul>

<div id="userchoice" style="border:1px #666666 solid; padding: 5px; margin:
            30px;">Make your selection please before continuing.</div><br/>

</div>

<script type="text/javascript">

function updateUi(elem, value) {

  // Create ajax object and set initial properties
  var ajax = new Ajax();
  ajax.responseType = Ajax.FBML;
  ajax.requireLogin = 1;
```

(continued)

Listing 6-1 *(continued)*

```
    // Event handler is triggered when a response is received from $callbackurl
    ajax.ondone = function(response) {

    document.getElementById(elem).setInnerFBML(response);
    }
      // params value to be passed to $callbackurl
    var params={"action": 'userchoice', "option": value};

    // Call server with the supplied params
    ajax.post('<?=$callbackurl?>', params);
}

</script>
```

Figure 6-8 shows the initial FBML canvas page. When users click either of the first two options, their response is, shall we say, rejected (see Figure 6-9). When users reluctantly decide on the pencil, they can continue (Figure 6-10).

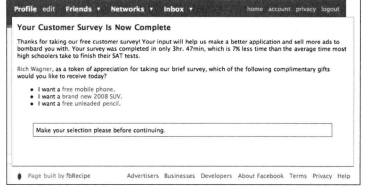

Figure 6-8: This innocent-looking FBJS canvas page . . .

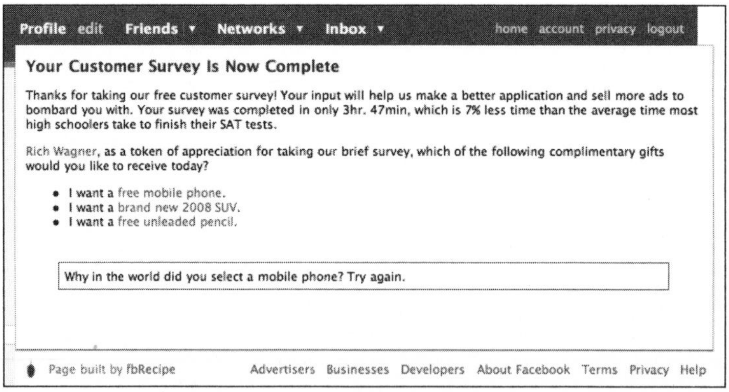

Figure 6-9: . . . hides an under-handed use of AJAX.

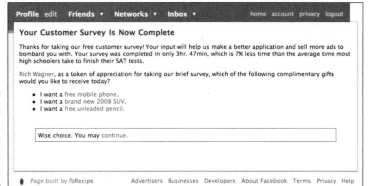

Figure 6-10:
A free
pencil is
better than
nothing.

Chapter 7

"Goin' API" with Facebook Developer Tools

. . . .

. . . .

Ask an experienced carpenter about a set of tools he recommends, and chances are good that you will get a passionate, opinionated response. After all, he spends hundreds of hours a year working with his tools; they become an extension of who he is as a professional craftsman. He doesn't want to simply use just any set of tools.

In the same way, experienced Web developers have an editor and a set of development tools that they are every bit as passionate about as the carpenter is of his table saw. These software tools enable the developer to get the job done quickly, efficiently, and with fewer bugs.

Facebook had this thought in mind when it came to the release of the Facebook Platform — providing not just the extensions developers need, but also the testing tools they need to make their apps work. You can use these tools to quickly discover and test API functionality outside of an application.

The suite includes the following tools:

> ✔ **API Test Console:** Use to make test calls to the Facebook API outside of your app.

> ✔ **FBML Test Console:** Use to test out FBML markup code.

> ✔ **Feed Preview Console:** Use the Feed Preview to see exactly how the feed story looks prior to actually sending it out.

Additionally, Firebug, a third-party script debugger (available at `www.get firebug.com`), is used for debugging Facebook JavaScript (FBJS). The following sections discuss all of these in greater detail.

Working with the API Test Console

The API Test Console (see Figure 7-1) is used to interact with the main Facebook programming interface. You can use it to call any of the available methods. To display this console, go to `http://developers.facebook.com/tools.php?api`.

The input boxes are provided on the left side of the page, and the raw results of the call are provided in the box on the right. Here are the main inputs:

- The User ID field displays the user ID of the currently logged-in user (you). This is a read-only field.

- The Application drop-down box displays a list of your applications and the Test Console. The results of the call are always displayed in the right-side box, regardless of the Application value. However, this box is useful when you are testing application-specific methods (such as `users.isAppAdded`).

- The Response Format drop-down list enables you to toggle among the three output formats: XML, JSON, and Facebook PHP Client.

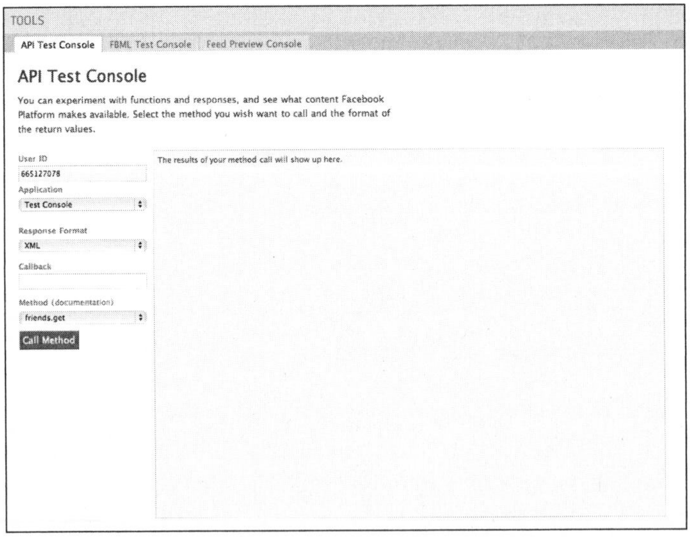

Figure 7-1:
The API Test
Console.

✔ The Callback field enables you to specify a JSONP callback function. (JSONP allows you to define a function in your application to handle the results of the Facebook API call.)

✔ The Method drop-down box lists each of the methods available.

The User ID, Application, Response Format, Callback, and Method boxes are displayed for every method. If the method has additional parameters, they are displayed below the Method drop-down list box. For example, although the `friends.get` method (see Figure 7-1) needs no additional parameters, `pages.getInfo` provides input for four (see Figure 7-2).

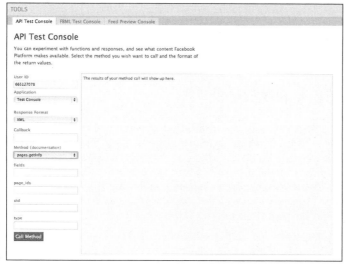

Figure 7-2: Parameter values are specified using the input boxes.

Using the API Test Console, suppose you want to check and see whether two users are friends. To do so, you can select `friends.areFriends` from the Method drop-down box. The `uid1` and `uid2` parameter boxes are displayed below the Method. Enter two user IDs in these boxes and click the Call Method button.

The XML results are displayed in the output box, as shown in Figure 7-3. You can switch the Response Format value to display the result in JSON or Facebook PHP Client.

See Chapter 3 for full details on how to work with the Facebook API.

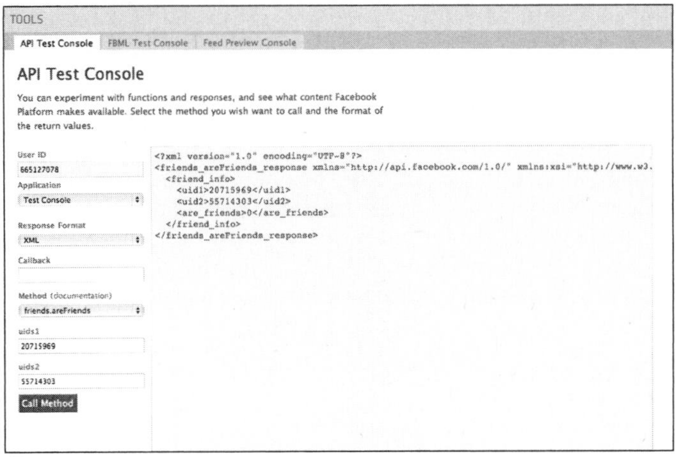

Figure 7-3:
Displaying
the results
of a method
call in the
API Test
Console.

FBML Test Console

The FBML Test Console is a utility that you can use to enter Facebook Markup Language (FBML) markup code in a code box and then instantly see the results displayed in a preview box along with the HTML code that is generated. Perhaps most significant is that the console allows you to render results in any of the possible output contexts, including the following:

- ✔ Profile box (wide or narrow)
- ✔ Canvas
- ✔ E-mail
- ✔ Notification
- ✔ Request
- ✔ Feed (title or body)
- ✔ Mobile device

To display the FBML Test Console, go to http://developers.facebook.com/tools.php?fbml. Figure 7-4 shows the console.

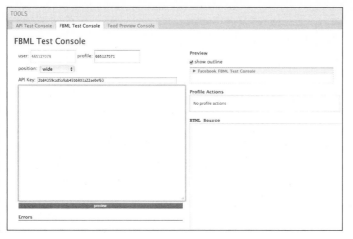

Figure 7-4:
The FBML
Test
Console is
the official
play area
for FBML
coders.

Several input controls are available:

- ✔ The User field displays your user ID. This entry is read-only.

- ✔ The Profile field displays the profile content in which the FBML code will be rendered. By default, the current user ID is displayed. However, you can adjust this value.

- ✔ The Position field allows you to specify the output of your code: wide (profile box), narrow (profile box), canvas, e-mail, notification, request, feed title, feed body, or mobile.

- ✔ The API Key field is used to display an application API key. By default, it displays the API key for the Test Console. However, you can add the API key of your application.

- ✔ The box below the API Key field is used to enter FBML markup code.

After you have entered information in these spaces, click the Preview button to render the results. Figure 7-5 displays the output of a wide profile box.

Using the FBML Test Console helps you identify potential problems in your code before you put it into your application. For example, Figure 7-6 displays FBML markup code that produces an error when you try to render in a profile box.

Figure 7-5:
Testing the
FBML code.

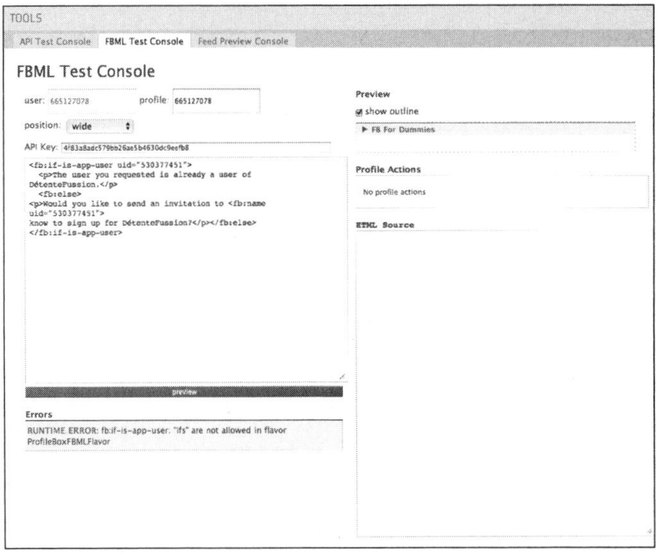

Figure 7-6:
`fb:if-*`
tags are not
allowed
in profile
boxes.

However, running the same code on a canvas page works fine, as shown in
Figure 7-7.

TOOLS

API Test Console   FBML Test Console   Feed Preview Console

FBML Test Console

user: 665127078   profile: 665127078

position: canvas

API Key: 4f83a8adc579bb26ae5b4630dc9eefb8

```
<fb:if-is-app-user uid="530377451">
  <p>The user you requested is already a user of
DétenteFussion.</p>
  <fb:else>
<p>Would you like to send an invitation to <fb:name
uid="530377451'/>
now to sign up for DétenteFussion?</p></fb:else>
</fb:if-is-app-user>
```

preview

Errors

Preview

☑ show outline

Would you like to send an invitation to Jordan Wagner

Profile Actions

No profile actions

HTML Source

```
<p>Would you like to send an invitation to <a
href="http://hs.facebook.com/profile.php?id=530377451"
onclick="(new Image()).src = '/ajax/ct.php?
app_id=6349917903&action_type=3&post_form_id=d7336354fb7eb127
024d64d0cbe3b0b7&position=3&' + Math.random();return
true;">Jordan Wagner</a></p>
```

Figure 7-7:
But
`fb:if-*`
tags work
fine when
rendered
on canvas
pages.

See Chapter 4 for full details on how to use FBML.

Feed Preview Console

Stories published using the `feed.publishTemplatizedAction` method
are an important part of any application to test thoroughly before you go live,
because you communicate with dozens or maybe even thousands of people
in the process. The Feed Preview Console allows you to experiment and preview a Mini-Feed story as well as the News Feed story that appears in the
friends of the user.

Go to http://developers.facebook.com/tools.php?feed to display the
Feed Preview Console, as shown in Figure 7-8.

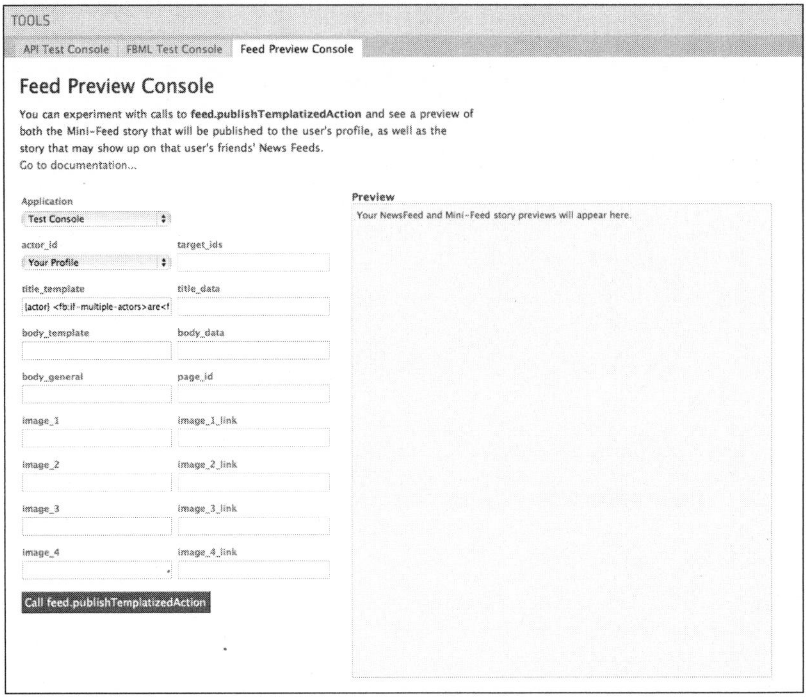

Figure 7-8:
The Feed
Preview
Console.

Several input fields are available, and most correspond to the parameters of `feed.publishTemplatizedAction`, as follows:

- The Application drop-down box displays the active application — either the Test Console or one of your applications.

- The Actor_id field allows you to select the user or page in which you would like to publish the Mini-Feed story.

- The Target_ids field is used to enter one or more user IDs that are directly linked to the story. (Normally optional, but required if you use `{target}` in the Title_template or Body_template field).

- The Title_template field contains the FBML markup that is used as the title for the story. The `{actor}` token must be included in this markup. Optionally, you can also add your own tokens and then associate values using the Title_data parameter (see the next bullet). This parameter is required.

- The Title_data field is used to display a JSON associative array (grouped in *token:substitution* pairs) that you want to have substituted into the Title_template field. (The array cannot substitute for `{actor}` and `{target}`.)

✔ The Body_template field contains the FBML markup for the story's body.

✔ The Body_data field, much like the Title_data field, contains a JSON associative array of values that you want to substitute into the Body_template field.

✔ The Body_general field provides additional markup to be displayed in the story's body.

✔ The Page_id field is used to specify a page ID when publishing to a Facebook page that has the app installed.

✔ The Image_*x* and Image_*x*_link fields provide a way to enter up to four images or image links.

After the story has been composed in these various fields, you can click the Call feed.publishTemplatizedAction button to preview both the News Feed and Mini-Feed stories in the Preview window. Figure 7-9 shows an example.

See Chapter 11 for more details on how to work with the `feed.publishTemplatizedAction` API call.

TOOLS

API Test Console | FBML Test Console | Feed Preview Console

Feed Preview Console

You can experiment with calls to **feed.publishTemplatizedAction** and see a preview of both the Mini-Feed story that will be published to the user's profile, as well as the story that may show up on that user's friends' News Feeds.
Go to documentation...

Application
[Test Console ⬦]

| actor_id | target_ids |
| [Your Profile ⬦] | 685578792 |

title_template | title_data
[actor] is a going to bike across the |

body_template | body_data
[actor] and [target] are going to ride |

body_general | page_id

image_1 | image_1_link

image_2 | image_2_link

image_3 | image_3_link

image_4 | image_4_link

[Call feed.publishTemplatizedAction]

Other actors (comma separated)

[Simulate aggregated story]

Preview

News Feed story

☐ Rich Wagner is a going to bike across the country with Jared Wagner.

Rich Wagner and Jared Wagner are going to ride from San Diego, CA to Charleston, SC this summer. Wanna come along?

Mini-Feed story

☐ Rich is a going to bike across the country with Jared Wagner.

Rich and Jared Wagner are going to ride from San Diego, CA to Charleston, SC this summer. Wanna come along?

Figure 7-9:
Previewing stories in the Feed Preview Console.

Debugging FBJS with Firebug

Although Facebook does not have an integrated testing console for FBJS, you can debug your FBJS code using Firebug, the popular JavaScript debugger that integrates with your Firefox browser. However, unlike the other experimental consoles, you need to work with your application files on your server.

Before continuing, go to `www.getfirebug.com` and download a free copy of Firebug. You must be using Firefox to download and install it.

After you have installed Firebug, you can activate it from the Firebox Tools menu (choose Tools➪Firebug➪Open Firebug). When you open your application, you can then debug the FBJS code by clicking Firebug's Script tab. You can set breakpoints and watch variables as you refine your Facebook JavaScript code. See Figure 7-10.

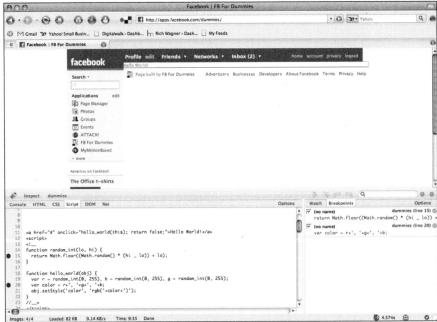

Figure 7-10: Firebug debugger tracks down FBJS bugs.

Part III
Developing Facebook Applications

The 5th Wave   By Rich Tennant

"Are you using that 'clone' app again?!"

In this part . . .

*N*ow that the introductions are over, it's time to apply what you learned. In this part, you are ready to dive into the key design, coding, and session management principles and techniques that you need to know to successfully code and deploy a Facebook application.

Chapter 8

Developing Facebook Canvas Pages

A Facebook page can be divided into three rectangular blocks — the top-most menu bar, the left sidebar, and the remaining frame known as the canvas page. Most all the interaction in Facebook takes place on the canvas page. When you view a profile, the profile shows up there. Or, when you run a Facebook app, it is presented inside the canvas page.

Although you cannot customize the menu bar or sidebar, you have free reign to do most anything you want inside the canvas page. From a technology perspective, you can either implement the canvas page using FBML or present an external Web site inside an iframe. (An *iframe*, or inline frame, is an element enabling you to embed another HTML page inside the main document.)

In this chapter, you explore how to work with and add an FBML framework to your canvas pages.

To FBML or iframe? That Is the Question

One of the strategic decisions that you need to make when you create your Facebook application is deciding whether to use FBML or an iframe for your canvas page. The issue is more than just an implementation detail. In fact, it gets to the heart of the goals for your application.

FBML embraces the Facebook Platform and enables your application to become part of Facebook itself. iframes, on the other hand, enable your Web application to function inside Facebook without coding an interface that works only inside a single context (Facebook).

The reasons for using FBML include the following:

- ✔ **Has a consistent look and feel:** When you use FBML, your application styles and controls automatically take on a Facebook look and feel, making it look identical to other Facebook apps. This consistency reduces the learning curve for your users and gives them instant familiarity and comfort with their surroundings.

- ✔ **Uses FBML elements:** FBML is filled with several tags, controls, and "widgets" that enable you to develop a rich app interface in minimal time.

  Want to add a dashboard navigation menu? With FBML, you simply need to add an `fb:dashboard` tag. With iframes, you need to code and style it all yourself.

- ✔ **May offer improved performance:** Facebook claims that performance is improved when you use FBML. However, that claim probably depends on the specifics of an application and is not necessarily a blanket statement.

On the other hand, reasons you should consider using an iframe approach include the following:

- ✔ **Enables existing apps to get up and running quicker:** If you have an existing Web app, you usually need to do very little to integrate into Facebook using an iframe approach. Your application can perform, more or less, as is within the confines of the iframe. If you port to FBML, you are going to have to rework a lot of the presentation code.

- ✔ **Makes it easier to maintain a common code base:** When you use FBML, you will probably need to branch your code base so that you can maintain a Facebook version, a stand-alone version, and perhaps a version that fits into another network, such as Bebo or OpenSocial. However, if you use an iframe approach, you will not need to replace more generic HTML with Facebook-specific FBML.

   Having said that, if you are going to integrate into various social networking environments, you need to be realistic. Some platform-specific presentation code must be performed, regardless of whether you use FBML. Therefore, the iframe approach is not necessarily a cure-all for portability.

- ✔ **Avoids JavaScript limitations:** The Facebook Platform does provide scripting support, but it is more restrictive than a native HTML environment. As a result, with iframes, you are not bound to the same restrictions for using JavaScript as you would be using FBML.

The decision you make will depend on your circumstances. But, if you are focused primarily on creating an app for the Facebook Platform, I highly recommend using FBML. (For more on working with iframe-based pages, see Chapter 10.)

Adding a Navigation Header Using FBML

When you browse the Facebook application directory, you get a variety of navigation headers, depending on whether the app takes an FBML or iframe approach as well as the extent to which the developer cared to emulate the Facebook environment. For example, consider the typical style of a Facebook app, such as Photos, as shown in Figure 8-1.

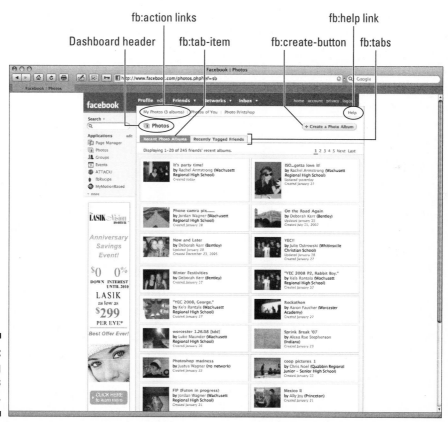

Figure 8-1: Navigating with Photos app.

However, although all Facebook apps fit inside the canvas area of the page, not all will model their navigation on the Facebook style. TripAdvisor's Local Picks app is one such example that uses an iframe approach and has a different look and feel for its navigation header (see Figure 8-2).

Other third-party apps aim to follow the Facebook approach using FBML tags, such as the CDs app (such as Figure 8-3), which essentially uses the same navigation controls as does Photos.

In the following sections, I walk you through creating a navigation header that emulates the Facebook look and feel.

Figure 8-2:
Local Picks app does not emulate the Facebook UI.

Figure 8-3:
CDs looks
like it could
be a built-in
Facebook
app.

Adding an fb:dashboard element

With FBML, you can add a Facebook navigation header to your application using a combination of FBML elements, including `fb:dashboard`, `fb:action`, `fb:create-button`, `fb:help`, `fb:tabs`, and `fb:tab-item`.

For example, suppose you want to create a new recipe application called fbRecipe. The structure for the application can include the following:

- ✔ Browsing sections for dinners, desserts, and appetizers
- ✔ Quick access to users' and friends' recipes
- ✔ A quick link to an online store for spices and other cooking ingredients
- ✔ A recipe discussion page
- ✔ A link to the app's About page

Following the Facebook conventions, I begin by adding an `fb:dashboard` element:

```
<fb:dashboard>
</fb:dashboard>
```

The `fb:dashboard` tag is used to render a dashboard header, which displays the title and icon of the application. It also serves as a container for any `fb:action`, `fb:create-button`, and `fb:help` tags you want to place on the page. In this example, I want to begin by placing three `fb:action` tags for the recipe and shopping links inside the dashboard container:

```
<fb:dashboard>
  <fb:action href="http://apps.facebook.com/dummies/myrecipes.php">My
          Recipes</fb:action>
  <fb:action href="http://apps.facebook.com/dummies/friends.php">Friends'
          Recipes</fb:action>
  <fb:action href="http://apps.facebook.com/dummies/shop.php">Shop for
          Ingredients</fb:action>
</fb:dashboard>
```

The `fb:action` element defines a link inside an `fb:dashboard` or a profile box's `fb:subtitle`. These will be placed above the application title, just below the Facebook top menu bar.

Next, the `fb:create-button` offers a highly visible way of performing the most common action in the app. In this case, adding a new recipe is the best candidate. I add the following inside the dashboard:

```
<fb:create-button
 href="http://apps.facebook.com/dummies/add.php">Add a new
 recipe</fb:create-button>
```

I add a Help link to provide quick access for users to get application assistance:

```
<fb:help href="http://apps.facebook.com/dummies/help.php">Help</fb:help>
```

Here's the completed dashboard code:

```
<fb:dashboard>
  <fb:action href="http://apps.facebook.com/dummies/myrecipes.php">My
          Recipes</fb:action>
  <fb:action href="http://apps.facebook.com/dummies/friends.php">Friends'
          Recipes</fb:action>
  <fb:action href="http://apps.facebook.com/dummies/shop.php">Shop for
          Ingredients</fb:action>
  <fb:help href="http://apps.facebook.com/dummies/help.php">Help</fb:help>
          <fb:create-button
           href="http://apps.facebook.com/dummies/add.php">Add a new
           recipe</fb:create-button>
</fb:dashboard>
```

Figure 8-4 shows the initial page with some dummy text, and Figure 8-5 displays the page with the dashboard header added.

Figure 8-4: Starter page.

Figure 8-5: fbRecipe's dashboard.

The `fb:dashboard` element does not enable you to customize the display of the application title and icon in the header. If you want greater flexibility, use the `fb:header` element (discussed in the section "Adding a header with fb:header," later in this chapter).

Adding a tab set with fb:tabs and fb:tab-item

A tab set is commonly used as a primary navigation device for applications with multiple views or modules. According to Facebook norms, tabs are placed underneath the dashboard header. In the fbRecipe app, I want to add several tabs, such as the home page and listings of dinners, desserts, and appetizers. I also want to add tabs for a discussion board and for the app's About page. To do so, I first add an `fb:tabs` element to serve as a container for the tabs:

```
<fb:tabs>
</fb:tabs>
```

Note that the order in which you place FBML tags in your source code generally dictates the display order. Therefore, if you place the `fb:tabs` element above `fb:dashboard`, the tab set will appear above the dashboard.

Each tab is added to the tab set using an `fb:tab-item` tag. It contains four attributes:

- `href`: Specifies the URL to link to (required).
- `title`: Declares the text to be displayed on the tab (required).
- `selected`: Indicates whether this tab is the active or selected tab in the set. If multiple tabs have `selected="true"`, Facebook chooses the first encountered and ignores the rest. (Optional; default is `false`.)
- `align`: Enables you to specify the left or right alignment of a tab. This attribute comes in handy when you want to place tabs on the right side of the page. (Optional; default is `left`.)

The first four are left-aligned, with the home page being the selected tab:

```
<fb:tabs>
   <fb:tab-item href='http://apps.facebook.com/dummies/index.php' title='Home'
            selected='true'/>
   <fb:tab-item href='http://apps.facebook.com/dummies/dinners.php'
            title='Dinners' />
   <fb:tab-item href='http://apps.facebook.com/dummies/desserts.php'
            title='Desserts'/>
   <fb:tab-item href='http://apps.facebook.com/dummies/apps.php'
            title='Appetizers'/>
</fb:tabs>
```

I'd like to right-align the final two tabs (using the `align="right"` attribute-value pair) to visually offset these from the other tabs:

```
<fb:tabs>
   <fb:tab-item href='http://apps.facebook.com/dummies/index.php' title='Home'
            selected='true'/>
   <fb:tab-item href='http://apps.facebook.com/dummies/dinners.php'
            title='Dinners'  selected='true'/>
   <fb:tab-item href='http://apps.facebook.com/dummies/desserts.php'
            title='Desserts'/>
   <fb:tab-item href='http://apps.facebook.com/dummies/apps.php'
            title='Appetizers'/>
   <fb:tab-item href='http://apps.facebook.com/dummies/discuss.php'
            title='Discuss' align="right"/>
   <fb:tab-item href='http://www.facebook.com/apps/application.php?id=6349917903'
            title='About fbRecipe' align="right" />
</fb:tabs>
```

Figure 8-6 displays the results.

Figure 8-6:
Tabs for the
fbRecipe
app.

Finally, the `fb:title` tag can be used to specify the title of the page inside the browser window (much like the `title` meta tag is used in a normal HTML page). Here's the code:

```
<fb:title>the ultimate recipe box you've never ever heard of</fb:title>
```

Facebook already specifies `Facebook | `*`YourAppName`* as the title of the page. Any text you place in the `fb:title` tag is appended to it. Therefore, the following text is the title for the fbRecipe home page:

```
Facebook | fbRecipe | the ultimate recipe box you've never ever heard of
```

All of this header code can then be included as part of each canvas page of the app, tweaking the `selected` attribute as needed for the tab items.

The full page listing is as follows:

```
<?php
require_once 'appinclude.php'
?>
<fb:title>the ultimate recipe box you've never ever heard of</fb:title>
<fb:dashboard>
    <fb:action href="http://apps.facebook.com/dummies/myrecipes.php">My
            Recipes</fb:action>
    <fb:action href="http://apps.facebook.com/dummies/friends.php">Friends'
            Recipes</fb:action>
    <fb:action href="http://apps.facebook.com/dummies/shop.php">Shop for
            Ingredients</fb:action>
    <fb:help href="http://apps.facebook.com/dummies/help.php">Help</fb:help>
    <fb:create-button href="http://apps.facebook.com/dummies/add.php">Add a new
            recipe</fb:create-button>
</fb:dashboard>
<fb:tabs>
    <fb:tab-item href='http://apps.facebook.com/dummies/index.php' title='Home'
            selected='true'/>
    <fb:tab-item href='http://apps.facebook.com/dummies/dinners.php'
            title='Dinners' />
```

```
  <fb:tab-item href='http://apps.facebook.com/dummies/desserts.php'
              title='Desserts'/>
  <fb:tab-item href='http://apps.facebook.com/dummies/apps.php'
              title='Appetizers'/>
  <fb:tab-item href='http://apps.facebook.com/dummies/discuss.php'
              title='Discuss' align="right"/>
  <fb:tab-item href='http://www.facebook.com/apps/application.php?id=6349917903'
              title='About fbRecipe' align="right" />
</fb:tabs>

<style>
 h1, p { margin: 10px;}
</style>


<h1>Welcome to fbRecipe</h1>
<p>Lorem ipsum dolor sit amet, consectetur adipisicing elit, sed do eiusmod tempor
              incididunt ut labore et dolore magna aliqua. Ut enim ad minim
              veniam, quis nostrud exercitation ullamco laboris nisi ut aliquip
              ex ea commodo consequat. Duis aute irure dolor in reprehenderit
              in voluptate velit esse cillum dolore eu fugiat nulla pariatur.
              Excepteur sint occaecat cupidatat non proident, sunt in culpa
              qui officia deserunt mollit anim id est laborum.</p>
```

See Chapter 10 for full details on working with styles.

Adding a header with fb:header

The `fb:header` tag is an alternative to the `fb:dashboard` tag for adding a header to your application. Although you cannot insert `fb:action` or `fb:help` links in an `fb:header`, `fb:header` does provide greater flexibility than `fb:dashboard` in terms of displaying your application title.

To modify your application title, specify it as content in the `fb:header` tag (see Figure 8-7):

```
<fb:header>fbRecipe, the recipe box for the masses</fb:header>
```

Figure 8-7:
Customized
application
title.

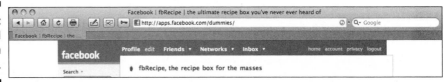

To remove the icon, use the `icon` attribute (see Figure 8-8):

```
<fb:header icon="false">fbRecipe, the recipe box for the masses</fb:header>
```

Figure 8-8:
Application
title sans
icon.

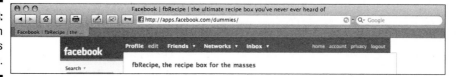

To add a border to the bottom of the header, use the `decoration` attribute, specifying `add_border`:

```
<fb:header decoration="add_border">fbRecipe, the recipe box for the
          masses</fb:header>
```

A `1px solid #ccc` border is displayed at the bottom of the header block, as shown in Figure 8-9. Note that, for style considerations, this option should not be used in combination with an `fb:tabs` set.

Figure 8-9:
A bottom
border can
be added
to the `fb:`
header.

To get rid of *all* the 20px padding surrounding the header, use the following code (see Figure 8-10):

```
<fb:header decoration="no_padding">fbRecipe, the recipe box for the
          masses</fb:header>
```

Figure 8-10:
Getting
rid of the
header
padding.

Or, to get rid of just the bottom 20px padding, use the following (see Figure 8-11):

```
<fb:header decoration="shorten">fbRecipe, the recipe box for the
            masses</fb:header>
```

Figure 8-11:
Eliminating the bottom padding with the `shorten` option.

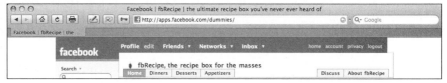

Finally, if you would like to add an image banner to the top of the canvas page, the `fb:header` element is often the best way to include it. Instead of adding text for the application title, use an `img` element instead. Be sure to use the `icon="false"` to prevent Facebook from overlaying the app icon on top of your banner image. Here's the code I used:

```
<fb:header icon="false"><img
            src="http://richwagnerwords.com/facebook/fbrecipe.png"/>
            </fb:header>
```

Figure 8-12 displays the results.

Figure 8-12:
The `fb:header` tag is ideal when you need to use an image header.

Creating an Editor Form Page

FBML provides a set of editor-related controls that enable you to quickly assemble a two-column data entry form on your canvas page. The `fb:editor` element serves as the form container for various controls (see Table 8-1).

Table 8-1	Editor Controls
FBML Element	**Description**
fb:editor	Renders a two-column form
fb:editor-button	Renders a submit button (the FBML equivalent of an input type="submit")
fb:editor-buttonset	Serves as a container for buttons inside an fb:editor element
fb:editor-cancel	Renders a Cancel button
fb:editor-custom	Serves as a container for FBML content
fb:editor-date	Renders a two-drop-down list box set for date selection (can only have one of these tags per page)
fb:editor-divider	Displays a horizontal line separator
fb:editor-month	Renders a month selector control
fb:editor-text	Renders a text control (the FBML equivalent of an input type="text")
fb:editor-textarea	Renders a multiline text control (the FBML equivalent of a textarea)
fb:editor-time	Renders a three-drop-down list box set for time selection

The fb:editor element combines aspects of the table and form elements from the HTML world. Like a table, it provides a two-column structure of one or more rows. But, like a form, it contains data-capturing elements that are submitted when a Submit button is clicked.

Each of the editor controls you place inside of fb:editor is positioned as a new row in the invisible table structure. The label attribute of the control is placed in the left column, and the control itself is rendered in the right.

The fb:editor element itself has three attributes:

✔ required: Specifies the URL that the form is being submitted to (required).

✔ width: Determines the width (in pixels) of the editor form. (Optional; defaults to 425 pixels.)

✔ labelwidth: Indicates the pixel width of the label column. (Optional; defaults to 75.)

The `fb:editor` tag is automatically centered on the canvas page. So, if you want to adjust its position, you can play with the lengths of the `width` and `labelwidth` controls.

To demonstrate, consider an editor page to be added to fbRecipe for adding a new recipe. Here are the data elements I want to capture:

- Name of the recipe, best captured using the standard `fb:editor-text` control.

- Category of the recipe (appetizer, dinner, dessert, or other), which is best displayed as a traditional `select` drop-down list (because no equivalent `fb:editor-*` controls exist).

- Ingredients and Directions are memo-type fields that can be captured with the `fb:editor-textarea` control.

- Serving size, like recipe category, is best displayed as a `select` drop-down list.

To create this editor form, I begin by defining the `fb:editor` element:

```
<fb:editor action="http://www.facebook.com/apps/add.php?addnew">
</fb:editor>
```

I added the `action` attribute, but I'll hold off specifying the `width` and `labelwidth` until later.

An `fb:editor-text` tag is added to capture the recipe name:

```
<fb:editor-text label="Name" name="name" value=""/>
```

To add the `select` drop-down box, I need to enclose it in an `fb:editor-custom` element. Inside this control, I can then add a standard HTML element:

```
<fb:editor-custom label="Category">
  <select name="type">
    <option value="0" selected="true">Appetizer</option>
    <option value="1">Dinner</option>
    <option value="2">Dessert</option>
    <option value="3">Other</option>
  </select>
</fb:editor-custom>
```

The `fb:editor-custom` element can be used to contain other familiar HTML elements too, including password fields, radio buttons, and check boxes. The label attribute value of `fb:editor-custom` is displayed in the label column, and the HTML control is rendered on the right.

The ingredients to a recipe are captured using a memo-style field, the
`fb:editor-textedit` tag:

```
<fb:editor-textarea label="Ingredients" name="ingredients"/>
```

The recipe directions are also captured using an `fb:editor-textedit`.
However, I also want to add a special note to users that I want to be dis-
played above the memo box. To do so, I add text inside an `fb:editor-custom` tag. Here are both lines:

```
<fb:editor-custom><em>Please be as descriptive as possible to help fellow
            fbRecipians:</em></fb:editor-custom>
<fb:editor-textarea label="Directions" name="directions"/>
```

The serving size is displayed using a `select` drop-down box, wrapped inside
an `fb:editor-custom` tag:

```
<fb:editor-custom label="Serving Size">
        <select name="size">
            <option value="1">1</option>
            <option value="2">2</option>
             <option value="4" selected="true">4</option>
            <option value="2">6</option>
            <option value="2">8</option>
        </select>
</fb:editor-custom>
```

Finally, no Web form is complete without buttons. Facebook editor forms use
an `fb:editor-buttonset` tag that serves as a container for buttons (`fb:editor-button`, `fb:editor-cancel`) that you want to place. Each of the
buttons is rendered next to each other in the order in which they appear in
the source code. For this example, I would like to include an Add and a
Cancel button:

```
    <fb:editor-buttonset>
        <fb:editor-button value="Add"/>
        <fb:editor-cancel />
    </fb:editor-buttonset>
```

The `fb:editor-button` element serves as a Submit button for the form. The
optional `value` attribute indicates the text to appear on the button when
rendered. The `fb:editor-cancel` element displays `Cancel` when no value
attribute is specified.

Here's the full source code to the editor form:

```
<fb:editor action="http://www.facebook.com/apps/add.php?addnew" width="400"
            labelwidth="80">
  <fb:editor-text label="Name" name="name" value=""/>
  <fb:editor-custom label="Category">
```

```
      <select name="type">
        <option value="0" selected="true">Appetizer</option>
        <option value="1">Dinner</option>
        <option value="2">Dessert</option>
        <option value="3">Other</option>
      </select>
    </fb:editor-custom>
    <fb:editor-textarea label="Ingredients" name="ingredients"/>
    <fb:editor-custom><em>Please be as descriptive as possible to help fellow
                fbRecipians:</em></fb:editor-custom>
    <fb:editor-textarea label="Directions" name="directions"/>
    <fb:editor-custom label="Serving Size">
      <select name="size">
        <option value="1">1</option>
        <option value="2">2</option>
        <option value="4" selected="true">4</option>
        <option value="2">6</option>
        <option value="2">8</option>
      </select>
    </fb:editor-custom>
    <fb:editor-buttonset>
      <fb:editor-button value="Add"/>
      <fb:editor-cancel />
    </fb:editor-buttonset>
  </fb:editor>
```

Figure 8-13 shows the results when the form is displayed in the browser.

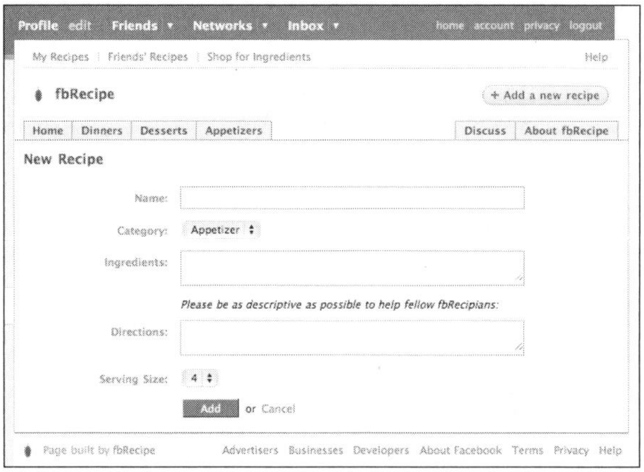

Figure 8-13:
Facebook's
`fb:`
`editor-*`
controls
make it
easy to
quickly
create
forms.

Chapter 9

Creating Content for Profile Pages

• •

In This Chapter

▶ Knowing what profile boxes and action links are

▶ Setting up default settings for your profile FBML

▶ Pushing content to the profile using the Facebook API

▶ Working with content in the profile box

▶ Creating profile action links

• •

*A*lthough Facebook applications can be launched from the left sidebar, there is little you can do to distinguish your app from others, unless you can design a killer 16x16 icon! However, a user's profile page is a different story. Effective use of a profile box and profile action links can do far more than serve as a mere application launcher. Instead, your app can become embedded in a user's Facebook experience and become indistinguishable from Facebook itself.

Back in the initial application development walk-through in Chapter 3, I introduce you to the basics of adding content to an application's profile box. However, in this chapter, you dive deeper and explore how to use FBML to create worthwhile content for profile boxes and action links.

Discovering Profile Boxes and Action Links

Outside of the application canvas page and news stories you publish, you can interact with users and potential users through the profile box and profile action links.

The next two sections discuss these two features in detail.

Profile box

A well-thought-out *profile box* is a user's primary point of contact with your application. It should enable the user to provide summary or latest information about the app. It should also provide one-click access to the most common tasks of the app.

Consider a few different approaches. Taking the "kitchen sink" approach, iLike (see Figure 9-1) displays personalized content and allows users to perform a wide variety of tasks, such as edit settings, view artists liked by the user, find upcoming shows, play a music challenge, and more.

In contrast, Where I've Been does nearly the opposite (see Figure 9-2), showing no personalized content inside the profile box. In fact, the profile box merely serves as a gateway to the application itself.

If iLike's profile box throws everything at you and Where I've Been throws only a little, Introplay's Workout Olympiad is an example (see Figure 9-3) of a profile box that fits comfortably in between. It provides up-to-date personalized summary workout data and a quick link to the most common task performed with the app.

Figure 9-1: iLike takes the "kitchen sink" approach to the profile box.

Figure 9-2:
Where I've
Been does
not display
updated
data.

Figure 9-3:
Personalized
content
displayed in
the Workout
Olympiad
app.

No matter which option you choose, keep in mind that the content displayed should reflect how your users would want to be represented in their profile boxes. Workout Olympiad, for example, would probably have few users if it added jibes like "This loser has not worked out in a week" or "Jeesh, Rich is ranked 122. Is that his age?" You should also present your application in an attractive light, encouraging viewers to install your app.

Profile action links

Profile action links are displayed below a Facebook user's photo on the profile page (see Figure 9-4). These links enable users to quickly access a function of your application. Facebook permits you to add a profile action link to Facebook users who have not installed your app. The action link is not visible to the user who has not installed your app, but is visible to users who have the app installed and view the profile of the user who hasn't.

Figure 9-4:
Profile
action links.

Configuring the Default Profile Settings

When you configure your application via the My Applications module of the Developer Home (www.facebook.com/developers/apps.php), you can set the default settings of your profile box and actions. When you click the Edit Settings link on your application listing, the Edit application page is displayed. In the Installation Options section, the following three options are associated with the profile:

✔ **Default FBML:** This option allows you to supply initial FBML content for your application. This hardcoded method works well if you do not need to display personalized content. However, if you do need to display such content, you will want to use the `profile.setFBML` API call.

Here are three other tips to keep in mind when working with default FBML for your profile box:

- The default FBML content is displayed to both application users and nonusers and is generally a good place to add an invitation link.

- The default FBML is cached, so when you make changes, content is not updated immediately. You will typically need to wait some time before your new changes appear.

Who sees what?

Exactly what is displayed in a user's profile for your profile box depends on both the profile owner and the viewer. When a viewer who has not installed your app views the profile of an application user, the `fb:wide` or `fb:` narrow content is displayed. However, if the viewer is a fellow app user, Facebook will also display any `fb:profile-action` items on the profile as well.

> • Any line breaks placed inside the Default FBML edit box are
>   replaced with <br /> tags.

✔ **Default Action FBML:** This enables you to provide a default action link
for users. (Handy if you have a common action that users perform in
your app.)

✔ **Default Profile Box Column:** This specifies whether the profile box
should be wide or narrow by default.

The default FBML you set up in the application configuration page is used
inside the profile box unless you specifically update it inside your application.

Pushing Profile Content with profile.setFBML

You can update a profile box or profile action link using the Facebook API
method `profile.setFBML`. The method in PHP looks like this:

```
$facebook->api_client->profile_setFBML($markup, $uid, $profile, $profile_action,
          $mobile_profile)
```

Several optional parameters are available:

✔ `$markup`: Is an attribute that is being phased out, so simply set it to
`null`.

✔ `$uid`: Specifies the user ID or page ID. (If `null`, the logged-in user is
assumed.)

✔ `$profile`: Specifies the FBML markup for the profile box.

✔ `$profile_action`: Indicates the content for a profile action link.

✔ `$mobile_profile`: Provides content for mobile devices.

Using `profile.setFBML`, the profile box of the current user can be updated
with the following code:

```
$fbml = 'Welcome <fb:name uid="loggedinuser" useyou="false"/> to fbRecipe, the
          way recipes were meant to be.';
$facebook->api_client->profile_setFBML(null,null,$fbml);
```

Figure 9-5 shows the results in the profile box.

Figure 9-5:
Updating
the profile
box content.

I walk you through how to use `profile.setFBML` to create action links in the section "Adding Action Links to a User Profile," later in this chapter.

To ensure that your profile box is updated, you should tie the updating of the profile box or action links to events inside your application. Consider, for example, the fbRecipe app. When a new recipe is entered, I could add the following content to the profile box:

```
View your new recipe.
You now have x recipes in your recipe box.
```

You cannot update the profile box dynamically when the profile loads — in other words, you can't get the profile to call your application when a user loads the page. Instead, you have to push content to users based on events happening in your application, not what's happening on a user's profile page.

Introplay's Workout Olympiad, for example, updates its profile box when a user enters workout info through its Facebook app UI. However, because users can also enter workout data from the main Introplay Web site (`www.introplay.com`) — totally outside of Facebook — Introplay also updates a Facebook user's profile box at that time as well.

In addition to updating the profile based on user-based events, you can also have a background process that periodically performs updates based on external events. For example, five days before a major holiday, the fbRecipe app could add a reminder to the profile box:

```
Thanksgiving is right around the corner. Find the perfect pumpkin pie recipe.
```

If it is an external app, you should trigger the update even if the user is working outside the Facebook implementation.

Working with Content in the Profile Box

Several FBML tags are specifically for adding content in a profile box. The `fb:subtitle` tag is used to display a title for the profile box. The `fb:action` tag, which is normally placed in a canvas page's dashboard header (see Chapter 8), can also be placed in the `fb:subtitle` tag.

The `fb:wide` element is used to define content to be rendered when the profile box is displayed in the wide column of a profile. The `fb:narrow` tag does the same for the narrow column.

The `fb:user-table` element displays a user table, displaying a square thumbnail and name for each user (defined by `fb:user-item`).

Consider a PHP-based example that uses these FBML tags to produce a mock profile box. To begin, I use the `<<<EndHereDoc` marker to declare a multiline string, assigned to a variable called `$fbml`:

```
$fbml = <<<EndHereDoc

EndHereDoc;
```

Inside this block, I add content specifically for the wide profile box by enclosing FBML content in `fb:wide` tags:

```
<fb:wide>
<fb:subtitle seeallurl="http://apps.facebook.com/dummies/index.php?seeall" >
  <fb:action href="http://apps.facebook.com/dummies/add.php">Add new
             recipe</fb:action>
  <fb:action href="http://apps.facebook.com/dummies/share.php">Share
             recipe</fb:action>
  fbRecipe box
 </fb:subtitle>
<p>Wide profile boxes rule!</p>
<p>Exchange recipes with your fbRecipe-toting friends:</p>
<fb:user-table cols="6">
   <fb:user-item uid="693048091" />
   <fb:user-item uid="530377451" />
   <fb:user-item uid="753980204" />
   <fb:user-item uid="685578792" />
   <fb:user-item uid="778763940 " />
   <fb:user-item uid="18601493" />
   <fb:user-item uid="20715969" />
   <fb:user-item uid="55700210" />
   <fb:user-item uid="55713606" />
   <fb:user-item uid="55714303" />
 </fb:user-table>
</fb:wide>
```

I want to point out several tags. The `fb:subtitle` tag defines an optional `seeallurl` attribute, which specifies a URL to jump to if the user wants to see everything by clicking a See All link in the subtitle bar. Two `fb:action` links are enclosed in the `fb:subtitle` element. These links appear on the right side of the subtitle bar (to the left of the See All link).

After the paragraph content, the block contains an `fb:user-table` definition, which specifies to render all the `fb:user-item` tags in a six-column grid.

When the profile box is displayed in the right wide column, all that FBML content will be rendered.

However, suppose that I'd like to change the content if the user moves the profile box to the narrow column in the profile. In this case, I specify custom content using the `fb:narrow` element, with a focus on minimizing width:

```
<fb:narrow>
<fb:subtitle>fbRecipe box</fb:subtitle>
<p>Narrow profile boxes rule!</p>
<p>Exchange recipes with your fbRecipe-toting friends:</p>
<fb:user-table cols="3">
   <fb:user-item uid="693048091" />
   <fb:user-item uid="530377451" />
   <fb:user-item uid="753980204" />
```

```
     <fb:user-item uid="685578792" />
     <fb:user-item uid="778763940 " />
     <fb:user-item uid="18601493" />
     <fb:user-item uid="20715969" />
     <fb:user-item uid="55700210" />
     <fb:user-item uid="55713606" />
     <fb:user-item uid="55714303" />
   </fb:user-table>
 </fb:narrow>
```

The `fb:subtitle` tag in this context is stripped down to the basics, offering just a subtitle caption. The additional links have been removed. What's more, the `fb:user-table cols` attribute is changed to display user items in a three-grid table.

The code for the entire file is shown here:

```
<?php
require_once 'appinclude.php';

$fbml = <<<EndHereDoc
<fb:wide>
<fb:subtitle seeallurl="http://apps.facebook.com/dummies/index.php?seeall" >
  <fb:action href="http://apps.facebook.com/dummies/add.php">Add new
             recipe</fb:action>
  <fb:action href="http://apps.facebook.com/dummies/share.php">Share
             recipe</fb:action>
  fbRecipe box
 </fb:subtitle>
<p>Wide profile boxes rule!</p>
<p>Exchange recipes with your fbRecipe-toting friends:</p>
<fb:user-table cols="6">

   <fb:user-item uid="693048091" />
   <fb:user-item uid="530377451" />
   <fb:user-item uid="753980204" />
   <fb:user-item uid="685578792" />
   <fb:user-item uid="7787163940" />
   <fb:user-item uid="18601493" />
   <fb:user-item uid="20715969" />
   <fb:user-item uid="55700210" />
   <fb:user-item uid="55713606" />
   <fb:user-item uid="55714303" />
 </fb:user-table>
</fb:wide>
<fb:narrow>
<fb:subtitle seeallurl="http://apps.facebook.com/dummies/index.php?seeall" >
  fbRecipe box
 </fb:subtitle>
<p>Narrow profile boxes rule!</p>
<p>Exchange recipes with your fbRecipe-toting friends:</p>
```

```
<fb:user-table cols="3">
   <fb:user-item uid="693048091" />
   <fb:user-item uid="530377451" />
   <fb:user-item uid="753980204" />
   <fb:user-item uid="685578792" />
   <fb:user-item uid="778763940" />
   <fb:user-item uid="18601493" />
   <fb:user-item uid="20715969" />
   <fb:user-item uid="55700210" />
   <fb:user-item uid="55713606" />
   <fb:user-item uid="55714303" />
 </fb:user-table>
</fb:narrow>
EndHereDoc;

$facebook->api_client->profile_setFBML(null,null,$fbml);

echo "<p>Amazing content was added to the profile box</p>";
?>
```

Figures 9-6 and 9-7 display the content in wide and narrow profile boxes, respectively.

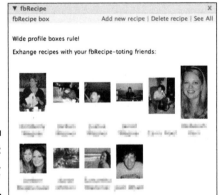

Figure 9-6: "Open wide, profile box."

Consider a second, more refined example in which I want to present the following information and action items in a profile box:

- ✔ Add a new recipe
- ✔ Share a recipe with a friend
- ✔ View a thumbnail listing of the latest recipes of the current user
- ✔ View all recipes of the current user
- ✔ View a thumbnail listing of the friends of the current user who are also app users

Figure 9-7:
A narrow-
minded
profile box.

Because I am rendering the latest recipes and friends/app users in a tabular structure (which has a fixed width), I need to have both a wide and narrow version to ensure proper display.

Looking first at the wide profile box, I begin by defining two `fb:action` links on the `fb:subtitle var`, but don't add a subtitle:

```
<fb:wide>
<fb:subtitle>
  <fb:action href="http://apps.facebook.com/dummies//add.php">Add new
          recipe</fb:action>
  <fb:action href="http://apps.facebook.com/dummies//share.php">Share
          recipe</fb:action>
 </fb:subtitle>
```

Next, I want to add a listing of the last seven recipes of the current user. A header is included that adds a thin gray line underneath it:

```
<p style="border-bottom:solid #333333 thin"><strong><fb:name uid="loggedinuser"
          possessive="true" firstnameonly="true" useyou="false"/> latest
          recipes</strong></p>
```

An HTML table is then used to present thumbnail images of the last seven recipes. Because of the width of the wide profile box, I can add each of these in a single row. These images are linked to the actual recipe listing in the app. Here's the table code:

```
<table border="0" cellspacing="1">
<tr>
  <td><a href="http://apps.facebook.com/dummies//recipes?14231"><img
          src="http://richwagnerwords.com/facebook/rimages//14231.jpg">
          </a></td>
  <td><a href="http://apps.facebook.com/dummies//recipes?17753"><img
          src="http://richwagnerwords.com/facebook/rimages//17753.jpg">
          </a></td>
  <td><a href="http://apps.facebook.com/dummies//recipes?20669"><img
          src="http://richwagnerwords.com/facebook/rimages//20669.jpg">
          </a></td>
  <td><a href="http://apps.facebook.com/dummies/recipes?21694"><img
          src="http://richwagnerwords.com/facebook/rimages//21694.jpg">
          </a></td>
  <td><a href="http://apps.facebook.com/dummies/recipes?24087"><img
          src="http://richwagnerwords.com/facebook/rimages//24087.jpg">
          </a></td>
  <td><a href="http://apps.facebook.com/dummies/recipes?26692"><img
          src="http://richwagnerwords.com/facebook/rimages//26692.jpg">
          </a></td>
  <td><a href="http://apps.facebook.com/dummies/recipes?29420"><img
          src="http://richwagnerwords.com/facebook/rimages//29420.jpg">
          </a></td>
</tr>
</table>
```

In a real-world setting, this table would be generated on the fly based on a database query.

Next, the thumbnail listing of friends who are also app users is displayed using the `fb:user-table` and `fb:user-item` tags that I describe earlier:

```
<p style="margin-top:2px;"><a
          href="http://apps.facebook.com/dummies//viewall.php">View all of
          <fb:name uid="loggedinuser" possessive="true" firstnameonly=
          "true" useyou="false"/> recipes</a></p>

<p style="border-bottom:solid #333333 thin"><strong><fb:name uid="loggedinuser"
          possessive="true" firstnameonly="true" useyou="false"/> friends
          who also cook</strong></p>
<fb:user-table cols="6">
   <fb:user-item uid="693048091" />
   <fb:user-item uid="530377451" />
   <fb:user-item uid="753980204" />
   <fb:user-item uid="685578792" />
   <fb:user-item uid="778763940 " />
```

```
    <fb:user-item uid="18601493" />
    <fb:user-item uid="20715969" />
    <fb:user-item uid="55700210" />
    <fb:user-item uid="55713606" />
    <fb:user-item uid="55714303" />
  </fb:user-table>
</fb:wide>
```

In the `fb:narrow` block, the profile box structure is tweaked to account for the narrow width, using three rows for the latest recipes table and changing the `fb:user-table cols` attribute to 3:

```
<fb:narrow>
<fb:subtitle>
  <fb:action href="http://apps.facebook.com/dummies//add.php">Add new
             recipe</fb:action>
  <fb:action href="http://apps.facebook.com/dummies//share.php">Share
             recipe</fb:action>
 </fb:subtitle>

<p style="border-bottom:solid #333333 thin"><strong><fb:name uid="loggedinuser"
             possessive="true" firstnameonly="true" useyou="false"/> latest
             recipes</strong></p>
<table border="0" cellspacing="1">
<tr>
  <td><a href="http://apps.facebook.com/dummies//recipes?14231"><img
             src="http://richwagnerwords.com/facebook/rimages//14231.jpg">
             </a></td>
  <td><a href="http://apps.facebook.com/dummies//recipes?17753"><img
             src="http://richwagnerwords.com/facebook/rimages//17753.jpg">
             </a></td>
  <td><a href="http://apps.facebook.com/dummies//recipes?20669"><img
             src="http://richwagnerwords.com/facebook/rimages//20669.jpg">
             </a></td>
</tr>
<tr>
  <td><a href="http://apps.facebook.com/dummies/recipes?21694"><img
             src="http://richwagnerwords.com/facebook/rimages//21694.jpg">
             </a></td>
  <td><a href="http://apps.facebook.com/dummies/recipes?24087"><img
             src="http://richwagnerwords.com/facebook/rimages//24087.jpg"></a>
             </td>
  <td><a href="http://apps.facebook.com/dummies/recipes?26692"><img
             src="http://richwagnerwords.com/facebook/rimages//26692.jpg">
             </a></td>
</tr>
<tr>
  <td><a href="http://apps.facebook.com/dummies/recipes?29420"><img
             src="http://richwagnerwords.com/facebook/rimages//29420.jpg">
             </a></td>
</tr>
</table>
```

```
<p style="margin-top:2px;"><a
          href="http://apps.facebook.com/dummies//viewall.php">View all of
          <fb:name uid="loggedinuser" possessive="true" firstnameonly="true"
          useyou="false"/> recipes</a></p>

<p style="border-bottom:solid #333333 thin"><strong><fb:name uid="loggedinuser"
          possessive="true" firstnameonly="true" useyou="false"/> friends
          who also cook</strong></p>
<fb:user-table cols="3">
   <fb:user-item uid="693048091" />
   <fb:user-item uid="530377451" />
   <fb:user-item uid="753980204" />
   <fb:user-item uid="685578792" />
   <fb:user-item uid="778763940 " />
   <fb:user-item uid="18601493" />
   <fb:user-item uid="20715969" />
   <fb:user-item uid="55700210" />
   <fb:user-item uid="55713606" />
   <fb:user-item uid="55714303" />
 </fb:user-table>
</fb:narrow>
```

This code could then be wrapped inside a PHP function named `republish_current_user_profile()`. The code listing below shows the full source for this example:

```
<?php
require_once 'appinclude.php';

republish_current_user_profile();

function republish_current_user_profile() {
  global $facebook;

  $fbml = <<<EndHereDoc
<fb:fbml version="1.1">
<fb:visible-to-owner>
  Hello <fb:name uid="loggedinuser" useyou="false" firstnameonly="true" />, this
          is your very own box.
  You win a free antique recipe box! You are special!
</fb:visible-to-owner>
<fb:fbml>
<fb:wide>
<fb:subtitle>
  <fb:action href="http://apps.facebook.com/dummies/add.php">Add new
          recipe</fb:action>
  <fb:action href="http://apps.facebook.com/dummies/share.php">Share
          recipe</fb:action>
 </fb:subtitle>
<p style="border-bottom:solid #333333 thin"><strong><fb:name uid="loggedinuser"
          possessive="true" firstnameonly="true" useyou="false"/> latest
          recipes</strong></p>
```

```
<table border="0" cellspacing="1">
<tr>
  <td><a href="http://apps.facebook.com/dummies/recipes?14231"><img
            src="http://richwagnerwords.com/facebook/rimages/14231.jpg">
            </a></td>
  <td><a href="http://apps.facebook.com/dummies/recipes?17753"><img
            src="http://richwagnerwords.com/facebook/rimages/17753.jpg">
            </a></td>
  <td><a href="http://apps.facebook.com/dummies/recipes?20669"><img
            src="http://richwagnerwords.com/facebook/rimages/20669.jpg">
            </a></td>
  <td><a href="http://apps.facebook.com/dummies/recipes?21694"><img
            src="http://richwagnerwords.com/facebook/rimages/21694.jpg">
            </a></td>
  <td><a href="http://apps.facebook.com/dummies/recipes?24087"><img
            src="http://richwagnerwords.com/facebook/rimages/24087.jpg">
            </a></td>
  <td><a href="http://apps.facebook.com/dummies/recipes?26692"><img
            src="http://richwagnerwords.com/facebook/rimages/26692.jpg">
            </a></td>
  <td><a href="http://apps.facebook.com/dummies/recipes?29420"><img
            src="http://richwagnerwords.com/facebook/rimages/29420.jpg">
            </a></td>
</tr>
</table>

<p style="margin-top:2px;"><a
            href="http://apps.facebook.com/dummies//viewall.php">View all
            of <fb:name uid="loggedinuser" possessive="true"
            firstnameonly="true" useyou="false"/> recipes</a></p>

<p style="border-bottom:solid #333333 thin"><strong><fb:name uid="loggedinuser"
            possessive="true" firstnameonly="true" useyou="false"/> friends
            who also cook</strong></p>
<fb:user-table cols="6">
   <fb:user-item uid="693048091" />
   <fb:user-item uid="530377451" />
   <fb:user-item uid="753980204" />
   <fb:user-item uid="685578792" />
   <fb:user-item uid="778763940 " />
   <fb:user-item uid="18601493" />
   <fb:user-item uid="20715969" />
   <fb:user-item uid="55700210" />
   <fb:user-item uid="55713606" />
   <fb:user-item uid="55714303" />
 </fb:user-table>
</fb:wide>

<fb:narrow>
<fb:subtitle>
  <fb:action href="http://apps.facebook.com/dummies//add.php">Add new
            recipe</fb:action>
```

```
  <fb:action href="http://apps.facebook.com/dummies//share.php">Share
          recipe</fb:action>
 </fb:subtitle>

<p style="border-bottom:solid #333333 thin"><strong><fb:name uid="loggedinuser"
          possessive="true" firstnameonly="true" useyou="false"/> latest
          recipes</strong></p>
<table border="0" cellspacing="1">
<tr>
  <td><a href="http://apps.facebook.com/dummies/recipes?14231"><img
          src="http://richwagnerwords.com/facebook/rimages/14231.jpg">
          </a></td>
  <td><a href="http://apps.facebook.com/dummies/recipes?17753"><img
          src="http://richwagnerwords.com/facebook/rimages/17753.jpg">
          </a></td>
  <td><a href="http://apps.facebook.com/dummies/recipes?20669"><img
          src="http://richwagnerwords.com/facebook/rimages/20669.jpg">
          </a></td>
</tr>
<tr>
  <td><a href="http://apps.facebook.com/dummies/recipes?21694"><img
          src="http://richwagnerwords.com/facebook/rimages/21694.jpg">
          </a></td>
  <td><a href="http://apps.facebook.com/dummies/recipes?24087"><img
          src="http://richwagnerwords.com/facebook/rimages/24087.jpg">
          </a></td>
  <td><a href="http://apps.facebook.com/dummies/recipes?26692"><img
          src="http://richwagnerwords.com/facebook/rimages/26692.jpg">
          </a></td>
</tr>
<tr>
  <td><a href="http://apps.facebook.com/dummies/recipes?29420"><img
          src="http://richwagnerwords.com/facebook/rimages/29420.jpg">
          </a></td>
</tr>
</table>
<p style="margin-top:2px;"><a
          href="http://apps.facebook.com/dummies//viewall.php">View all of
          <fb:name uid="loggedinuser" possessive="true" firstnameonly=
          "true" useyou="false"/> recipes</a></p>

<p style="border-bottom:solid #333333 thin"><strong><fb:name uid="loggedinuser"
          possessive="true" firstnameonly="true" useyou="false"/> friends
          who also cook</strong></p>
<fb:user-table cols="3">
   <fb:user-item uid="693048091" />
   <fb:user-item uid="530377451" />
   <fb:user-item uid="753980204" />
```

```
   <fb:user-item uid="685578792" />
   <fb:user-item uid="778763940 " />
   <fb:user-item uid="18601493" />
   <fb:user-item uid="20715969" />
   <fb:user-item uid="55700210" />
   <fb:user-item uid="55713606" />
   <fb:user-item uid="55714303" />
 </fb:user-table>
</fb:narrow>

EndHereDoc;
  $facebook->api_client->profile_setFBML(null,null,$fbml);
}

?>
```

Figures 9-8 and 9-9 show the profile box in both wide and narrow views.

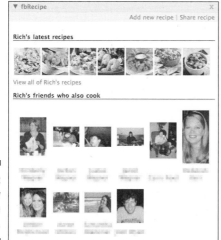

Figure 9-8:
Wide view
of the
profile box.

See Chapter 4 for tips on using the `fb:visible-to-*` tags to display content according to the person viewing it.

Figure 9-9:
Narrow
profile box.

Adding Action Links to a User Profile

The `profile.setFBML` API call is also used to add profile action links. The only difference is the parameter you specify:

```
$facebook->api_client->profile_setFBML($markup, $uid, $profile, $profile_action,
        $mobile_profile)
```

The `$profile_action` parameter should include FBML content that is enclosed in the `fb:profile-action` tags. The content inside this tag is then turned into a profile action button under the user's profile photo.

To create a profile action link for the current user using PHP, you can enter the following:

```
function getRecipeCount($user){
  return 10; // Hardcoded example
}
$total_count=getRecipeCount($user);
$fbml ='<fb:profile-action
            url="http://apps.facebook.com/dummies/myrecipes.php">View my
            recipes ('.$total_count.')</fb:profile-action>';
$facebook->api_client->profile_setFBML(null,null,null,$fbml);
```

The `getRecipeCount()` function returns the number of recipes that the specified user has in the system and assigns it to `$total_count`. The `$fbml` variable contains the `fb:profile-action` tag and its content. This variable is then used in the call to the `profile.setFBML` function.

The text of a profile action link should no more than 28 to 30 characters.

Figure 9-10 displays the profile action link.

Figure 9-10:
Profile
action link.

View Photos of Me (5)
Where I've Traveled (20)
See Rich's FunWall
View Books (4)
Who calls you a Top Friend
View My Countdowns (1)
View your Movies (8)
Edit My Where I've Been Map
Advanced Search
View my recipes (19)
Edit My Profile

When a user clicks the link, Facebook adds an `id` parameter to the target URL, passing along the user ID. Therefore, the following is passed to the app when I click it:

```
http://apps.facebook.com/dummies//myrecipes.php?id=665127078
```

Chapter 10

Seamless Styles: Styling Your Facebook Application

In This Chapter

▶ Adding CSS styles into FBML markup

▶ Using external CSS style sheets with your apps

▶ Defining styles for profile boxes

▶ Using `fb:ref` for defining style sheets

▶ Adding Facebook styles to iframe canvas pages

***U**nlike the styling free-for-all at alternative sites like MySpace, Facebook has always been known for its stricter adherence to design standards and for its refusal to offer style customization for individual profiles. Although some users and even developers may lament for more individual expression, the advantages of structure seem to outweigh the disadvantages of stylistic anarchy.

Still, Facebook's design restrictions don't mean you can't have any style at all. In this chapter, you discover how to add styles to your application, including FBML canvas pages as well as profile boxes. And, if you are implementing an iframe-based application, I show you how you can use CSS styles to emulate the look and feel of FBML pages.

Adding Styles to Your FBML

When you develop an FBML canvas page or render content for a profile box, your application already takes on the base default styles of Facebook, such as fonts. The FBML markup tags (such as `fb:tab-item` or `fb:action`) that you add also automatically take on a visual style when they are displayed. As a result, you can actually get a long way without adding style code to your application.

However, if your application has any degree of complexity, you will very likely run into situations in which you do need to apply CSS styles to your content.

You can do that either inline (as a `style` attribute), embedded (as a `style` tag), or as an external style sheet.

Using inline styles

Like a typical HTML file, you can add CSS styles to your FBML using the `style` attribute or the `style` element.

To define a style for a specific element, simply add the `style` attribute. In the following PHP-based example, using a `style` attribute, the top margin and font color are specified for the `div` that is rendered on a canvas page:

```
$uids1 = array( 20715969, 55713606, 696951095);
$uids2 = array( 705671487, 55714303, 549572223);
$friendsMatch = $facebook->api_client->friends_areFriends($uids1, $uids2);

echo "<div style='margin-top: 20px; color: #666666;'>";
echo "<ul>";
echo "<li>Are <fb:name uid=\"{$friendsMatch[0]['uid1']}\" useyou=\"false\" />
            and <fb:name uid=\"{$friendsMatch[0]['uid2']}\" useyou=\"false\"
            /> friends? {$friendsMatch[0]['are_friends']}</li>";
echo "<li>Are <fb:name uid=\"{$friendsMatch[1]['uid1']}\" useyou=\"false\" />
            and <fb:name uid=\"{$friendsMatch[1]['uid2']}\" useyou=\"false\"
            /> friends? {$friendsMatch[1]['are_friends']}</li>";
echo "<li>Are <fb:name uid=\"{$friendsMatch[2]['uid1']}\" useyou=\"false\" />
            and <fb:name uid=\"{$friendsMatch[2]['uid2']}\" useyou=\"false\"
            /> friends? {$friendsMatch[2]['are_friends']}</li>";
echo "</ul>";
echo "</div>";
```

Using embedded styles

You can also include a `style` element in your FBML content block and have it used in the rendering of the page. To illustrate, for the following profile box, FBML uses a `style` element to define the styles for `table` and `td` and the `:hover` pseudo-class:

```
$fbml = <<<HERE
<fb:narrow>
<style>
  table{
     margin: 0px;
     left: 0px;
```

```
    width: 198px;
    border: none;
  }

  td{
    width: 65px;
    text-align: center;
    vertical-align: top;
    border: 1px solid #666666;
    padding: 2px;
  }

  td:hover{
    background-color: #3B5998;
  }
</style>
<table>
  <tr>
    <td>
      <img src="http://www.richwagnerwords.com/speeddial/1.png"/><br />
      <fb:profile-pic uid="{$dial_friends[0]['fid']}" size="square"
          linked="true" />
      <fb:name uid="{$dial_friends[0]['fid']}" useyou="false" />
    </td>
    <td>
      <img src="http://www.richwagnerwords.com/speeddial/2.png"/><br />
      <fb:profile-pic uid="{$dial_friends[1]['fid']}" size="square"
          linked="true" />
      <fb:name uid="{$dial_friends[1]['fid']}" useyou="false" />
    </td>
    <td>
      <img src="http://www.richwagnerwords.com/speeddial/3.png"/><br />
      <fb:profile-pic uid="{$dial_friends[2]['fid']}" size="square"
          linked="true" />
      <fb:name uid="{$dial_friends[2]['fid']}" useyou="false" />
    </td>
  </tr>
</table>
</fb:narrow>
HERE;

$facebook->api_client->profile_setFBML(null,null,$fbml);
```

Note that you have to implement pseudo-classes like :hover in a specific way for profile box FBML. You cannot add pseudo-class styles as an inline style (using the style attribute). Instead, you need to define their style properties in an embedded style element inside the fb:wide or fb:narrow elements.

Including external style sheets

As shown in the previous sections, FBML supports the use of the `style` attribute and tag within FBML canvas and profile pages. However, at least at the time of this writing, FBML does not permit the use of the `link` tag or allow `@import` rules to include external `.css` style sheets with your FBML code.

However, a work-around is available — embedding the style sheet on the server side. For example, using PHP, you can embed an external style sheet by doing the following:

```
<style>
<?php echo htmlentities(file_get_contents('global.css', true)); ?>
</style>
```

If the `.css` file is in the same directory as the PHP source file, you can drop the second Boolean parameter (which optionally searches for the file in the included path).

Specifying Wide and Narrow Styles for Profile Boxes

When you are creating styles for the profile box, you will likely find occasion in which you want to customize the style properties based on whether the profile box is displayed in wide or narrow format.

The general rule of thumb is to define generic styles outside the `fb:wide` and `fb:narrow` elements and then embed styles inside of them that are appropriate only for those layout contexts.

To use different styles for the wide and narrow profiles, you may find it helpful to actually define a narrow and wide class to better organize your code. For example:

```
<style>
    .toolbar { font-weight:bold; padding: 5px; margin: 3px; }
    .narrow .toolbar { width: 40px; }
    .wide .toolbar { width: 120px; }
</style>
<fb:wide>
  <div class='wide'>
     <div class='toolbar'>
         Extended content
     </div>
```

```
    </div>
  </fb:wide>
  <fb:narrow>
    <div class='narrow'>
      <div class='toolbar'>
          Skinny content
      </div>
    </div>
  </fb:narrow>
```

Using fb:ref to Load CSS in a Profile Box

You can use the `fb:ref` tag to load CSS styles into a profile box. The `fb:reg` tag references FBML from a handle defined using `fbml.setRefHandle` or from a URL.

I have not talked about `fb:ref` or `fbml.setRefHandle`, so let me begin by showing you how this works. The `fbml.setRefHandle` is called with the following syntax in PHP:

```
$facebook->api_client->fbml_setRefHandle("$handle", "markup")
```

The `$handle` variable is associated with FBML code (the `$fbml` variable). When you create a handle, you register it with Facebook servers. Then, when the content it points to is requested, Facebook serves up the FBML associated with the handle. You can use the handle in multiple places within your application to reference identical FBML content by referencing it with the `fb:ref` tag.

However, perhaps the principal advantage of using `fb:ref` is its ability to update all user profiles *en masse*. You can make one call to `fbml.set RefHandle` to update all profiles rather than being forced to update each and every user. Additionally, when you are using `fb:ref`, you can make one call to `fbml.setRefHandle` to update the profile rather than re-rendering the entire profile using `profile.setFBML`.

For example, if you would like to use `fb:ref` to load CSS styles, you could begin by registering a handle called `my_css_styles`:

```
$fbml = <<<EndHereDoc
<style>
#top { position: relative; width: 100px; margin: 0 auto;
  text-align: center;
}
</style>
EndHereDoc;
$facebook->api_client->fbml_setRefHandle("my_css_styles",$fbml);
```

You can then add an `fb:ref` tag to the profile box markup:

```
<fb:ref handle="my_css_styles" />
<fb:wide>
  Extended content
</fb:wide>
<fb:narrow>
  Skinny connect
</fb:narrow>
```

Facebook caches the latest update of the `my_css_styles` handle and renders it when the `fb:ref` is encountered. When you want to update the `my_css_styles` content, simply call `fbml.setRefHandle` from your app or from a backend process that runs periodically.

What's more, instead of using a handle, you can also assign FBML content by specifying a URL as an attribute of `fb:ref`:

```
<fb:ref url="http://www.richwagnerwords.com/facebook/global.css" />
```

Facebook caches the content the first time it encounters the reference. When you want to update it, you call `fbml.refreshRefUrl`:

```
$facebook->api_client-
          >fbml_refreshRefUrl("http://www.richwagnerwords.com/facebook/
          global.css");
```

Going Native: Emulating Facebook Styles

One of the advantages of working with FBML canvas pages is that many of the Facebook styles come along for free — making it easy to create a seamless look and feel simply by adding FBML tags to your code. However, if you need to implement an iframe-based canvas page, you can find your app resembling a second-class citizen — looking much different than the Facebook environs. However, because Facebook is built on top of Web standards, you can use the same technologies to emulate Facebook inside your iframe. In the following sections, I show you how to use CSS and HTML to re-create some of the Facebook elements you will likely want to implement on an iframe page.

Even if you are using FBML pages, you may still find these sections useful, because some of the controls I emulate have no FBML equivalent (such as the buttons or two-column lists).

In general, I try to follow the naming conventions of FBML tags. So, when a matching CSS style exists for an FBML tag like `fb:dashboard`, I name the corresponding class style `fb-dashboard`. When no FBML equivalent is available, I usually fall back to Facebook-style sheet-naming conventions.

Alternatively, you can always view the source of a Facebook page and check out the actual Facebook style sheets and see how its pages are styled.

You can save time typing in all the code by downloading the `pseudo_face book.css` style sheet and `iframe_example.php` at this book's companion Web site.

Setting the basic formatting styles

Regardless of the elements you will include on your canvas page, you want to be sure to begin by defining the basic formatting styles for the fonts, sizing, links, and so on. These are shown here:

```css
/* Base styles */
body {
  background: #fff;
  font-family: "Lucida Grande", Tahoma, Verdana, Arial, sans-serif;
  font-size: 11px;
  margin: 0px;
  padding: 0px;
  text-align: left;
}

h1, h2, h3, h4, h5 { font-size: 13px; color: #333; margin: 0px; padding: 0px; }

h1 { font-size: 14px; }

h4, h5 { font-size: 11px; }

p {
  font-family: "Lucida Grande", Tahoma, Verdana, Arial, sans-serif;
  font-size: 11px;
  text-align: left;
}

a { color: #3b5998; text-decoration: none; }

a:hover { text-decoration: underline; }

img { border: 0px; }

select {
  border: 1px solid #BDC7D8;
  font-family: "Lucida Grande", Tahoma, Verdana, Arial, sans-serif;
  font-size: 11px;
  padding: 2px;
}

td, td.label { font-size: 11px; text-align: left; }
```

Next, for page content, I define a `canvas_content` class:

```
.canvas_content { margin: 10px 20px 5px 10px; }
```

The following HTML boilerplate markup is then added to the page to display the basic styles:

```
<div class="canvas_content">
    <h1>This is an h1 header.</h1>
    <h2>This is an h2 header.</h2>
    <h3>This is an h3 header.</h3>
    <h4>This is an h4 header.</h4>
    <h5>This is an h5 header.</h5>
    <h6>This is an h6 header.</h6>
    <p>This is a normal paragraph.</p>
    <ul>
        <li>Item 1</li>
        <li>Item 2</li>
        <li>Item 3</li>
        <li>Item 4</li>
        <li>Item 5</li>
    </ul>
    <br />
</div>
```

Figures 10-1 shows the iframe page.

Figure 10-1:
Basic text styles with Facebook emulation.

Looking at the Facebook color palette

Facebook uses four major colors in its color palette. As you design your UI, you want to be sure to use these to better emulate the look of Facebook. These include white and four shades of blue. Here are the colors' hex values: hex values: #ffffff (white), #d8dfea (lightest blue), #afbdd4 (lighter blue), #6d84b4 (darker blue), and #3b5998 (darkest blue).

Emulating the Facebook dashboard

On FBML pages, you can use the `fb:dashboard` element to define a dashboard region on the canvas page that contains the application title and icon as well as any `fb:action`, `fb:help`, or `fb:create-button` tags that you want to include. For this sample page, I am going to re-create a dashboard with three action links, one Help button, and a Create button. I begin by defining the dashboard as a `div` at the spot in which I want it to appear on the page:

```
<div class="fb-dashboard">
</div>
```

Inside the dashboard `div`, I begin by enclosing the three action links in a container `div` called `fb-actions`. Inside, I add three `a` links along with `span` elements to define the pipe spacer. I also add a `div` named `fb-help` to house the help link:

```
<div class="fb-links clearfix">
  <div class="fb-actions">
      <a href="#">Action Link 1</a>
      <span class="pipe">|</span>
      <a href="#">Action Link 2</a>
      <span class="pipe">|</span>
      <a href="#">Action Link 2</a>
  </div>
  <div class="fb-help"><a href="#">Help</a></div>
</div>
```

Don't worry about the `clearfix` class style just yet. I explain that later.

Also inside the dashboard `div`, I need to add the series of elements that appear just below the action links and help — the application icon, title, and a Create button. Here's the code:

```
<div class="fb-titlebar clearfix">
    <h2 style="background-image:
        url('http://static.ak.facebook.com/images/icons/
        photo.gif?55:25796')">My iframe Application</h2>
    <div class="fb-create-button-wrapper">
      <a href="#" class="fb-create-button">
        <div class="tr">
          <div class="bl">
            <div class="br">
              <span>Create Something</span>
            </div>
          </div>
        </div>
      </a>
    </div>
</div>
```

The h2 header displays the icon as a background image, which for this example I simply reference a built-in Facebook graphic. Following Facebook style convention, the `fb-create-button-wrapper` div is used to define the Create button. This wrapper contains a set of `div`s and a `span`, each of which is used to emulate the unique look of the button.

The following styles transform that HTML markup into a dashboard that closely emulates the kind you would create on an FBML page:

```
.fb-dashboard { padding: 10px 10px 0px; }

.fb-dashboard .fb-links { padding: 0px 10px 5px; border-bottom: solid 1px #ccc;
                          }

.fb-dashboard .fb-links .fb-actions { float: left; }

.fb-dashboard .fb-links .fb-help { float: right; }

.fb-dashboard .fb-links .pipe { padding: 0px 7px; color: #aaa; }

.fb-dashboard .fb-links form { display: inline; overflow: hidden; width: 0px; }

.fb-dashboard .fb-titlebar { padding: 10px 10px 12px; }

.fb-dashboard .fb-titlebar h2 {
      background-repeat: no-repeat;
      background-position: 1px 8px;
      float: left;
      font-size: 14px;
      padding: 7px 0px 7px 24px;
}
.fb-dashboard .fb-create-button-wrapper {
  float: right;
  margin: 7px 0px 0px 10px;
  background: url(http://www.facebook.com/images/new_media_button_active.gif)
              no-repeat bottom;

/* fb-create-button */

.fb-create-button {
  display: block;
  float: left;
  color: #777;
  text-decoration: none;
  background: url(http://www.facebook.com/images/new_media_button.gif) no-
              repeat;
}
```

```
.fb-create-button .tr { background:
           url(http://www.facebook.com//images/new_media_button.gif) no-
           repeat top right; }

.fb-create-button .bl { background:
           url(http://www.facebook.com//images/new_media_button.gif) no-
           repeat bottom left; }
.fb-create-button .br { background:
           url(http://www.facebook.com//images/new_media_button.gif) no-
           repeat bottom right; }

.fb-create-button span {
  background: url(http://www.facebook.com/images/new_media_button_plus.gif) no-
           repeat 9px center;
  color: #333;
  font-size: 11px;
  font-weight: bold;
  display: block;
  padding: 3px 9px 5px 22px;
  text-shadow: white 0px 1px 1px;
}

.fb-create-button:hover { text-decoration: underline; }

.fb-create-button:active,
.fb-create-button:active .tr,
.fb-create-button:active .bl,
.fb-create-button:active .br { background-image:
           url(http://www.facebook.com/images/new_media_button_active.gif); }
```

Note that I am referencing a Facebook image to match the look and feel of the
Create button. In each of the cases in which graphics are used in the styles,
I reference the Facebook URL of the actual resource.

I also define the `clearfix` class, which is used by the `fb-links` and
`fb-titlebar div` elements. The `clearfix` class is a utility class used
by Facebook to achieve subtle formatting tweaks. Here's the code:

```
.clearfix:after { content: "."; display: block; clear: both; visibility: hidden;
           line-height: 0; height: 0; }

.clearfix { display: inline-block; }

html[xmlns] .clearfix { display: block; }

* html .clearfix { height: 1%; }
```

Figure 10-2 shows the homemade dashboard on an iframe page.

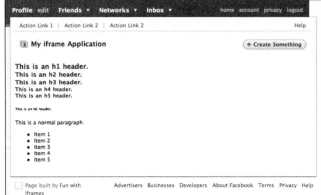

Figure 10-2:
The
dashboard —
Is it live or is
it Memorex?

Creating your own navigation tabs

The familiar blue, gray, and white navigation tabs are one of the more ubiquitous visual elements of any Facebook application. You can re-create them in your iframe by using a combination of HTML and CSS.

The `fb:tabs` container can be re-created using a `div`, and then left- and right-aligned tabs are placed inside separate `div` elements (usually added to the page just after the dashboard code):

```
<div class="fb-tabs clearfix">
<center>
  <div class="left_tabs">
  </div>
  <div class="right_tabs">
  </div>
</center>
</div>
```

The individual tabs are then re-created using bulleted list items. For example, the following code defines three left-aligned tabs and two right-aligned tabs:

```
<div class="fb-tabs clearfix">
<center>
  <div class="left_tabs">
    <ul class="fb-tabitems clearfix">
      <li><a href="#" class="selected">NavbarLink1</a></li>
      <li><a href="#">NavbarLink2</a></li>
      <li><a href="#">NavbarLink3</a></li>
    </ul>
  </div>
```

```
    <div class="right_tabs">
      <ul class="fb-tabitems clearfix">
        <li><a href="#">NavbarLink1Right</a></li>
        <li><a href="#">NavbarLink2Right</a></li>
      </ul>
    </div>
  </center>
</div>
```

Note that the first tab item is assigned to the `selected` class, which indicates that it will be the selected tab when the page is rendered.

The following CSS code is used to emulate the Facebook look and feel:

```
.fb-tabs { border-bottom: 1px solid #898989; padding: 3px 0; }

.fb-tabs .left_tabs { float: left; padding-left: 10px; }

.fb-tabs .right_tabs { float: right; padding-right: 10px; }

.fb-tabitems {
  display: inline;
  list-style: none;
  margin: 0;
  padding: 0;
  text-align: center;
}

.fb-tabitems li {
  display:inline;
  padding: 2px 0px 3px;
  background: #f1f1f1 url(http://www.facebook.com/images/components/toggle_
             tab_gloss.gif) top left repeat-x;
}

.fb-tabitems li a {
  border: 1px solid #898989;
  color: #333;
  font-weight: bold;
  padding: 2px 8px 3px 9px;
}

.fb-tabitems li a small { font-size: 11px; font-weight: normal; }

.fb-tabitems li a:focus { outline: 0px; }

.fb-tabitems li.first a { border:1px solid #898989; }

.fb-tabitems li a.selected {
  background: #6d84b4;
  border: 1px solid #3b5998;
  border-left: 1px solid #5973a9;
  border-right: 1px solid #5973a9;
```

```
  color: #fff;
  margin-left: -1px;
}
.fb-tabitems li.last a.selected {
  margin-left:-1px;
  border-left:1px solid #5973a9;
  border-right:1px solid #36538f;
}
.fb-tabitems li.first a.selected {
  margin: 0;
  border-left: 1px solid #36538f;
  border-right: 1px solid #5973a9;
}

.fb-tabitems li.first.last a.selected { border: 1px solid #36538f; }

.fb-tabitems li a.selected:hover { text-decoration: none; }
```

Figure 10-3 shows the newly created dashboard and navigation tabs.

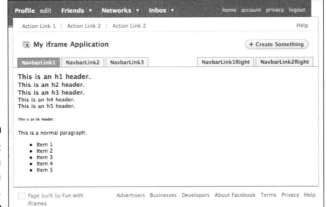

Figure 10-3:
Navigation
tabs on an
iframe page.

Creating a subtitle region

Beneath the navigation tabs region, some Facebook apps provide a subtitle region, which usually contains a caption or perhaps links to other pages if you are displaying multipage listings (such as in the Photos app).

No FBML tags exist to render this section in an FBML page, but here's how you can define it in HTML:

```
<div class="subtitle clearfix">
  <div class="caption">This is a place for captions and subtitles.</div>
</div>
```

The CSS for these two `div` elements is as follows:

```
.subtitle {
  border-bottom: 1px solid #D8DFEA;
  clear: both;
  padding: 11px 20px 0px;
  color: black;
  font-weight: normal;
  line-height: normal; }
.subtitle .caption {
  color: #333;
  float: left;
  padding-top: 3px;
  padding-bottom: 4px;
}
```

As Figure 10-4 shows, the iframe page now contains a full header section that looks like an FBML-generated page.

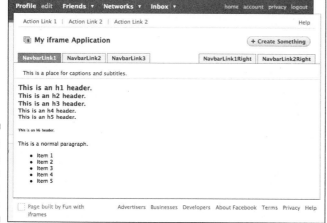

Figure 10-4:
Adding a subtitle header to a page.

Emulating Facebook buttons

Facebook uses several different sizes or styles of buttons throughout its UI, but I show you how to emulate two of them: A standard input button and a "link button" are used, for example, on the Register for Facebook startup page.

The input button is defined using the standard HTML element:

```
<input type="button" class="inputbutton" value="Do Action"/>
```

The CSS class `inputbutton` defines the border and font settings for the button:

```
.inputbutton {
  border-style: solid;
  border-top-width: 1px;
  border-left-width: 1px;
  border-bottom-width: 1px;
  border-right-width: 1px;
  border-top-color: #D9DFEA;
  border-left-color: #D9DFEA;
  border-bottom-color: #0e1f5b;
  border-right-color: #0e1f5b;
  background-color: #3b5998;
  color: #ffffff;
  font-size: 11px;
  font-family: "Lucida Grande", Tahoma, Verdana, Arial, sans-serif;
  padding: 2px 15px 3px 15px;
  text-align: center;
}
```

The link button is slightly more involved, because it uses a set of `div`s and an a link to re-create the Facebook look:

```
<div>
  <a href="#" class="link_btn_style reg_btn_style">
    <div>
      <div>
        <div>
          <span class="btn_text">Click Me</span>
        </div>
      </div>
    </div>
  </a>
</div>
```

The CSS used to style the link button uses a set of selectors to format the `div`, `link`, and `span` elements:

```
a.link_btn_style {
  color: #fff;
  font-size: 13px;
  outline: none;
  display:block;
  height:25px;
}

html[xmlns] a.link_btn_style { display:table; }

a.link_btn_style div,
a.link_btn_style span {
  cursor:pointer;
  float:left;
```

```
  line-height:15px;
  padding: 0px 0px 2px 0px;
  background-repeat: no-repeat;
  background-position: bottom left;
}

a.link_btn_style div div {
  padding:0px 2px 0px 0px;
  background-position: top right;
}

a.link_btn_style div div div {
  padding:0px;
  background-position: top left;
}

a.link_btn_style span.btn_text {
  display:block;
  margin:2px -2px -2px 2px;
  padding:2px 19px 5px 17px;
  background-position: bottom right;
}

* html a.link_btn_style span { position:relative; }

a.reg_btn_style div {
    background-image:
        url(http://www.facebook.com/images/welcome/btn_register_signup_
        active_bg.gif);
}

a.reg_btn_style span.btn_text {
  color:#fff;
  font-weight:normal;
}

a.reg_btn_style:link div,
a.reg_btn_style:link span,
a.reg_btn_style:visited div,
a.reg_btn_style:visited span {
  background-image:
            url(http://www.facebook.com//images/welcome/btn_register_signup_
            bg.gif);
}

a.reg_btn_style:active div,
a.reg_btn_style:active span {
  background-image:
            url(http://www.facebook.com//images/welcome/btn_register_signup_
            active_bg.gif);
}
```

Figure 10-5 shows these two buttons on the iframe page.

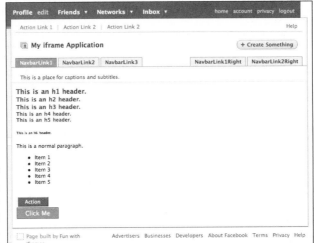

Figure 10-5:
Facebook-
looking
buttons.

Creating two-column lists

Facebook makes use of a two-column list structure inside some of its apps. Even if you are using an FBML page, no FBML tag equivalents exist, so to re-create this look on your canvas page, you need to go the custom route.

The two-column list can be created using a table structure in HTML. Check out the code:

```
<div>
  <table class="lists" cellspacing="0" border="0">
  <tr>
    <th><h4>List 1</h4><a href="#">See All</a></th>
    <th class="spacer"></th>
    <th><h4>List 2</h4><a href="#">See All</a></th>
  </tr>
  <tr>
     <td class="list">
      <div class="list_item clearfix">
      Aenean felis purus, ullamcorper sed, laoreet quis, porttitor et,
          mauris. Donec blandit dictum dui. Cras magna erat, sagittis vitae,
          ornare quis, dignissim eget, orci. Sed viverra nisl nec erat. Ut
          vulputate. Sed vitae elit sed nisi condimentum fringilla. Proin
          dapibus dui ac tellus.
      </div>
    </td>
    <td class="spacer"></td>
    <td class="list">
```

```
        <div class="list_item clearfix">
          Nulla in tellus tempor mauris euismod bibendum. Vestibulum metus quam,
             tincidunt sed, gravida pretium, vulputate a, augue. Maecenas
             tempus metus a nulla. Nullam sollicitudin, lorem ut ultricies
             ultricies, est ipsum vulputate nunc, vel feugiat mi sem in erat.
          </div>
        </td>
      </tr>
      <tr>
      <td class="see_all"><div><a href="#">See all List 1's</a></div></td>
      <td class="spacer"></td>
      <td class="see_all"><div><a href="#">See all List 2's</a></div></td>
      </tr>
      </table>
    </div>
```

The following CSS styles define the look for each of the various list elements:

```
.lists th { background: #6d84b4; text-align: left; padding: 5px 10px; }
.lists .spacer {
  background: none;
  border: none;
  padding: 0px;
  margin: 0px;
  width: 10px;
}

.lists th h4 { float: left; color: white; }
.lists th a { float: right; font-weight: normal; color: #d9dfea; }
.lists th a:hover { color: white; }

.lists td {
  margin:0px 10px;
  padding:0px;
  vertical-align:top;
  width:306px;
}

.lists .list {
  background: white none repeat scroll 0%;
  border-color: -moz-use-text-color #BBBBBB;
  border-style: none solid;
  border-width: medium 1px;
}
.lists .list .list_item { border-top:1px solid #E5E5E5; padding: 10px; }
.lists .list .list_item.first { border-top: none; }
.lists .see_all {
  background: white none repeat scroll 0%;
  border-color: -moz-use-text-color #BBBBBB rgb(187, 187, 187);
  border-style: none solid solid;
```

```
    border-width: medium 1px 1px;
    text-align: left;
}
.lists .see_all div { border-top:1px solid #E5E5E5; padding:5px 10px; }
```

The full listing of the CSS/HTML source code is available on this book's companion Web site.

Figure 10-6 displays the two-column list.

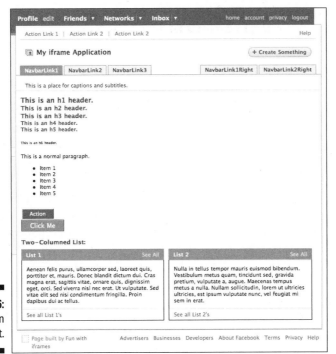

Figure 10-6: Two-column list.

Chapter 11

Hear Ye, Hear Ye: Communicating with the News Feed and Notifications

In This Chapter

▶ Publishing a News Feed story to the current user

▶ How to simultaneously publish a Mini-Feed story and News Feed story to friends

▶ Creating templatized actions

▶ Sending notifications to users

f you build it, they will come. That strategy may have worked for Ray Kinsella in *Field of Dreams,* but it is not a practical solution for Facebook application developers. For better or worse, you cannot simply develop a killer app and expect people to gravitate toward it each time they come to Facebook. The constant fear of all app developers is that users install their app, place it on their sidebar, and then quickly forget about it and never launch it again.

Because Facebook is a social environment in which users are always interacting with one another, people are constantly in each other's "business" — a status message update, a new friend, a new app installed, and so on. Therefore, one of the keys to any app that is able to achieve significant viral growth is leveraging the social network to build user loyalty and spread the news to non-users of the app.

In this chapter, you discover how to communicate effectively with users and their friends through news stories and notifications.

Before beginning this chapter, you may find it helpful to examine your application and identify specific actions that users perform that are "story worthy." Then, as you read through the chapter, you can determine the appropriate publishing method for that particular user action.

Publishing a News Feed Story to Current Users

The `feed.publishStoryToUser` API call can be used to publish a News Feed story to current users. (See Chapter 1 for more info on the News Feed.) The method is called in PHP using the following syntax:

```
feed_publishStoryToUser($title, $body, $image_1, $image_1_link, $image_2,
                $image_2_link, $image_3, $image_3_link, $image_4, $image_4_link)
```

`$title` is required, but the remaining parameters are optional. Here's more information on each of them:

✔ The `$title` parameter declares the title of the News Feed story. The title length must be 60 characters or fewer of visible text. You can include one a link in the title, but no more than one.

✔ The `$body` parameter specifies content for the story and can be a maximum of 200 visible characters. You can include a links and old-style b and i tags.

✔ The image-related attributes allow you to define up to four 75x75 pixel image links for your story. The image source can either be a Facebook PID (photo ID) or the URL of an image you have granted Facebook permission to cache.

The `feed.publishStoryToUser` returns a 1 when successful or 0 when an error has occurred.

There are a couple of usage notes when using `feed.publishStoryToUser`:

✔ As Table 11-1 shows, you can only call this method once every 12 hours for a given user. However, for development and testing purposes, there are no restrictions to publishing to your own News Feed.

✔ Your story is not guaranteed to show up in the user's News Feed. Based on Facebook's algorithms, its appearance is related to the number of competing stories and the "relative quality" of the news stories.

Table 11-1	Publishing Restrictions
Method	**Restriction**
feed.publishStoryToUser	1 story per user in a 12-hour period (unlimited to developer's user ID).
feed.publishActionOfUser	10 stories per user in a rolling 48-hour window. (Developers are limited to the same restriction.)
feed.publishTemplatizedAction	10 stories per user or page in a rolling 48-hour window. (Developers are limited to the same restriction.)
notifications.send	40 notifications (non-invitation) to a user's notifications page per day; 20 invites per user in a day.

Here's a PHP-based example using `feed.publishStoryToUser`:

```
$title = 'Your <a href="http://apps.facebook.com/dummies/recipes?14231">Buried
         Treasure Dip recipe</a> has been approved and is ready for
         sharing';
$story = 'We just wanted to let you know that Chef Cosma Crammer loved your
         recipe so much that he has stolen your idea and called it his own
         for his upcoming book <i>Best Recipes I Never Knew</i>.';
$image1 = 'http://richwagnerwords.com/facebook/rimages/14231.jpg';
$image1_link = 'http://apps.facebook.com/dummies/recipes?14231';
$success = $facebook->api_client->feed_publishStoryToUser($title, $story,
         $image1, $image1_link);
```

The `$title` contains the one permissible a link, whereas the `$story` uses an i tag (em tags are not allowed). One image link is specified.

Figure 11-1 shows the story after it is published in the News Feed.

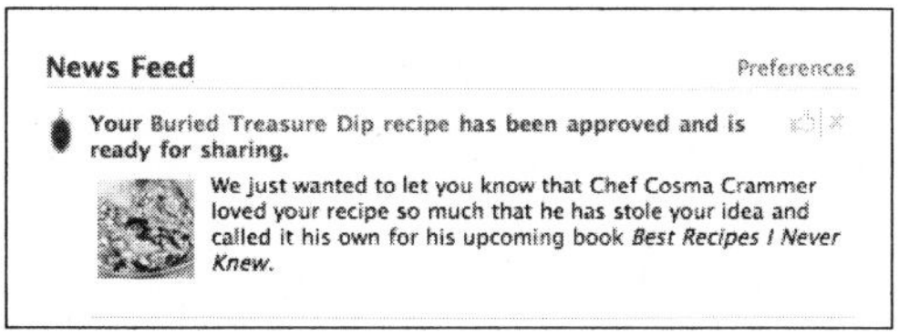

Figure 11-1:
Publishing a
story to the
current
user.

Here's a second example in which a PID is used in place of an image URL:

```
$result = $facebook->api_client->feed_publishStoryToUser('You did something
        newsworthy', '<b>You</b> performed an <i>amazing</i> feat of
        human strength and endurance today.', 2856699047694594574,
        'http://www.facebook.com/profile.php?id=665127078');

if ( $result[0] == 1 ) {
  echo "News Feed story was successfully published. Let's celebrate.";
}
else {
   echo "Unable to publish News Feed story. Isn't that awful news?";
}
```

Publishing Actions to a User's Mini-Feed and Friends' News Feed

The Mini-Feed contains a summary of the actions of a Facebook user, whereas the News Feed presents action-based stories about a Facebook user and friends of the user. However, you may often want to publish to a user's Mini-Feed of his or her recent activity, while letting app-installed friends of the user know as well through a News Feed story. You can use the `feed.publishActionOfUser` to do both at the same time.

The syntax and parameters for the method are nearly identical to that of the `feed.publishStoryToUser` call described earlier in the chapter in the "Publishing a News Feed Story to Current Users" section. In PHP, the syntax looks like this:

```
$facebook->api_client->feed_publishActionOfUser($title, $body, $image_1,
        $image_1_link, $image_2, $image_2_link, $image_3, $image_3_link,
        $image_4, $image_4_link)
```

The `$title` parameter is required, whereas others are optional. Although the parameters are the same as with `feed.publishStoryToUser`, there are some differences to the content you are permitted to place inside of them. Take a look at the details:

✔ The `$title` parameter declares the title of the story. Excluding markup tags, the title length must be 60 characters or fewer. You are limited to the FBML tags permitted. Specifically, you can include one `a` link, one `fb:userlink` (with the user ID of the person performing the action), and one or more `fb:name` tags.

If no `fb:userlink` tag is contained in your `$title` content, Facebook automatically adds it to the start of the title.

✔ The `$body` parameter specifies content for the story and can be a maximum of 200 visible characters. You can include a links, `fb:userlink` and `fb:name` FBML tags, and the old-school b and i formatting tags.

✔ The image-related attributes allow you to define up to four 75x75 pixel image links for your story. The image source can either be a Facebook PID (photo ID) or the URL of an image you have granted Facebook permission to cache.

When using `feed.publishActionOfUser`, remember the following:

✔ You can call this method up to ten times for a given user within a 48-hour window. As a developer, you have the same restriction.

✔ Although your story appears in the Mini-Feed of the user, it is not guaranteed to show up in his or her friends' News Feed. Based on Facebook's algorithms, its appearance is related to the number of competing stories and the quality of the stories relative to each other.

The `feed.publishActionOfUser` returns a 1 when successful or 0 when an error has occurred.

Consider the following PHP example:

```
$title = '<fb:userlink uid="665127078"/> is sharing <a
          href="http://apps.facebook.com/dummies/recipes?14231">Crazy
          Louie\'s Potato Chip Dip recipe</a> with <fb:name uid="530377451"
          /> and <fb:name uid="685578792" />';
$story = 'We just wanted to let you know that, with the blessings of Master Chef
          Cosmoo Crammer, <fb:userlink uid="665127078"/> is now willing to
          share his beloved recipes on fbRecipe. <a
          href="http://apps.facebook.com//dummies">Click here to share your
          recipes with Cosmoo too.</a>';
$image1 = 'http://richwagnerwords.com/facebook/rimages/14231.jpg';
$image1_link = 'http://apps.facebook.com/dummies/recipes?14231';

$result = $facebook->api_client->feed_publishActionOfUser($title, $story,
          $image1, $image1_link);

if ( $result[0] == 1 ) {
  echo "Your story was successfully published. Let's celebrate.";
}
else {
    echo "Unable to publish story. Isn't that awful news?";
}
```

This example uses `fb:userlink` and `fb:name` tags in the `$title` parameter, connecting the user with app friends who were the recipients of his action.

Figure 11-2 shows the story as published on the user's Mini-Feed.

Figure 11-2:
Mini-Feed
story just
published.

Facebook is expected to phase out `feed.publishActionOfUser` over time, so I recommend that you use `feed.publishTemplatizedAction` instead. This method is discussed more fully in the next few sections.

Rolling Up Your Sleeves: Publishing Templatized Actions

If `feed.publishActionOfUser` is a relatively straightforward way to publish a story to the Mini-Feed and News Feed, think of `feed.publish TemplatizedAction` as its "industrial strength" counterpart. It is more complicated to assemble what Facebook calls a "templatized action," but it is also a more powerful way to publish. Here's why:

- ✔ **Story aggregation.** `feed.publishTemplatizedAction` enables two or more stories published to be aggregated, which increases the chances of it being displayed in News Feeds. In other words, if two users have the same exact story published for each of them, aggregation combines them up into one story that includes both users in the story.

- ✔ **Publish to non-app users.** This method allows you to optionally publish to the News Feeds of all friends of the user, not just those who have installed your app. (The `feed.publishActionOfUser` call, in contrast, only publishes to app user friends.) You can also publish to Pages as well.

- ✔ **Token support.** This method supports variables known as *tokens*, which enable you to more compose more flexible messages. I show you how these work in the section, "Working with tokens," later in this chapter.

Exploring the template parameters

Check out the PHP version of the call:

```
$facebook->api_client->feed_publishTemplatizedAction($title_template,
        $title_data,
        $body_template, $body_data, $body_general,
        $image_1, $image_1_link,
        $image_2, $image_2,
        $image_3, $image_3_link,
        $image_4, $image_4_link,
        $target_ids, $page_actor_id)
```

This method allows you to publish a Mini-Feed story to the logged-in user (or to a Facebook Page) and simultaneously publish a News Feed story to friends of the user about the action.

The method has several parameters. `$title_template` is the only one required. Others are optional. They are

✔ `$title_template` contains the FBML markup (60 visible characters or fewer) that is used as the title for the story. You can use `fb:name`, `fb:pronoun`, `fb:if-multiple-actors`, and a links tags, but no other markup tags are allowed.

An important distinction of `feed.publishTemplatizedAction` is the ability to use *tokens* (variables that are enclosed in squiggly brackets):

   • The `{actor}` token, which refers to the current user or Facebook page, must be included in the title.

   • The `{target}` token can be used to specify additional user(s) related to the story. The `$target_ids` parameter supplies the user IDs.

   • You can also add your own tokens and then specify corresponding values using the `$title_data` parameter.

Developers are permitted to publish stories only in which the `{actor}` plays an *active* role in the activity. For example, `Rich added a new recipe` is acceptable, but `Rich has a free recipe box waiting for him` is not.

✔ `$title_data` is used to declare a JSON associative array that corresponds to the tokens you defined in the `$title_template`. (However, the array cannot substitute for `{actor}` and `{target}`.)

✔ `$body_template` contains the markup for the story's body. The displayed content must be 200 characters or less. Permissible tags include `fb:userlink`, `fb:name`, `fb:pronoun`, `fb:if-multiple-actors`, a, b, and i. Once again, you can use tokens.

✔ `$body_data`, much like `$title_data`, contains a display a JSON associative array that you wish to have substituted into `$body_template`.

✔ `$body_general` provides additional markup to be displayed in the story's body.

The difference between this parameter and `$body_template` is that `$body_general` does not aggregate. Therefore, because this content does not need to match another story for aggregation to occur, this parameter is the spot in which you can place unique content for a given user.

✔ The `$image_x` and `$image_x_link` parameters provides a way to enter up to four image links.

✔ `$target_ids` is a comma-delimited list of user IDs that are directly linked to the story. (This parameter is required if you use `{target}` in `$title_template` or `$body_template`.)

✔ `$page_actor_id` is used to optionally specify a page ID when publishing to a Facebook page that has the app installed.

In order for two or more stories to aggregate, the following pieces of the story must be identical:

✔ `$title_template`

✔ `$title_data`

✔ `$body_template`

✔ `$body_data`

✔ `$target_ids`

When stories are aggregated, `{actor}` takes on the names of all of the users in the stories.

You are limited to calling `feed.publishTemplatizedAction` ten times for each user or Page in a rolling 48-hour window.

Working with tokens

One of the powerful aspects of `feed.publishTemplatizedAction` is the ability to use tokens, making it easy for you to create content templates that are easy to use from story to story. For example:

```
{actor} added a new recipe.
{actor} is throwing a pie at {target}.
{actor} made a cake for {target}.
```

The one potential gotcha that can arise when stories are aggregated, how-ever, is subject-verb agreement. For example, suppose the following two sto-ries are combined into a single news item:

```
Jordan is throwing pie at Josh.
Jared is throwing a pie at Josh.
```

With the template defined above, the following aggregated title would be generated:

```
Jordan and Jared is throwing a pie at Josh.
```

To the rescue, the `fb:if-multiple-actors` allows you to specify alternate content when multiple actors are used in an aggregated story. Here's how the template would look:

```
{actor} <fb:if-multiple-actors>are<fb:else>is</fb:else></fb:if-multiple-actors>
          throwing a pie at {target}.
```

Now, when aggregated, the template displays grammar that would make any English teacher proud:

```
Jordan and Jared are throwing a pie at Josh.
```

The `{actor}` and `{target}` tokens are reserved. The `{actor}` receives its value from the current session ID (current user) or the `$page_actor_id` (if the actor is a Facebook Page). The `{target}` token receives its value from the `$target_ids` parameter. However, consider the following template:

```
{actor} made a {recipe} for {holiday}.
```

The `{recipe}` and `{holiday}` tokens are variables that I am defining specif-ically for use with my news story. The `$title_data` and `$body_data` para-meters are used for passing this data to Facebook. The values for these two parameters must be in the form of a JSON-encoded associative array:

```
{"recipe":"California Grits","holiday":"Festivus"}
```

In PHP, you can define using the `json_encode()` function as

```
$title_data = json_encode(array(
    'recipe' => 'California Grits',
    'holiday' => 'Festivus',
));
```

Exploring the fbRecipe template

Consider a full example of `feed.publishTemplatizedAction` using the sample `fbRecipe` app. I'll begin by defining the template title, using tokens:

```
$title_template = '{actor} <fb:if-multiple-
            actors>are<fb:else>is</fb:else></fb:if-multiple-actors> sharing
            {recipe} with {target} for {holiday}';
```

The `fb:if-multiple-actors` tag is included to ensure subject-verb agreement, regardless of the number of actors in an aggregated story.

The `{actor}` is always replaced by the current user, whereas the `{target}` is specified with the `$target_ids` parameter. I include two user IDs in the comma-delimited list:

```
$target_ids = '530377451,685578792';
```

The data represented by the `{recipe}` and `{holiday}` tokens are defined in the `$title_data` parameter:

```
$title_data = json_encode(array(
    'recipe' => 'Crazy Louie\'s Potato Chip Dip recipe',
    'holiday'  => 'New Year\'s Eve'
));
```

The `$body_template` provides a full description of the story:

```
$body_template = 'We just wanted to let you know that, with the blessings of
            Master Chef Cosmoo Crammer, {actor} <fb:if-multiple-
            actors>are<fb:else>is</fb:else></fb:if-multiple-actors> sharing
            his beloved recipes on fbRecipe. <a
            href="http://apps.facebook.com/dummies">Click here to join
            fbRecipe and share your recipes with the Great Cosmoo too.</a>';
```

One image link is defined:

```
$image1 = 'http://richwagnerwords.com/facebook/rimages/14231.jpg';
$image1_link = 'http://apps.facebook.com/dummies/recipes?14231';
```

The API call is then made using each of the defined parameters:

```
$result = $facebook->api_client->feed_publishTemplatizedAction($title_template,
            $title_data, $body_template, '', '', $image_1, $image_1_link,
            null, null, null, null, null, null, $target_ids, null);
```

Here's the complete listing for this example:

```
$title_template = '{actor} is sharing {recipe} with {target} for {holiday}';
$title_data = json_encode(array(
    'recipe' => 'Crazy Louie\'s Potato Chip Dip recipe',
    'holiday'  => 'New Year\'s Eve'
));
$body_template = 'We just wanted to let you know that, with the blessings of
                Master Chef Cosmoo Crammer, {actor} <fb:if-multiple-
                actors>are<fb:else>is</fb:else></fb:if-multiple-actors> sharing
                his beloved recipes on fbRecipe. <a
                href="http://apps.facebook.com/dummies">Click here to join
                fbRecipe and share your recipes with the Great Cosmoo too.</a>';
$image1 = 'http://richwagnerwords.com/facebook/rimages/14231.jpg';
$image1_link = 'http://apps.facebook.com/dummies/recipes?14231';
$target_ids = '530377451,685578792';

$result = $facebook->api_client->feed_publishTemplatizedAction($title_template,
                $title_data, $body_template, '', '', $image_1, $image_1_link,
                null, null, null, null, null, null, $target_ids, null);

if ( $result[0] == 1 ) {
  echo "Your story was successfully published. Let's celebrate.";
}
else {
    echo "Unable to publish story. Isn't that awful news?";
}
```

Figure 11-3 shows the story when it shows up in the Mini-Feed.

Figure 11-3:
Template
story.

Registering your story template

Facebook also allows you to register a news story template. When you register, your stories become eligible for being distributed to non-users of your
application. In addition, registered story templates are monitored by
Facebook so they can measure how engaged users are in your stories
(through the thumb's up and x buttons). You can register up to ten story
templates for each application.

To register a news story template, go to the My Applications page (www.facebook.com/developers/apps.php). In your application listing, click the Feed Templates link. (See Figure 11-4.)

Feed Templates link

Figure 11-4:
Begin here
to register
your news
story
templates.

On the following page, click the Register New Template link. The Register Feed Story Templates page is displayed (see Figure 11-5).

Figure 11-5:
Defining
the story
template
to be
registered.

Tips for getting published

Like it or not, the stories you work so hard to compose are not guaranteed to be displayed on the News Feed of your user's friends. Your chances of success depend on a top-secret Facebook algorithm. However, to increase your chances, consider these tips:

✔ Register your story template with Facebook. Only stories that are published using registered templates have a chance at being displayed to friends who do not have your application installed.

✔ When you add a link to your story, you should not take the user to a page that requires a login. A login prompt usually discourages users from following through on the link and may cause them to click the dreaded X (Close) button.

✔ Make sure your content is worthwhile to users and not just NFN — News Feed Noise.

Enter the content in the Title Template and Body Template boxes. If you would like to have your news story considered for publication to non-users of your app, be sure to click the check box near the bottom of this page. Click Submit.

Sending Notifications

Facebook provides a way to notify users of your application or friends of theirs through its `notifications.send` API call. The function in PHP looks like this:

```
$facebook->api_client->notifications_send($to_ids, $notification)
```

The `$to_ids` parameter is a comma-delimited of user IDs. The users must be users of the application or friends of the current user. The `$notification` parameter is the FBML content to be displayed.

When you send a message to other users, the current user's name is added to the start of the notification. If you just send to the current user, the name is not added.

Here's how to send a notification to the current user:

```
$facebook->api_client->notifications_send( null, 'Your <a
        //href="http://apps.facebooks.com/dummies//newrecipe.php">new
        recipe</a> is ready for viewing.');
```

Figure 11-6 shows the results in the Notifications list.

Figure 11-6:
Notification
sent from
application.

Here's how to send a notification to a list of others:

```
$facebook->api_client->notifications_send(array(530377451,685578792, 665127078),
            ': My <a
            href="http://apps.facebooks.com/dummies//newrecipe.php">new
            recipe</a> is available for viewing.');
```

Figure 11-7 shows the result in the current user's notification list, including a notification that a message was sent on the user's behalf. Figure 11-8 shows the message in the friend's list.

Figure 11-7:
Notification
to the
current
user.

Figure 11-8:
Notification
to a friend.

Chapter 12

Tying It All Together: Speed Dial Application

● ●

In This Chapter

▶ Scoping out the application

▶ Using FBML and the Facebook API inside PHP

▶ Designing the canvas page UI

▶ Rendering the profile box content

▶ Publishing notifications and News Feed stories

● ●

*T*hroughout this book, I progressively explore the various technologies in which you need to become proficient if you are going to build applications for the Facebook Platform. However, now it is time for me to roll up my sleeves and walk through an entire application, tying together a MySQL database, PHP app server, and the Facebook Platform.

The app explored in the case study in this chapter is called Speed Dial. It is inspired by *Seinfeld*'s famous Speed Dial episode, in which Jerry notices that he is on his girlfriend Valerie's Speed Dial and begins to obsess over his position on it. Speed Dial allows users to add their friends to their own profile's Speed Dial, creating a "relationship barometer," to borrow the words of Jerry.

Coming Up with a Basic Vision

Several profile-based third-party apps on Facebook extend the functionality offered by the basic Friends profile box. In watching an old rerun of the Speed Dial episode *Seinfeld* one day, however, I decided that it would be a fun idea to take this "relationship barometer" and transform it into a social networking app.

I envisioned the primary user interaction with Speed Dial as a profile box. The UI would be a square grid of ranked friends that visually looked like buttons on a phone. Most of the fun of the app is simply the ranking of friends on the dial, but I wanted to add some basic functionality, including the ability to jump to the friend's profile, to poke the friend, and to go to the friend's wall.

In a further nod to the television episode, I wanted to add a Poison Control spot in which a user could place a secret friend. (If you've seen the *Seinfeld* episode, you will recall that the stepmom of Jerry's girlfriend places Jerry under the Poison Control Speed Dial button.) A Poison Control image (the gagging green face of Mr. Yuk) would take the place of the user, but still link to the secret friend.

The app's canvas page would be kept as simple as possible and be used simply for configuring the Speed Dial itself, such as adding, reordering, and removing friends. It would also have a space for inviting friends.

Perhaps the biggest decision I had to make at the design stage was trying to determine whether to use an FBML or iframe page. I wanted to use FBML to leverage the tight Facebook integration that you get with FBML to speed and simplify development. However, I envisioned a drag-and-drop interface for configuring the Speed Dial and knew that I'd have to go with an iframe solution if I went that direction.

I conducted a drag-and-drop proof of concept during the design stage, but felt like the UI that I came up with was not all that much easier to use than a forms-based solution that I could implement using FBML. Therefore, in the end, I ended up opting for FBML.

At the design stage, make sure you fully think through the FBML versus iframe decision. The decision you make has major implications for how your application turns out, or at least how it is implemented.

Setting Up Speed Dial in Facebook

After you have the basic design goals and objectives determined, your next step in any Facebook application is setting up the application inside of the My Application area at `www.facebook.com/developers/apps.php`. If you have worked through this book in order, you know by now that most of these options are fairly straightforward.

Perhaps the key decision to make in setting up your application is deciding on the Canvas Page URL. I tried for `http://apps.facebook.com/speeddial`, but it was already taken — evidently another Facebook developer had a similar idea! So, I opted for the hyphenated solution instead: `http://apps.facebook.com/speed-dial`.

Figure 12-1 shows the base options for Speed Dial.

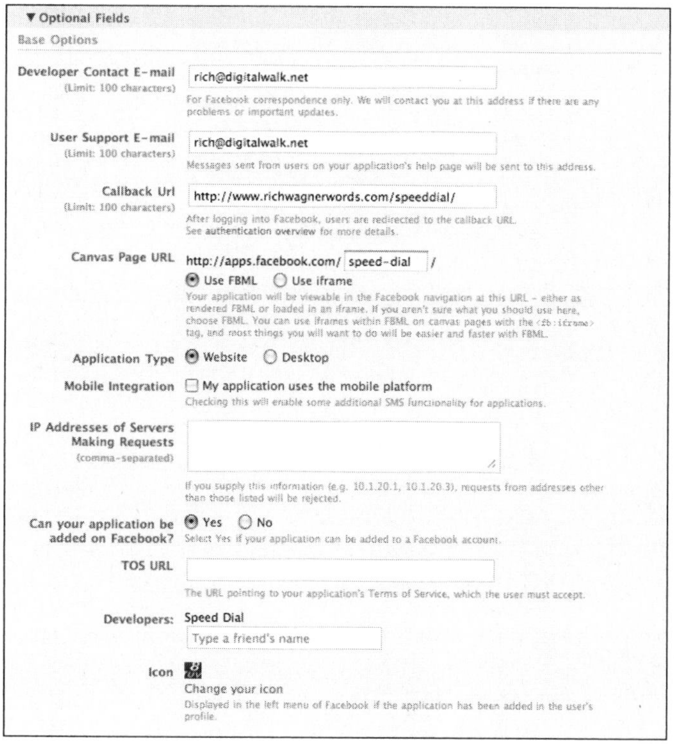

Figure 12-1: Base options for Speed Dial.

In the Installation Options section are a few noteworthy options to speak of:

✔ Although it makes more sense for users to add Speed Dial to their profile instead of a Facebook page, there is no reason technically why a page could not add it, so I enabled the option for both users and pages.

✔ The Post-Add URL should be an `apps.facebook.com` URL, not my own domain.

✔ Because the profile box content is the heart of the app and will be rendered immediately when the user first views Speed Dial, I choose not to add Default FBML.

✔ However, I have only one default profile action (Edit My Speed Dial) for version 1.0, so I am going to add the FBML code here.

✔ I specify Narrow as the Default Profile Box Column. For Speed Dial, this setting is equivalent. I decided during the design stage that the "phone dial" interface should be rendered only in narrow mode, not wide.

✔ The Developer Mode box should be checked during the coding and testing stage.

Figure 12-2 displays the Installation options.

Figure 12-2:
Installation
options for
Speed Dial.

The Integration Points section is used to connect various optional parts of the application to Facebook. The only integration point I am concerned about at this point is the Side Nav URL, as shown in Figure 12-3. This URL must be the canvas page URL (apps.facebook.com/myapp), not a separate domain.

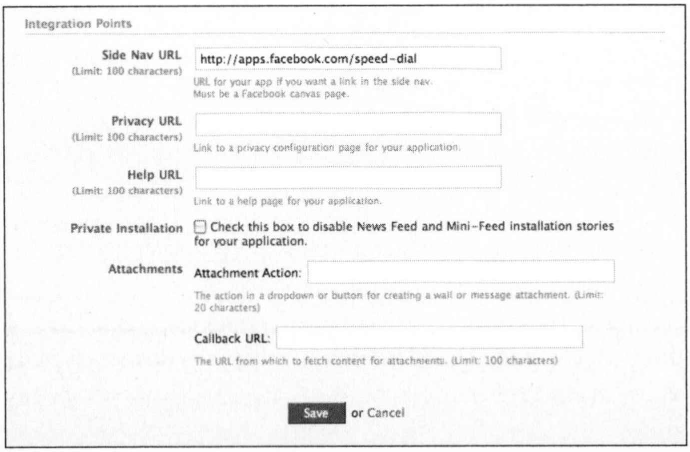

Figure 12-3:
Integration
points
options for
Speed Dial.

After I click Save, I am brought back to the main My Applications window, shown in Figure 12-4. From there, the API key and secret key are displayed. I will need that info when I begin to code my application.

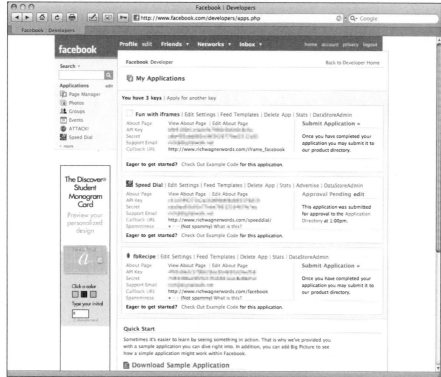

Figure 12-4:
Speed Dial
shown in
the My
Applications
page.

Creating the Speed Dial Database

As I mention at the start of the chapter, Speed Dial is a PHP-based application that uses a MySQL backend database. The data the app needs to store is quite basic, consisting of four fields in a table named `speeddial`. The fields are as follows:

- User ID of the current user (`bigint`).
- Friend ID of the user assigned to the Speed Dial (`bigint`).
- Ranking of the user (value between 1-12) (`tinyint`).
- Thumbnail, which indicates the thumbnail image to display. For now, 0 indicates the default user picture and 1 indicates the Poison Control image. A future version may add additional thumbnails (`tinyint`).

The SQL for creating the database table is shown below:

```
CREATE TABLE speeddial (
   uid bigint(20) NOT NULL default '0',
   fid bigint(20) NOT NULL,
   ranking tinyint(4) NOT NULL,
   thumbnail tinyint(4) NOT NULL default '0',
   PRIMARY KEY  (uid,fid)
) ENGINE=MyISAM DEFAULT CHARSET=latin1;
```

Structuring the PHP Source Code

In structuring the source code for Speed Dial, I divided it up into several different source files, as follows:

- ✔ appinclude.php contains global variable declarations and the basic Facebook login routine.

- ✔ db.php defines all of the MySQL database routines.

- ✔ display.php defines all of the main routines associated with the canvas page.

- ✔ index.php serves as the main application file.

- ✔ invite.php contains the routines used for the Invite Friends module.

- ✔ profile.php defines all of the functions for rendering the profile box.

- ✔ publish.php contains routines for sending notifications or publishing News Feed stories.

By dividing up the source code across several files by app module, the source code becomes easy to navigate and make sense of.

Figure 12-5 shows the basic architecture of Speed Dial.

Setting Up the Canvas Page

The profile box may be intended as the primary UI of Speed Dial, but because of the architecture of the Facebook Platform, an app's profile box can't drive the application itself. The FBML content for the profile box, after all, is cached by Facebook. It must be generated by Speed Dial elsewhere. As a result, the Speed Dial's canvas page becomes the primary driver of all application activity.

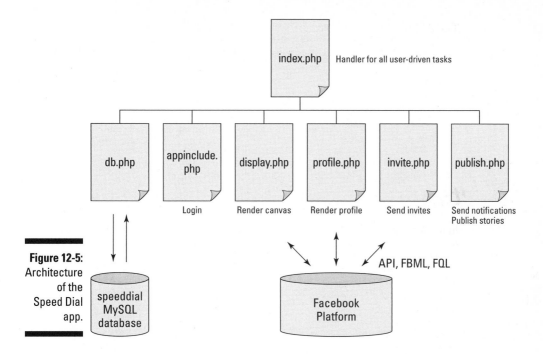

Figure 12-5:
Architecture
of the
Speed Dial
app.

Speed Dial's canvas page is the `index.php` source file. As the first step in coding, I'll add includes to the other app files:

```php
<?php
include_once 'appinclude.php';
include_once 'db.php';
include_once 'display.php';
include_once 'profile.php';
include_once 'publish.php';
```

I get back to the canvas page UI of `index.php` in a moment, but I first need to connect to Facebook and enable login. To do that, I start by discussing `appinclude.php`.

Connecting to Facebook

The first activity in any Facebook application is to connect to instantiate a Facebook object and then log in to Facebook. Fortunately, this code is boilerplate for most any application. You simply need to substitute the app-specific keys and URLs. (See Chapter 2 for another example.)

At the same time, I need to define the database user name and password that my database routines will use later on. Here's the initial source code that I am housing inside of `appinclude.php` (substitute actual values for my place-holders below):

```php
<?php
require_once '../facebook-platform/client/facebook.php';

$APP_API_KEY = 'i_place_my_api_key_here';
$APP_SECRET = 'i_place_my_secret_key_here';
$APP_CALLBACK_URL = 'http://www.richwagnerwords.com/speeddial/';
$APP_ROOT_URL = 'http://apps.facebook.com/speed-dial/';

$DB_IP = 'localhost';
$DB_USER = 'my_db_user_name_here';
$DB_PASS = 'my_db_password_here';
$DB_NAME = 'my_db_name_here';

// Connect to Facebook, retrieve user
$facebook = new Facebook($APP_API_KEY, $APP_SECRET);
$user = $facebook->get_loggedin_user();
$is_logged_out = !$user;

// Exception handler for invalid session_keys
try {
  // If app is not added, then attempt to add
  if (!$facebook->api_client->users_isAppAdded()) {
    $facebook->redirect($facebook->get_add_url());
  }
} catch (Exception $ex) {
  // Clear out cookies for app and redirect user to a login prompt
  $facebook->set_user(null, null);
  $facebook->redirect($APP_CALLBACK_URL);
}
?>
```

Building the Canvas Page

The user interface for the canvas page needs to be able to enable the user to perform the following activities:

- Look up a friend and add him to a specific spot on the Speed Dial.

- Remove a friend or all friends from the Speed Dial.

- Assign a friend the Poison Control thumbnail.

- Preview the Speed Dial.

- Invite friends to join Speed Dial.

Constructing the page header

There is a logical division for all of the activities from the previous list — configure and invite modes. As a result, a two-tab navigation scheme was most appropriate using `fb:tabs`. I also added an `fb:dashboard` to display the app name and icon, even though I don't have immediate use for `fb:action` links at this time.

The `render_canvas_header()` function, placed inside of `display.php`, is used to render the header. The `$invite` parameter indicates which tab is selected:

```php
function render_canvas_header($invite) {
  global $APP_ROOT_URL;

  echo '<fb:dashboard>';
  echo '</fb:dashboard>';

  echo '<fb:tabs>';
  if (!$invite) {
    echo '<fb:tab-item href="' . $APP_ROOT_URL . 'index.php" title="Set Your
          Speed Dial" selected="true" />';
    echo '<fb:tab-item href="' . $APP_ROOT_URL . 'invite.php" title="Invite
          Friends" />';
  }
  else {
    echo '<fb:tab-item href="' . $APP_ROOT_URL . 'index.php" title="Set Your
          Speed Dial" />';
    echo '<fb:tab-item href="' . $APP_ROOT_URL . 'invite.php" title="Invite
          Friends" selected="true"/>';
  }

  echo '</fb:tabs>';

  echo '<div style="padding: 10px 20px 20px"></div>';
}
```

The `index.php` file calls this routine as its first step in generating the UI for the page:

```php
render_canvas_header(false);
```

I then use some FBML to provide a user-specific greeting as a header in `index.php`:

```html
<h3>Welcome <fb:name uid="loggedinuser" firstnameonly="true" useyou="false"
          capitalize="true"/> to Speed Dial, the Relationship Barometer
          </h3>
<br />
```

Adding a friend

The interface for adding a friend to the Speed Dial needs to have three controls — a friend picker, a placement selector, and a submit button. Facebook has different friend picker controls available through FBML, but unfortunately, the most visual one, `fb:multi-friend-input`, can be used only inside an `fb:request-form`. I could have created my own control from scratch, but for now I'm content with the `fb:friend-selector` element. This element provides a predictive friend selector input that a user can quickly use to find a friend. This control has two disadvantages, however. First, a user can't browse through all friends, but needs to know the friend's name or the start of the name first. Second, the friend's thumbnail picture is not displayed like it is in `fb:multi-friend-input`. Nonetheless, given the simplicity of the FBML tag and its UI cleanliness, I opted for `fb:friend-selector` in spite of its drawbacks. I then use a normal `select` element for obtaining the placement value. Here's the form code in `index.php`:

```
<form method="post" action="http://apps.facebook.com/speed-
    dial/index.php">
  <h4>Add a Friend</h4>
  <p>First, select a friend:</p>
  <fb:friend-selector idname="friend_picked"/>
  <br />
  <p>Then pick your friend's placement on the speed dial:</p>
  <select name="placement">
    <option value ="1">1</option>
    <option value ="2">2</option>
    <option value ="3">3</option>
    <option value ="4">4</option>
    <option value ="5">5</option>
    <option value ="6">6</option>
    <option value ="7">7</option>
    <option value ="8">8</option>
    <option value ="9">9</option>
    <option value ="10">* Asterisk</option>
    <option value ="11">0</option>
    <option value ="12"># Pound sign</option>
  </select>
    <input class="inputbutton" value="Add" type="submit"/>
</form>
```

Note that I need to account for the asterisk and pound sign keys of the Speed Dial. For simplicity, I simply assign a value of 1-12.

The input is assigned a CSS class of `inputbutton`, which I define later to emulate a blue Facebook submit button.

The `action` parameter in the form calls itself (the `index.php` file).
Therefore, I need to add a handler for the form at the top of the source file.
Here's the code:

```
if (isset($_POST['friend_picked'])) {
  $fid = $_POST['friend_picked'];
  $place = $_POST['placement'];
  add_dial_friend($user, $fid, $place, 0);
}
```

This handler assigns the form values to variables and uses them in calling a
database routine called `add_dial_friend()`, which is in the `db.php` file.
This routine calls a basic routine that gets a database connection. Both of
these functions are shown below:

```
function get_db_conn() {
  $conn = mysql_connect($GLOBALS['DB_IP'], $GLOBALS['DB_USER'],
              $GLOBALS['DB_PASS']);
  mysql_select_db($GLOBALS['DB_NAME'], $conn);
  return $conn;
}

function add_dial_friend($uid, $fid, $ranking, $thumbnail) {
  $conn = get_db_conn();
  $query = "DELETE FROM speeddial WHERE uid=$uid AND 'ranking'=$ranking";
  mysql_query($query, $conn);
  $query = "INSERT INTO 'richwagn_speeddial'.'speeddial' ('uid', 'fid',
              'ranking', 'thumbnail') VALUES ('$uid', '$fid', '$ranking',
              '$thumbnail')";
  mysql_query($query, $conn);
}
```

Getting a list of dial friends

Each time the `index.php` file loads, it makes a call to a database routine to
get the list of friends currently on the Speed Dial. This array, called
`$dial_friends`, is used in several parts of the app. Here's the call:

```
$dial_friends = get_dial_friends($user);
```

The `get_dial_friends()` function inside of `db.php` makes a `SQL SELECT`
call and returns the result set back as an array:

```
function get_dial_friends($uid) {
  $conn = get_db_conn();
  $query = "SELECT uid, fid, ranking, thumbnail FROM speeddial WHERE uid=$uid
              ORDER BY ranking";
```

```
$result = mysql_query($query, $conn);
$dial_friends = array();
while ($row = mysql_fetch_assoc($result)) {
  $dial_friends[] = $row;
}
return $dial_friends;
}
```

Previewing the Speed Dial

The canvas page (index.php) also needs to have a preview for the Speed Dial. This previewer needs to be able to show what the actual Speed Dial will look like in the profile box. However, it also provides links that enable a user to remove a friend or else assign the Poison Control designation to a friend. Here's the basic HTML added to index.php that is used to display the Speed Dial grid:

```
<table class="speeddial" border='0' cellpadding='1' width='198px'>
  <tr>
    <?php render_cell( 1) ?>
    <?php render_cell( 2) ?>
    <?php render_cell( 3 ) ?>
  </tr>
  <tr>
    <?php render_cell( 4 ) ?>
    <?php render_cell( 5 ) ?>
    <?php render_cell( 6 ) ?>
  </tr>
  <tr>
    <?php render_cell( 7 ) ?>
    <?php render_cell( 8 ) ?>
    <?php render_cell( 9 ) ?>
  </tr>
  <tr>
    <?php render_cell( 10 ) ?>
    <?php render_cell( 11 ) ?>
    <?php render_cell( 12 ) ?>
  </tr>
</table>
```

As you can see, I am going to render each of the cells using a routine called render_cell() that I add to display.php. Check out the routine before I walk you through it:

```
function render_cell($index) {
 global $dial_friends;
 global $APP_ROOT_URL;
 global $APP_CALLBACK_URL;

 $total_friends = count($dial_friends);
```

```
for ($i=0; $i<=$total_friends; $i++) {
  $match = false;
  if ( $dial_friends[$i]['ranking'] == $index ) {
    $match = true;
    $f_index = $i;
    break;
  }
}
echo "<td>";
echo "<img src=\"$APP_CALLBACK_URL/$index.png\" /><br />";
if ( !$match ) {
  echo "<img src=\"$APP_CALLBACK_URL/q_default.gif\" />";
  echo "(None) <br />";
}
else {
    if ( $dial_friends[$f_index]['thumbnail'] == 1 ) {
      echo "<img src=\"$APP_CALLBACK_URL/toxic.jpg\" />";
    }
    else {
      echo "<fb:profile-pic uid=\"{$dial_friends[$f_index]['fid']}\"
            size='square' linked='true' />";
    }
    echo "<fb:name uid=\"{$dial_friends[$f_index]['fid']}\" useyou=\"false\"
            /><br />";
    echo "<a class=\"icons\"
            href=\"{$APP_ROOT_URL}index.php?action=delete&fid={$dial_friends
            [$f_index]['fid']}\"  title=\"Remove from Speed Dial\"\"><img
            src=\"$APP_CALLBACK_URL/del.gif\"/></a>";
    echo "<a class=\"icons\"
            href=\"{$APP_ROOT_URL}index.php?action=pc&fid={$dial_friends
            [$f_index]['fid']}&place={$index} title=\"Upgrade to Poison
            Control\"\"><img src=\"$APP_CALLBACK_URL/toxic-sm.gif\" /></a>";
  }
  echo "</td>";
}
```

The `for` loop at the start of the function is used to find the specific friend
whose ranking matches the table cell. If no match is found, the function renders the cell contents as an unassigned spot. Otherwise, the friend's thumbnail image is added. (However, if the friend has the Poison Control
designation, the `toxic.jpg` image is used instead.)

The final two `echo` statements render two icon links: One calls a remove friend
command and the other calls the Poison Control action. Notice that the action-
specific values are added to the HREF attributes for these links. The `index.php`
file needs to add handlers for these parameters being passed to it. I cover that in
the "Processing user actions" section later in this chapter.

Resetting the Speed Dial

Although most of the friend activity of the Speed Dial can be added by the add friend form (see the "Adding a friend" section earlier in this chapter) and by the remove and Poison Control links in the previewer (see the previous section, "Previewing the Speed Dial"), there are a couple additional functions that should be added — the ability to clear the entire Speed Dial, and the ability to unassign the Poison Control designation. These can be accomplished using links on the canvas page (index.php) that specify the action as part of the URL, as follows:

```
<p><a href="http://apps.facebook.com/speed-
          dial//index.php?action=clearpc">Unassign the Poison Control</a>
          icon for now.</p>

<p><a href="http://apps.facebook.com/speed-
          dial//index.php?action=clearall">Remove all your friends</a> and
          start over. No soup for anyone!</p>
```

Processing user actions

Although the add friend form has its own handler already discussed earlier in the "Adding a friend" section, the action links called in the canvas page need to have a separate handler at the top of the index.php page. Here's the code:

```
// Handlers for action links
$action = $_REQUEST['action'];
$fid_actor = (int) $_REQUEST['fid'];
$place = (int) $_REQUEST['place'];

// Delete friend
if ( $action == 'delete' ) {
  remove_dial_friend($user, $fid_actor);
}
// Add as Poison Control
elseif ( $action == 'pc' ) {
  clear_thumbnail($user);
  remove_dial_friend($user, $fid_actor);
  add_dial_friend($user, $fid_actor, $place, 1);
}
// Clear all friends
elseif ( $action == 'clearall' ) {
  clear_dial($user);
}
// Clear Poison Control icon
elseif ( $action == 'clearpc' ) {
  clear_thumbnail($user);
}
```

When the `delete` action is called, a `remove_dial_friend()` function in `db.php` is executed:

```
function remove_dial_friend($uid, $fid) {
  $conn = get_db_conn();
  $query = "DELETE FROM speeddial WHERE 'uid'='$uid' AND 'fid'='$fid'";
  mysql_query($query, $conn);
}
```

When the `pc` action is called to add the Poison Control designation, the `clear_thumbnail()` function in `db.php` is first called, which resets the thumbnail values for the user's Speed Dial:

```
function clear_thumbnail($uid) {
  $conn = get_db_conn();
  $query = "UPDATE speeddial SET 'thumbnail'=0 WHERE 'thumbnail'=1 AND
            'uid'='$uid'";
  mysql_query($query, $conn);
}
```

Back in `index.php`, the friend in question is then re-added with the updated thumbnail value:

```
clear_thumbnail($user);
add_dial_friend($user, $fid_actor, $place, 1);
```

When the `clearall` action is called, the `clear_dial()` function from `db.php` is called, which removes all of the friends of the user from the `speeddial` database:

```
function clear_dial($uid) {
  $conn = get_db_conn();
  $query = "DELETE FROM speeddial WHERE 'uid'=$uid ";
  mysql_query($query, $conn);
}
```

Finally, when the `clearpc` action is called, the `clear_thumbnail()` routine is called.

Assembling the canvas page UI

So far, I've coded all of the core functionality for the canvas page, but need to assemble it in usable manner. In considering the different UI options for the main canvas page, a two-column list style seemed to work best (see `wiki.developers.facebook.com/index.php/Facebook_Styles` for more details). According to the two-column list style, I enclosed all of these controls inside of a table. Here's the code in `index.php`:

```
<h3>Welcome <fb:name uid="loggedinuser" firstnameonly="true" useyou="false"
            capitalize="true"/> to Speed Dial, the Relationship Barometer
            </h3>
<br />

<div>
  <table class="lists" cellspacing="0" border="0">
  <tr>
    <th>
      <h4>Barometerize Your Friends</h4>
    </th>
    <th class="spacer"></th>
    <th>
      <h4>Your Speed Dial</h4>
    </th>
  </tr>
  <tr>
    <td class="list">
        <div class="list_item clearfix">
            <form method="post" action="http://apps.facebook.com/speed-dial/">
            <h4>Add a Friend</h4>
            <p>First, select a friend:</p>
            <fb:friend-selector idname="friend_picked"/>
            <br />
            <p>Then pick your friend's placement on the speed dial:</p>
            <select name="placement">
              <option value ="1">1</option>
              <option value ="2">2</option>
              <option value ="3">3</option>
              <option value ="4">4</option>
              <option value ="5">5</option>
              <option value ="6">6</option>
              <option value ="7">7</option>
              <option value ="8">8</option>
              <option value ="9">9</option>
              <option value ="10">* Asterisk</option>
              <option value ="11">0</option>
              <option value ="12"># Pound sign</option>
          </select>
            <input class="inputbutton" value="Add" type="submit"/>
          </form>
          <br/>

            <h4>Pick your Special Friend</h4>
            <p>Click the <img
            src="http://www.richwagnerwords.com/speeddial/toxic-sm.gif"/>
            button under your friend's picture to assign a friend to the
            coveted Poison Control spot.</p>

            <p><a href="http://apps.facebook.com/speed-
            dial//index.php?action=clearpc">Unassign the Poison Control</a>
            icon for now.</p>
```

```
        <h4>Remove a Friend</h4>
        <p>Click the <img
        src="http://www.richwagnerwords.com/speeddial/del.gif"/> button
        under your friend's picture to delete him or her from your speed
        dial.</p>

        <p><a href="http://apps.facebook.com/speed-
        dial//index.php?action=clearall">Remove all your friends</a> and
        start over. No soup for anyone!</p>

        </div>
    </td>
    <td class="spacer"></td>
    <td class="list">
    <div class="list_item clearfix">
      <center>
        <table class="speeddial" border='0' cellpadding='1' width='198px'>
          <tr>
            <?php render_cell( 1) ?>
            <?php render_cell( 2) ?>
            <?php render_cell( 3 ) ?>
          </tr>
          <tr>
            <?php render_cell( 4 ) ?>
            <?php render_cell( 5 ) ?>
            <?php render_cell( 6 ) ?>
          </tr>
          <tr>
            <?php render_cell( 7 ) ?>
            <?php render_cell( 8 ) ?>
            <?php render_cell( 9 ) ?>
          </tr>
          <tr>
            <?php render_cell( 10 ) ?>
            <?php render_cell( 11 ) ?>
            <?php render_cell( 12 ) ?>
          </tr>
        </table>
      </center>
    </div>
  </td>
 </tr>
 </table>
</div>
```

See Chapter 10 for more details on the two-column list style.

Styling the UI

Several CSS styles are used to format these elements during rendering. The Speed Dial previewer table uses the following styles to resemble a phone dial:

```
.speeddial { margin:0 0; left:0px;}

.speeddial td {
  width: 65px;
  text-align:center;
  vertical-align: top;
  border: 1px solid #d8dfea;
  padding:2px;
}
```

The Add button is assigned the `inputbutton` class to emulate a Facebook button.

```
.inputbutton {
  border-style: solid;
  border-top-width: 1px;
  border-left-width: 1px;
  border-bottom-width: 1px;
  border-right-width: 1px;
  border-top-color: #D9DFEA;
  border-left-color: #D9DFEA;
  border-bottom-color: #0e1f5b;
  border-right-color: #0e1f5b;
  background-color: #3b5998;
  color: #ffffff;
  font-size: 11px;
  font-family: "Lucida Grande", Tahoma, Verdana, Arial, sans-serif;
  padding: 2px 15px 3px 15px;
  text-align: center;
}
```

The two-column list uses a set of styles to define its look and feel:

```
.lists th {
  background: #6d84b4;
  text-align: left;
  padding: 5px 10px;
}

.lists .spacer {
  background: none;
  border: none;
  padding: 0px;
  margin: 0px;
  width: 10px;
}
```

```
.lists th h4 { float: left; color: white; }
.lists th a { float: right; font-weight: normal; color: #d9dfea; }
.lists th a:hover { color: white; }

.lists td {
  margin:0px 10px;
  padding:0px;
  vertical-align:top;
  width:306px;
}

.lists td h4 {
  text-align:left;
  background-color: #e7e7e7;
  border: 1px solid #d8dfea;
  padding:2px;
  color: #333333;
  padding-top: 3px;
  padding-right: 10px;
  padding-bottom: 3px;
  padding-left: 10px;
  font-weight: bold;
  font-size: 11px;
  margin-top: 10px;
  margin-right: 0pt;
  margin-bottom: 0pt;
  margin-left: 0pt;

}

.lists .list {
  background:white none repeat scroll 0%;
  border-color:-moz-use-text-color #BBBBBB;
  border-color: #d8dfea;
  border-style:none solid solid;
  border-width:medium 1px 1px;
}

.lists .list .list_item { border-top:1px solid #E5E5E5; padding: 10px; }
.lists .list .list_item.first { border-top: none; }
.clearfix:after {
    content: ".";
    display: block;
    clear: both;
    visibility: hidden;
    line-height: 0;
    height: 0; }

.clearfix {
    display: inline-block; }
html[xmlns] .clearfix {
    display: block; }
* html .clearfix {
    height: 1%; }
```

Adding a random quote display

As a finishing touch to the canvas page UI, I would like to display a Speed Dial–related quote just under the page header. However, instead of a single quote, I'd like to display a random quote. To do so inside a Facebook app, I can take advantage of the `fb:random` tag, which renders content by randomly choosing a `fb:random-option` item based on the weights you provide. Here's the function in `display.php` that returns a random quote:

```
function get_random_quote() {
  $fbml .= "<fb:random>";
  $fbml .= "<fb:random-option weight=\"2\">\"You know uh, Valerie, I uh,
          couldn't help but notice that I'm on your
  speed dial.\" - Jerry</fb:random-option>";
  $fbml .= "<fb:random-option weight=\"1\">George: \"So you're on the speed
          dial?\" Jerry: \"After two dates!\"</fb:random-option>";
  $fbml .= "<fb:random-option weight=\"1\">\"Wha! You know, it's a pain to
          change that. You gotta lift up that
  plastic thing with a pen.\" - George</fb:random-option>";
  $fbml .= "<fb:random-option weight=\"1\">\"I had like a so-so date with
          Valerie, now I'm number nine on the
  speed dial.\" - Jerry</fb:random-option>";
  $fbml .= "<fb:random-option weight=\"3\">\"Yeah, this speed dial's like a
          relationship barometer.\" - Jerry </fb:random-option>";
  $fbml .= "<fb:random-option weight=\"1\">\"It's taken me thirteen years to
          climb up to the top of that
  speed dial, and I don't intend to lose my spot to you.\" - Mrs.
          Hamilton</fb:random-option>";
  $fbml .= "<fb:random-option weight=\"1\">\"You know, in the year two-thousand,
          we'll all be on speed dial. You'll
  just have to think of a person, they'll be talking to you.\" -
          Kramer</fb:random-option>";
  $fbml .= "<fb:random-option weight=\"1\">\"Uuh, I can't believe she did this
          again. That's it! She's off the
  speed dial completely!\" - Valerie</fb:random-option>";
  $fbml .= "<fb:random-option weight=\"1\">\"Wow, poison control? That's even
          higher than number one!\" - Jerry</fb:random-option>";
  $fbml .= "<fb:random-option weight=\"2\">\"I can't help thinking that maybe
          there's someone in your life who deserves [the number one spot]
          more. Someone you've known, you know, more than a week.\" -
          Jerry</fb:random-option>";
  $fbml .= "<fb:random-option weight=\"2\">\"My stepmother got to you, didn't
          she?...Uuh, I can't believe she did this again. That's it! She's
          off the speed dial completely!\" - Valerie</fb:random-option>";
  $fbml .= "<fb:random-option weight=\"2\">\"Why don't I put you on my speed-
          dial?\" - Mrs. Hamilton</fb:random-option>";
  $fbml .= "</fb:random>";
  return $fbml;
}
```

Some of the quotes are weighted higher than others based on the weight attribute of the `fb:random-option`.

In the `index.php`, the following code is provided to display the random quote:

```
<div class="q_owner"><span class ="q"><?php echo str_replace( "\"", "",
                get_random_quote() ); ?></span></div>
```

Facebook uses graphical quotation marks when it displays quotes in certain parts of its UI (such as the Events app). I am going to emulate that through the following styles, both of which call the Facebook quote mark image as a `background-image`:

```
.q_owner {
    background-color: transparent;
    background-image: url(http://www.facebook.com/images/start_quote_small.gif);
    background-repeat: no-repeat;
    padding-top: 0px;
    padding-right: 0px;
    padding-bottom: 5px;
    padding-left: 18px;
    width: 400px;
}

.q_owner span.q {
    color: #555555;
    background-color: transparent;
    background-image: url(http://www.facebook.com/images/end_quote_small.gif);
    background-repeat: no-repeat;
    background-position: center right;
    padding-top: 2px;
    padding-right: 16px;
    padding-bottom: 2px;
    padding-left: 0px;
}
```

As you can see from the `fb:random` declaration, the quotes themselves contain quotation marks. A `str_replace()` call is used to remove these quotes in favor of the graphical ones. (I use the character-based quotation marks in the profile box later.)

Adding a page footer

The final part of the canvas page is to add a standard footer. I do this with a routine contained in display.php:

```
function render_canvas_footer() {
  echo '<br/><p>Speed Dial v.0.1. Beta. Please <a
          href="http://www.facebook.com/apps/application.php?id=7727364217">
          post your feedback here</a>.</p>';
  echo '<p>Learn how to build Speed Dial in <a
          href="http://www.amazon.com/Building-Facebook-Applications-
          Dummies-Computer/dp/0470277955">Building Facebook Applications For
          Dummies</a>.</p>';
  echo '</div>';
}
```

Figure 12-6 shows the completed canvas page.

Figure 12-6:
Fully
assembled
Speed Dial
canvas
page.

Setting the Profile Box Content

Although the canvas page is fully operational, the real intent of Speed Dial is to display the Speed Dial on the user's profile. Therefore, the next step is to take the information gathered in the canvas page and render it in the profile box. The actual content that I want to display in the profile box is similar, but not identical, to the previewer shown in the canvas page.

Additionally, the way in which the canvas page and profile box content are both rendered is different. For the canvas page, I render the FBML either using literal FBML markup or through the PHP echo command. However, with the profile box, I need to pass an FBML string to the profile.setFBML() API call and then Facebook does the rendering.

The get_profile_fbml() function compiles the FBML content for use with the profile. An fb:narrow element contains the Speed Dial itself and a random quote. I don't want to display the Speed Dial inside fb:wide, so I add a quote and provide instructions to move it to the narrow column. Here's the code in profile.php:

```php
function get_profile_fbml() {

  $fbml .= "<fb:narrow>";
  $fbml .= "<style>";
  $fbml .= " table {margin:-10px 0px 0px -5px;}";
  $fbml .= " td { border: 1px solid #d8dfea; padding: 0px; width: 80px; text-
             align: center; vertical-align: top; }";
  $fbml .= "</style>";
  $fbml .= "<table>";
  $fbml .= "<tr>";
  $fbml .=   get_cell_contents(1);
  $fbml .=   get_cell_contents(2);
  $fbml .=   get_cell_contents(3);
  $fbml .=   "</tr>";
  $fbml .= "<tr>";
  $fbml .=   get_cell_contents(4);
  $fbml .=   get_cell_contents(5);
  $fbml .=   get_cell_contents(6);
  $fbml .=   "</tr>";
  $fbml .= "<tr>";
  $fbml .=   get_cell_contents(7);
  $fbml .=   get_cell_contents(8);
  $fbml .=   get_cell_contents(9);
  $fbml .=   "</tr>";
  $fbml .= "<tr>";
  $fbml .=   get_cell_contents(10);
  $fbml .=   get_cell_contents(11);
  $fbml .=   get_cell_contents(12);
  $fbml .=   "</tr>";
  $fbml .=   "</table>" ;
```

```
$fbml .= "<p style=\"color:#6d84b4;margin-top:5px;\"><strong>Random Speed Dial
        Quote:</strong></p>";
$fbml .= "<p style=\"color:#6d84b4;\">" . get_random_quote() . "</p>";
$fbml .=  "</fb:narrow>";
$fbml .= "<fb:wide>";
$fbml .= "<p style=\"color:#6d84b4;margin-top:5px;\"><strong>Random Speed Dial
        Quote:</strong></p>";
$fbml .= "<p style=\"color:#6d84b4; text-align: center;\">" .
        get_random_quote() . "</p> <br /> <br />";
$fbml .= "<p style=\"text-align: center;\">Move profile box to narrow column
        to view speed dial. </p>";
$fbml .=  "</fb:wide>";

return $fbml;
}
```

The get_cell_contents() function in profile.php is similar to the
canvas page's render_cell() function, but specific to the needs of the profile box:

```
function get_cell_contents($index) {
 global $dial_friends;
 global $APP_ROOT_URL;
 global $APP_CALLBACK_URL;

$total_friends = count($dial_friends);

 for ($i=0; $i<=$total_friends; $i++) {
   $match = false;
   if ( $dial_friends[$i]['ranking'] == $index ) {
     $match = true;
     $f_index = $i;
     break;
   }
 }

 $fbml .= "<td>";
 $fbml .= "<img src=\"$APP_CALLBACK_URL/$index.png\" /><br />";
 if ( !$match ) {
   $fbml .= "<img src=\"$APP_CALLBACK_URL/q_default.gif\" />";
   $fbml .= "(None) <br />";
 }
 else {
    if ( $dial_friends[$f_index]['thumbnail'] == 1 ) {
      $fbml .= "<img src=\"$APP_CALLBACK_URL/toxic.jpg\" />";
      $fbml .= "<a href=\"http://www.facebook.com/profile.php?id={$dial_friends
          [$f_index]['fid']}\">Poison Control</a><br />";
    }
    else {
      $fbml .= "<fb:profile-pic uid=\"{$dial_friends[$f_index]['fid']}\"
          size='square' linked='true' />";
```

```
        $fbml .= "<fb:name uid=\"{$dial_friends[$f_index]['fid']}\"
            useyou=\"false\" /><br />";
    }
    $fbml .= "<a href=\"http://www.facebook.com/poke.php?id={$dial_friends
        [$f_index]['fid']}\" style=\"margin-right:3px;\"><img
        src=\"$APP_CALLBACK_URL/poke.gif\" /></a>";
    $fbml .= "<a href=\"http://www.facebook.com/wall.php?id={$dial_friends
        [$f_index]['fid']}\"><img src=\"$APP_CALLBACK_URL/wall.gif\"
        /></a> <br />";
}

$fbml .= "</td>";
return $fbml;
}
```

Underneath the thumbnail of the friend, a poke and wall action links are provided. All of the content is returned to the calling `get_profile_fbml()`
function as a string.

The `get_profile_fbml()` and `get_cell_contents()` functions do the
work of assembling the profile box content. The `render_profile_box()` in
`display.php` is the one that actually calls the `profile.setFBML` function:

```
function render_profile_box() {
 global $facebook;

 $fbml = get_profile_fbml();
 $facebook->api_client->profile_setFBML(null, null, $fbml);
}
```

One of the key questions for any app is when to update the profile box. For
some apps, it makes sense to have a chron program running that updates the
profile box of a user based on time. However, with Speed Dial, it makes the
most sense to update the profile box anytime a user makes a change to his
Speed Dial. I could call `render_profile_box()` when `index.php` loads,
but that is not as efficient as adding it to the data-changing handlers in
`index.php`:

```
if (isset($_POST['friend_picked'])) {
  $fid = $_POST['friend_picked'];
  $place = $_POST['placement'];
  add_dial_friend($user, $fid, $place, 0);
  render_profile_box();
}

// Handlers for action links
$action = $_REQUEST['action'];
$fid_actor = (int) $_REQUEST['fid'];
$place = (int) $_REQUEST['place'];
```

```
// Delete friend
if ( $action == 'delete' ) {
  remove_dial_friend($user, $fid_actor);
  render_profile_box();


}
// Add as Poison Control
elseif ( $action == 'pc' ) {
  clear_thumbnail($user);
  add_dial_friend($user, $fid_actor, $place, 1);
  render_profile_box();
}
// Clear all friends
elseif ( $action == 'clearall' ) {
  clear_dial($user);
  render_profile_box();
}
// Clear Poison Control icon
elseif ( $action == 'clearpc' ) {
  clear_thumbnail($user);
  render_profile_box();
}
```

Figures 12-7 and 12-8 show the profile box in both the narrow and wide columns of the profile page.

Figure 12-7:
Speed Dial
in the profile
page.

Figure 12-8:
Speed Dial
is not
designed for
the wide
column.

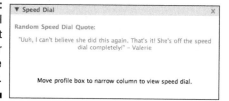

Sending Notifications and Publishing a News Feed Story

Some of the functionality of Speed Dial lends itself to notifications and News Feed stories. The trick is determining what sort of communication is appropriate for a given user action. I decided that I would send a notification to a friend when she is added to a user's Speed Dial or is assigned the Poison Control designation. Here's the `notify_friend()` function, contained in `publish.php`:

```
function notify_friend($fid, $action, $ranking) {
  global $facebook;
  global $user;

  if ($action == 'add') {
    $fbml = 'added you to spot $ranking on <fb:pronoun uid="' . $user . '"
           useyou="false" possessive="true"/> speed dial.';
  }
  else if ($action == 'pc' ) {
    $fbml = 'secretly placed you under the Poison Control label on <fb:pronoun
           uid="' . $user . '" useyou="false" possessive="true"/> speed
           dial.';
  }
  try {
    $facebook->api_client->notifications_send($fid, $fbml);
  }
  catch (Exception $ex) {
    // maybe do something
  }
}
```

Because Facebook places a limit to the number of notifications an app can send a day, the `notifications.send()` call is wrapped inside of a `try/catch` block.

I also set up a templatized action in `publish.php` by calling `feed.publish TemplatizedAction()` based on the action that the user performs:

```php
// Publish a news story related to a Speed Dial event
function publish_news_story( $target_id, $action, $ranking) {
  global $facebook;
  global $APP_ROOT_URL;

  if ($action == 'add') {
    $title_template = '{actor} added {target} to spot {ranking} on  <fb:pronoun
            uid="actor" useyou="false" possessive="true"/> speed dial.';
    $title_data = json_encode(array(
      'ranking' => $ranking,
    ));
  }
  else if ($action == 'delete' ) {
    $title_template = '{actor} removed {target} from <fb:pronoun uid="actor"
            useyou="false" possessive="true"/> speed dial.';
    $title_data = null;
  }
  else if ($action == 'pc' ) {
    $title_template = '{actor} secretly placed {target} under the Poison Control
            label on <fb:pronoun uid="actor"  useyou="false"
            possessive="true"/> speed dial.';
    $title_data = null;
  }
  else if ($action == 'clearall' ) {
    $title_template = '{actor} cleared all friends from <fb:pronoun uid="actor"
            useyou="false" possessive="true"/> speed dial.';
    $title_data = null;
  }
  else if ($action == 'clearpc' ) {
    $title_template = '{actor} unassigned the coveted Poison Control label from
            <fb:pronoun uid="actor" useyou="false" possessive="true"/> speed
            dial.';
    $title_data = null;
  }

  // Wrap in an exception handler in case the max is reached
  try {
      $facebook->api_client->feed_publishTemplatizedAction($title_template,
            $title_data, $body_template, '', '', null, null, null, null, null,
            null, null, null, $target_id, null);
  }
  catch (Exception $ex) {
    // maybe do something
  }
}
```

However, the act of publishing News Feed stories is something that you probably want to massage and tweak based on how the people are using your application. For example, after coding the above routine, I found that publishing for each of these events was simply too much. Therefore, for now, I decided to publish a News Feed story only when the Poison Control designation is assigned.

These two functions are called in the data-changing handlers of index.php:

```php
if (isset($_POST['friend_picked'])) {
  $fid = $_POST['friend_picked'];
  $place = $_POST['placement'];
  add_dial_friend($user, $fid, $place, 0);
  render_profile_box();
  notify_friend($fid, 'add', $place);
}

// Handlers for action links
$action = $_REQUEST['action'];
$fid_actor = (int) $_REQUEST['fid'];
$place = (int) $_REQUEST['place'];

// Delete friend
if ( $action == 'delete' ) {
  remove_dial_friend($user, $fid_actor);
  render_profile_box();

}
// Add as Poison Control
elseif ( $action == 'pc' ) {
  clear_thumbnail($user);
  add_dial_friend($user, $fid_actor, $place, 1);
  render_profile_box();
  publish_news_story( $fid_actor, $action, $place);
  notify_friend($fid_actor, $action, $place);
}
// Clear all friends
elseif ( $action == 'clearall' ) {
  clear_dial($user);
  render_profile_box();
}
// Clear Poison Control icon
elseif ( $action == 'clearpc' ) {
  clear_thumbnail($user);
  render_profile_box();
}
```

Facebook app development is iterative. Therefore, I make changes to the story publishing triggers as time goes on.

Adding an Invitation Page

The final component of the Speed Dial application is a page for inviting users. This page is displayed when a user clicks the Invite Users tab. The `fb:request-form` tag is ideal for quickly constructing an invitation form. However, before doing so, I need to gather a list of current users of Speed Dial who are friends of the user and exclude these people from the invitation form. To do so, I slip into FQL mode and use a query in `invite.php`:

```php
$result_set = $facebook->api_client->fql_query("SELECT uid FROM user WHERE
            has_added_app=1 and uid IN (SELECT uid2 FROM friend WHERE uid1 =
            $user)");
$exclude_list = "";

// Build a delimited list of users...
if ($result_set) {
  for ( $i = 0; $i < count($result_set); $i++ ) {
    if ( $exclude_list != "" )
      $exclude_list .= ",";
    $exclude_list .= $result_set[$i]["uid"];
  }
}
```

I then use some boilerplate code in `invite.php` to do the rest, only changing the content of the invitation message and the `fb:request-form` attribute values:

```php
$sNextUrl = urlencode("&refuid=".$user);

$invfbml = <<<FBML
<fb:name uid="$user" firstnameonly="true"/> invites you to add Speed Dial, the
            most Seinfeld-like app on Facebook.
<fb:req-choice url="http://www.facebook.com/add.php?api_key=$APP_API_KEY&next=
            $sNextUrl" label="Add Speed Dial" />
FBML;
?>

<fb:request-form type="Speed Dial" action="http://apps.facebook.com/speed-dial"
            content="<?=htmlentities($invfbml)?>" invite="true">
  <fb:multi-friend-selector showborder="false" actiontext="Invite your friends
            to use Speed Dial."  exclude_ids="<?=$exclude_list?>">
</fb:request-form>
```

Figure 12-9 shows the invitation form in action.

Figure 12-9:
Invitation
form.

Prepping the About Page

The final UI portion of the Speed Dial app to take care of is the About page, as shown in Figure 12-10. As I discuss in Chapter 15, add an app logo and descriptive information. The About page is an important component of making your application successful.

Figure 12-10:
Speed Dial's
About page.

Exploring the Full Source Files

Listings 12-1 through 12-7 show the full source code for the Speed Dial application.

Listing 12-1: index.php

```php
<?php
/*
 *  Speed Dial v0.1
 *    Copyright (C) 2008 Rich Wagner
 *
 *
 * THIS MATERIAL IS PROVIDED AS IS, WITH ABSOLUTELY NO WARRANTY EXPRESSED
 * OR IMPLIED.  ANY USE IS AT YOUR OWN RISK.
 *
 * Permission is hereby granted to use or copy this program for any
 * purpose, provided the above notices are retained on all copies.
 * Permission to modify the code and to distribute modified code is
 * granted, provided the above notices are retained, and a notice that
 * the code was modified is included with the above copyright notice.
 */
```

```php
include_once 'appinclude.php';
include_once 'db.php';
include_once 'display.php';
include_once 'profile.php';
include_once 'publish.php';

//
// Processing parameters
//

// Handler for Add a Friend
if (isset($_POST['friend_picked'])) {
  $fid = $_POST['friend_picked'];
  $place = $_POST['placement'];
  add_dial_friend($user, $fid, $place, 0);
  render_profile_box();
  notify_friend($fid, 'add', $place);
}

// Handlers for action links
$action = $_REQUEST['action'];
$fid_actor = (int) $_REQUEST['fid'];
$place = (int) $_REQUEST['place'];

// Delete friend
if ( $action == 'delete' ) {
  remove_dial_friend($user, $fid_actor);
  render_profile_box();

}
// Add as Poison Control
elseif ( $action == 'pc' ) {
  clear_thumbnail($user);
  add_dial_friend($user, $fid_actor, $place, 1);
  render_profile_box();
  publish_news_story( $fid_actor, $action, $place);
  notify_friend($fid_actor, $action, $place);
}
// Clear all friends
elseif ( $action == 'clearall' ) {
  clear_dial($user);
  render_profile_box();
}
// Clear Poison Control icon
elseif ( $action == 'clearpc' ) {
  clear_thumbnail($user);
  render_profile_box();
}

$dial_friends = get_dial_friends($user);

render_canvas_header(false);
```

(continued)

```
?>

<style>

.speeddial { margin:0 0; left:0px;}

.speeddial td {
  width: 65px;
  text-align:center;
  vertical-align: top;
  border: 1px solid #d8dfea;
  padding:2px;
}

.icons { margin-top: 3px; }

/* Pseudo-Facebook element */

.inputbutton {
  border-style: solid;
  border-top-width: 1px;
  border-left-width: 1px;
  border-bottom-width: 1px;
  border-right-width: 1px;
  border-top-color: #D9DFEA;
  border-left-color: #D9DFEA;
  border-bottom-color: #0e1f5b;
  border-right-color: #0e1f5b;
  background-color: #3b5998;
  color: #ffffff;
  font-size: 11px;
  font-family: "Lucida Grande", Tahoma, Verdana, Arial, sans-serif;
  padding: 2px 15px 3px 15px;
  text-align: center;
}

/* Clearfix */

.clearfix:after {
    content: ".";
    display: block;
    clear: both;
    visibility: hidden;
    line-height: 0;
    height: 0; }

.clearfix {
    display: inline-block; }

html[xmlns] .clearfix {
    display: block; }

* html .clearfix {
    height: 1%; }
```

```
/* Based on 2-Column Lists style on
             http://wiki.developers.facebook.com/index.php/Facebook_Styles */

.lists th {
  background: #6d84b4;
  text-align: left;
  padding: 5px 10px;
}

.lists .spacer {
  background: none;
  border: none;
  padding: 0px;
  margin: 0px;
  width: 10px;
}

.lists th h4 { float: left; color: white; }
.lists th a { float: right; font-weight: normal; color: #d9dfea; }
.lists th a:hover { color: white; }

.lists td {
  margin:0px 10px;
  padding:0px;
  vertical-align:top;
  width:306px;
}

.lists td h4 {
  text-align:left;
  background-color: #e7e7e7;
  border: 1px solid #d8dfea;
  padding:2px;
  color: #333333;
  padding-top: 3px;
  padding-right: 10px;
  padding-bottom: 3px;
  padding-left: 10px;
  font-weight: bold;
  font-size: 11px;
  margin-top: 10px;
  margin-right: 0pt;
  margin-bottom: 0pt;
  margin-left: 0pt;

}

.lists .list {
  background:white none repeat scroll 0%;
  border-color:-moz-use-text-color #BBBBBB;
  border-color: #d8dfea;
  border-style:none solid solid;
```

(continued)

```
  border-width:medium 1px 1px;
}

.lists .list .list_item { border-top:1px solid #E5E5E5; padding: 10px; }
.lists .list .list_item.first { border-top: none; }

/* Based on quote display in Facebook Events */

.q_owner {
  background-color: transparent;
  background-image: url(http://www.facebook.com/images/start_quote_small.gif);
  background-repeat: no-repeat;
  padding-top: 0px;
  padding-right: 0px;
  padding-bottom: 5px;
  padding-left: 18px;
  width: 400px;
}

.q_owner span.q {
  color: #555555;
  background-color: transparent;
  background-image: url(http://www.facebook.com/images/end_quote_small.gif);
  background-repeat: no-repeat;
  background-position: center right;
  padding-top: 2px;
  padding-right: 16px;
  padding-bottom: 2px;
  padding-left: 0px;
}

</style>


<h3>Welcome <fb:name uid="loggedinuser" firstnameonly="true" useyou="false"
            capitalize="true"/> to Speed Dial, the Relationship Barometer</h3>
<br />

<div class="q_owner"><span class ="q"><?php echo str_replace( "\"", "",
            get_random_quote() ); ?></span></div>

<br />
<div>
  <table class="lists" cellspacing="0" border="0">
  <tr>
    <th>
      <h4>Barometerize Your Friends</h4>
    </th>
    <th class="spacer"></th>
    <th>
      <h4>Your Speed Dial</h4>
    </th>
```

```
</tr>
<tr>
    <td class="list">
        <div class="list_item clearfix">
            <form method="post" action="http://apps.facebook.com/speed-dial/">
            <h4>Add a Friend</h4>
            <p>First, select a friend:</p>
            <fb:friend-selector idname="friend_picked"/>
            <br />
            <p>Then pick your friend's placement on the speed dial:</p>
            <select name="placement">
              <option value ="1">1</option>
              <option value ="2">2</option>
              <option value ="3">3</option>
              <option value ="4">4</option>
              <option value ="5">5</option>
              <option value ="6">6</option>
              <option value ="7">7</option>
              <option value ="8">8</option>
              <option value ="9">9</option>
              <option value ="10">* Asterisk</option>
              <option value ="11">0</option>
              <option value ="12"># Pound sign</option>
            </select>
              <input class="inputbutton" value="Add" type="submit"/>
            </form>
            <br/>

             <h4>Pick your Special Friend</h4>
             <p>Click the <img
            src="http://www.richwagnerwords.com/speeddial/toxic-sm.gif"/>
            button under your friend's picture to assign a friend to the
            coveted Poison Control spot.</p>

             <p><a href="http://apps.facebook.com/speed-
            dial//index.php?action=clearpc">Unassign the Poison Control</a>
            icon for now.</p>

             <h4>Remove a Friend</h4>
             <p>Click the <img
            src="http://www.richwagnerwords.com/speeddial/del.gif"/> button
            under your friend's picture to delete him or her from your speed
            dial.</p>

             <p><a href="http://apps.facebook.com/speed-
            dial//index.php?action=clearall">Remove all your friends</a> and
            start over. No soup for anyone!</p>

        </div>
    </td>
    <td class="spacer"></td>
```

(continued)

```
        <td class="list">
        <div class="list_item clearfix">
          <center>
            <table class="speeddial" border='0' cellpadding='1' width='198px'>
              <tr>
                <?php render_cell( 1) ?>
                <?php render_cell( 2) ?>
                <?php render_cell( 3 ) ?>
              </tr>
              <tr>
                <?php render_cell( 4 ) ?>
                <?php render_cell( 5 ) ?>
                <?php render_cell( 6 ) ?>
              </tr>
              <tr>
                <?php render_cell( 7 ) ?>
                <?php render_cell( 8 ) ?>
                <?php render_cell( 9 ) ?>
              </tr>
              <tr>
                <?php render_cell( 10 ) ?>
                <?php render_cell( 11 ) ?>
                <?php render_cell( 12 ) ?>
              </tr>
            </table>
          </center>
        </div>
      </td>
    </tr>
    </table>
  </div>

<?php
  render_canvas_footer();
?>
```

Listing 12-2: appinclude.php

```
<?php
/*
 *  Speed Dial v0.1
 *    Copyright (C) 2008 Rich Wagner
 *
 *
 * THIS MATERIAL IS PROVIDED AS IS, WITH ABSOLUTELY NO WARRANTY EXPRESSED
 * OR IMPLIED.  ANY USE IS AT YOUR OWN RISK.
 *
 * Permission is hereby granted to use or copy this program for any
 * purpose, provided the above notices are retained on all copies.
 * Permission to modify the code and to distribute modified code is
 * granted, provided the above notices are retained, and a notice that
 * the code was modified is included with the above copyright notice.
 */
```

```php
require_once '../facebook-platform/client/facebook.php';

$APP_API_KEY = 'enter_api_key';
$APP_SECRET = 'enter_secret_key';
$APP_CALLBACK_URL = 'http://www.richwagnerwords.com/speeddial';
$APP_ROOT_URL = 'http://apps.facebook.com/speed-dial//';

$DB_IP = 'localhost';
$DB_USER = 'username';
$DB_PASS = password';
$DB_NAME = 'db_name';

// Connect to Facebook, retrieve user
$facebook = new Facebook($APP_API_KEY, $APP_SECRET);
$user = $facebook->get_loggedin_user();
$is_logged_out = !$user;

// Exception handler for invalid session_keys
try {
  // If app is not added, then attempt to add
  if (!$facebook->api_client->users_isAppAdded()) {
    $facebook->redirect($facebook->get_add_url());
  }
} catch (Exception $ex) {
  // Clear out cookies for app and redirect user to a login prompt
  $facebook->set_user(null, null);
  $facebook->redirect($APP_CALLBACK_URL);
}
?>
```

Listing 12-3: display.php

```php
<?php
/*
*   Speed Dial v0.1
*     Copyright (C) 2008 Rich Wagner
*
*
* THIS MATERIAL IS PROVIDED AS IS, WITH ABSOLUTELY NO WARRANTY EXPRESSED
* OR IMPLIED.  ANY USE IS AT YOUR OWN RISK.
*
* Permission is hereby granted to use or copy this program for any
* purpose, provided the above notices are retained on all copies.
* Permission to modify the code and to distribute modified code is
* granted, provided the above notices are retained, and a notice that
* the code was modified is included with the above copyright notice.
*/
```

(continued)

```
// Returns a random quote for display purposes using fb:random
function get_random_quote() {
  $fbml .= "<fb:random>";
  $fbml .= "<fb:random-option weight=\"2\">\"You know uh, Valerie, I uh,
            couldn't help but notice that I'm on your
  speed dial.\" - Jerry</fb:random-option>";
  $fbml .= "<fb:random-option weight=\"1\">George: \"So you're on the speed
            dial?\" Jerry: \"After two dates!\"</fb:random-option>";
  $fbml .= "<fb:random-option weight=\"1\">\"Wha! You know, it's a pain to
            change that. You gotta lift up that
  plastic thing with a pen.\" - George</fb:random-option>";
  $fbml .= "<fb:random-option weight=\"1\">\"I had like a so-so date with
            Valerie, now I'm number nine on the
  speed dial.\" - Jerry</fb:random-option>";
  $fbml .= "<fb:random-option weight=\"3\">\"Yeah, this speed dial's like a
            relationship barometer.\" - Jerry </fb:random-option>";
  $fbml .= "<fb:random-option weight=\"1\">\"It's taken me thirteen years to
            climb up to the top of that
  speed dial, and I don't intend to lose my spot to you.\" - Mrs.
            Hamilton</fb:random-option>";
  $fbml .= "<fb:random-option weight=\"1\">\"You know, in the year two-thousand,
            we'll all be on speed dial. You'll
  just have to think of a person, they'll be talking to you.\" -
            Kramer</fb:random-option>";
  $fbml .= "<fb:random-option weight=\"1\">\"Uuh, I can't believe she did this
            again. That's it! She's off the
  speed dial completely!\" - Valerie</fb:random-option>";
  $fbml .= "<fb:random-option weight=\"1\">\"Wow, poison control? That's even
            higher than number one!\" - Jerry</fb:random-option>";
  $fbml .= "<fb:random-option weight=\"2\">\"I can't help thinking that maybe
            there's someone in your life who deserves [the number one spot]
            more. Someone you've known, you know, more than a week.\" -
            Jerry</fb:random-option>";
  $fbml .= "<fb:random-option weight=\"2\">\"My stepmother got to you, didn't
            she?...Uuh, I can't believe she did this again. That's it! She's
            off the speed dial completely!\" - Valerie</fb:random-option>";
  $fbml .= "<fb:random-option weight=\"2\">\"Why don't I put you on my speed-
            dial?\" - Mrs. Hamilton</fb:random-option>";
  $fbml .= "</fb:random>";
 return $fbml;
}

// Renders the canvas header for the main page and invite page
function render_canvas_header($invite) {
  global $APP_ROOT_URL;

  echo '<fb:dashboard>';
  echo '</fb:dashboard>';

  echo '<fb:tabs>';
  if (!$invite) {
```

```php
    echo '<fb:tab-item href="' . $APP_ROOT_URL . 'index.php" title="Set Your
            Speed Dial" selected="true" />';
    echo '<fb:tab-item href="' . $APP_ROOT_URL . 'invite.php" title="Invite
            Friends" />';
    echo '</div>';
  }
  else {
    echo '<fb:tab-item href="' . $APP_ROOT_URL . 'index.php" title="Set Your
            Speed Dial" />';
    echo '<fb:tab-item href="' . $APP_ROOT_URL . 'invite.php" title="Invite
            Friends" selected="true"/>';
  }

  echo '</fb:tabs>';

  echo '<div style="padding: 10px 20px 20px">';
}

// Renders the footer
function render_canvas_footer() {
  echo '<br/><p>Speed Dial v.0.1. Early beta, so please <a
            href="http://www.facebook.com/apps/application.php?id=7727364217">
            post bugs here</a>.</p>';
  echo '<p>Learn how to build Speed Dial in <a
            href="http://www.amazon.com/Building-Facebook-Applications-
            Dummies-Computer/dp/0470277955">Building Facebook Applications For
            Dummies</a>.</p>';
  echo '</div>';
}

// Renders a Speed Dial cell for the canvas previewer (not for the profile box)
function render_cell($index) {
 global $dial_friends;
 global $APP_ROOT_URL;
 global $APP_CALLBACK_URL;

 $total_friends = count($dial_friends);

 for ($i=0; $i<=$total_friends; $i++) {
   $match = false;
   if ( $dial_friends[$i]['ranking'] == $index ) {
     $match = true;
     $f_index = $i;
     break;
   }
 }
 echo "<td>";
 echo "<img src=\"" . $APP_CALLBACK_URL . "//$index.png\" /><br />";
 if ( !$match ) {
   echo "<img src=\"" . $APP_CALLBACK_URL . "/q_default.gif\" />";
   echo "(None) <br />";
 }
```

(continued)

```
  else {
    if ( $dial_friends[$f_index]['thumbnail'] == 1 ) {
      echo "<img src=\"" . $APP_CALLBACK_URL . "/toxic.jpg\" />";
    }
    else {
      echo "<fb:profile-pic uid=\"{$dial_friends[$f_index]['fid']}\"
            size='square' linked='true' />";
    }
    echo "<fb:name uid=\"{$dial_friends[$f_index]['fid']}\" useyou=\"false\"
          /><br />";
    echo "<a class=\"icons\" href=\""   . $APP_ROOT_URL .
            "index.php?action=delete&fid={$dial_friends[$f_index]['fid']}\"
            title=\"Remove from Speed Dial\"\"><img src=\"" .
            $APP_CALLBACK_URL . "/del.gif\"/></a>";
    echo "<a class=\"icons\" href=\""   . $APP_ROOT_URL .
            "index.php?action=pc&fid={$dial_friends[$f_index]['fid']}&place=
            {$index} title=\"Upgrade to Poison Control\"\"><img src=\"" .
            $APP_CALLBACK_URL . "/toxic-sm.gif\" /></a>";
  }
  echo "</td>";
}

?>
```

Listing 12-4: db.php

```
<?php
/*
*   Speed Dial v0.1
*     Copyright (C) 2008 Rich Wagner
*
*
*
* THIS MATERIAL IS PROVIDED AS IS, WITH ABSOLUTELY NO WARRANTY EXPRESSED
* OR IMPLIED.  ANY USE IS AT YOUR OWN RISK.
*
* Permission is hereby granted to use or copy this program for any
* purpose, provided the above notices are retained on all copies.
* Permission to modify the code and to distribute modified code is
* granted, provided the above notices are retained, and a notice that
* the code was modified is included with the above copyright notice.
*/


//
// Database queries
//

function get_db_conn() {
  $conn = mysql_connect($GLOBALS['DB_IP'], $GLOBALS['DB_USER'],
            $GLOBALS['DB_PASS']);
```

```php
    mysql_select_db($GLOBALS['DB_NAME'], $conn);
    return $conn;
}

function get_dial_friends($uid) {
  $conn = get_db_conn();
  $query = 'SELECT uid, fid, ranking, thumbnail FROM speeddial WHERE uid=' .
            $uid . ' ORDER BY ranking';
  $result = mysql_query($query, $conn);
  $dial_friends = array();
  while ($row = mysql_fetch_assoc($result)) {
    $dial_friends[] = $row;
  }
  return $dial_friends;
}

function add_dial_friend($uid, $fid, $ranking, $thumbnail) {
  $conn = get_db_conn();
  $query = 'DELETE FROM speeddial WHERE uid=' . $uid . ' AND `ranking`=' .
            $ranking;
  mysql_query($query, $conn);
  $query = 'INSERT INTO `richwagn_speeddial`.`speeddial` (`uid`, `fid`,
            `ranking`, `thumbnail`) VALUES (\'' . $uid .' \', \'' . $fid .'\',
            \'' . $ranking .'\', \'' . $thumbnail .'\');';
  mysql_query($query, $conn);
}

function clear_thumbnail($uid) {
  $conn = get_db_conn();
  $query = 'UPDATE speeddial SET `thumbnail`=0 WHERE `thumbnail`=1 AND `uid`=' .
            $uid;
  mysql_query($query, $conn);
}

function remove_dial_friend($uid, $fid) {
  $conn = get_db_conn();
  $query = 'DELETE FROM speeddial WHERE `uid`=' . $uid . ' AND `fid`=' . $fid;
  mysql_query($query, $conn);
}

function clear_dial($uid) {
  $conn = get_db_conn();
  $query = 'DELETE FROM speeddial WHERE `uid`=' . $uid;
  mysql_query($query, $conn);
}

?>
```

Listing 12-5: profile.php

```php
<?php
/*
*  Speed Dial v0.1
*    Copyright (C) 2008 Rich Wagner
*
*
* THIS MATERIAL IS PROVIDED AS IS, WITH ABSOLUTELY NO WARRANTY EXPRESSED
* OR IMPLIED.  ANY USE IS AT YOUR OWN RISK.
*
* Permission is hereby granted to use or copy this program for any
* purpose, provided the above notices are retained on all copies.
* Permission to modify the code and to distribute modified code is
* granted, provided the above notices are retained, and a notice that
* the code was modified is included with the above copyright notice.
*/

//
// All functions are related to the profile and News Feed publishing
//

// Returns FBML content for specified cell in the Speed Dial table
function get_cell_contents($index) {
 global $dial_friends;
 global $APP_ROOT_URL;
 global $APP_CALLBACK_URL;

 $total_friends = count($dial_friends);

 for ($i=0; $i<=$total_friends; $i++) {
   $match = false;
   if ( $dial_friends[$i]['ranking'] == $index ) {
     $match = true;
     $f_index = $i;
     break;
   }
 }

 $fbml .= "<td>";
 $fbml .= "<img src=\"" . $APP_CALLBACK_URL . "//$index.png\" /><br />";
 if ( !$match ) {
   $fbml .= "<img src=\"" . $APP_CALLBACK_URL . "/q_default.gif\" />";
   $fbml .= "(None) <br />";
 }
 else {
    if ( $dial_friends[$f_index]['thumbnail'] == 1 ) {
      $fbml .= "<img src=\"" . $APP_CALLBACK_URL . "/toxic.jpg\" />";
      $fbml .= "<a
             href=\"http://www.facebook.com//profile.php?id={$dial_friends
             [$f_index]['fid']}\">Poison Control</a><br />";
    }
    else {
```

```
      $fbml .= "<fb:profile-pic uid=\"{$dial_friends[$f_index]['fid']}\"
              size='square' linked='true' />";
      $fbml .= "<fb:name uid=\"{$dial_friends[$f_index]['fid']}\"
              useyou=\"false\" /><br />";
    }
    $fbml .= "<a href=\"http://www.facebook.com/poke.php?id={$dial_friends
            [$f_index]['fid']}\" style=\"margin-right:3px;\"><img  src=\"" .
            $APP_CALLBACK_URL . "/poke.gif\" /></a>";
    $fbml .= "<a href=\"http://www.facebook.com/wall.php?id={$dial_friends
            [$f_index]['fid']}\"><img src=\"" . $APP_CALLBACK_URL .
            "/wall.gif\" /></a> <br />";
  }

  $fbml .= "</td>";
  return $fbml;
}


// Returns FBML content for the profile box
function get_profile_fbml() {

  $fbml .= "<fb:narrow>";
  $fbml .= "<style>";
  $fbml .= " table {margin:-10px 0px 0px -5px;}";
  $fbml .= " td { border: 1px solid #d8dfea; padding: 0px; width: 80px; text-
              align: center; vertical-align: top; }";
  $fbml .= "</style>";
  $fbml .= "<table>";
  $fbml .= "<tr>";
  $fbml .=  get_cell_contents(1);
  $fbml .=  get_cell_contents(2);
  $fbml .=  get_cell_contents(3);
  $fbml .=  "</tr>";
  $fbml .= "<tr>";
  $fbml .=  get_cell_contents(4);
  $fbml .=  get_cell_contents(5);
  $fbml .=  get_cell_contents(6);
  $fbml .=  "</tr>";
  $fbml .= "<tr>";
  $fbml .=  get_cell_contents(7);
  $fbml .=  get_cell_contents(8);
  $fbml .=  get_cell_contents(9);
  $fbml .=  "</tr>";
  $fbml .= "<tr>";
  $fbml .=  get_cell_contents(10);
  $fbml .=  get_cell_contents(11);
  $fbml .=  get_cell_contents(12);
  $fbml .=  "</tr>";
  $fbml .=  "</table>" ;
  $fbml .= "<p style=\"color:#6d84b4;margin-top:5px;\"><strong>Random Speed Dial
              Quote:</strong></p>";
```

(continued)

```php
    $fbml .= "<p style=\"color:#6d84b4;\">" . get_random_quote() . "</p>";
    $fbml .= "</fb:narrow>";
    $fbml .= "<fb:wide>";
    $fbml .= "<p style=\"color:#6d84b4;margin-top:5px;\"><strong>Random Speed Dial
              Quote:</strong></p>";
    $fbml .= "<p style=\"color:#6d84b4; text-align: center;\">" .
              get_random_quote() . "</p> <br /> <br />";
    $fbml .= "<p style=\"text-align: center;\">Move profile box to narrow column
              to view speed dial. </p>";
    $fbml .= "</fb:wide>";

  return $fbml;
}


// Renders the profile box
function render_profile_box() {
 global $facebook;

 $fbml = get_profile_fbml();
 $facebook->api_client->profile_setFBML(null, null, $fbml);
}

// Renders a profile action
function render_profile_action() {
  global $facebook;

  $fbml ='<fb:profile-action url="http://apps.facebook.com/speed-dial//">Edit My
            Speed Dial</fb:profile-action>';
  $facebook->api_client->profile_setFBML(null,null,null,$fbml);
}?>
```

Listing 12-6: publish.php

```php
<?php
/*
*  Speed Dial v0.1
*    Copyright (C) 2008 Rich Wagner
*
*
* THIS MATERIAL IS PROVIDED AS IS, WITH ABSOLUTELY NO WARRANTY EXPRESSED
* OR IMPLIED.  ANY USE IS AT YOUR OWN RISK.
*
* Permission is hereby granted to use or copy this program for any
* purpose, provided the above notices are retained on all copies.
* Permission to modify the code and to distribute modified code is
* granted, provided the above notices are retained, and a notice that
* the code was modified is included with the above copyright notice.
*/


//
// All functions are related to notifications and News Feed stories
//
```

```
function notify_friend($fid, $action, $ranking) {
  global $facebook;
  global $user;

  if ($action == 'add') {
    $fbml = 'added you to spot $ranking on <fb:pronoun uid="' . $user . '"
            useyou="false" possessive="true"/> speed dial.';
  }
 else if ($action == 'pc' ) {
    $fbml = 'secretly placed you under the Poison Control label on <fb:pronoun
            uid="' . $user . '" useyou="false" possessive="true"/> speed
            dial.';
 }
try {
 $facebook->api_client->notifications_send($fid, $fbml);
}
catch (Exception $ex) {
  // maybe do something
}
}

// Publish a news story related to a Speed Dial event
function publish_news_story( $target_id, $action, $ranking) {
  global $facebook;
  global $APP_ROOT_URL;

  if ($action == 'add') {
    $title_template = '{actor} added {target} to spot {ranking} on  <fb:pronoun
            uid="actor" useyou="false" possessive="true"/> speed dial.';
    $title_data = json_encode(array(
      'ranking' => $ranking,
    ));
  }
  else if ($action == 'delete' ) {
    $title_template = '{actor} removed {target} from <fb:pronoun uid="actor"
            useyou="false" possessive="true"/> speed dial.';
    $title_data = null;
  }
  else if ($action == 'pc' ) {
    $title_template = '{actor} secretly placed {target} under the Poison Control
            label on <fb:pronoun uid="actor"  useyou="false"
            possessive="true"/> speed dial.';
    $title_data = null;
  }
  else if ($action == 'clearall' ) {
    $title_template = '{actor} cleared all friends from <fb:pronoun uid="actor"
            useyou="false" possessive="true"/> speed dial.';
    $title_data = null;
  }
  else if ($action == 'clearpc' ) {
```

(continued)

```
    $title_template = '{actor} unassigned the coveted Poison Control label from
            <fb:pronoun uid="actor" useyou="false" possessive="true"/> speed
            dial.';
    $title_data = null;
  }

  // Wrap in an exception handler in case the max is reached
  try {
      $facebook->api_client->feed_publishTemplatizedAction($title_template,
            $title_data, $body_template, '', '', null, null, null, null, null,
            null, null, null, $target_id, null);
  }
  catch (Exception $ex) {
    // maybe do something
  }
}?>
```

Listing 12-7: invite.php

```php
<?php
/*
*  Speed Dial v0.1
*    Copyright (C) 2008 Rich Wagner
*
*
* THIS MATERIAL IS PROVIDED AS IS, WITH ABSOLUTELY NO WARRANTY EXPRESSED
* OR IMPLIED.  ANY USE IS AT YOUR OWN RISK.
*
* Permission is hereby granted to use or copy this program for any
* purpose, provided the above notices are retained on all copies.
* Permission to modify the code and to distribute modified code is
* granted, provided the above notices are retained, and a notice that
* the code was modified is included with the above copyright notice.
*/

include_once 'appinclude.php';
include_once 'db.php';
include_once 'display.php';
include_once 'profile.php';

render_canvas_header(true);

$result_set = $facebook->api_client->fql_query("SELECT uid FROM user WHERE
            has_added_app=1 and uid IN (SELECT uid2 FROM friend WHERE uid1 =
            $user)");
$exclude_list = "";

//  Build a delimited list of users...
if ($result_set) {
  for ( $i = 0; $i < count($result_set); $i++ ) {
    if ( $exclude_list != "" )
```

```
        $exclude_list .= ",";
      $exclude_list .= $result_set[$i]["uid"];
  }
}


// Construct a next url for referrals
$sNextUrl = urlencode("&refuid=".$user);

// Build your invite text
$invfbml = <<<FBML
<fb:name uid="$user" firstnameonly="true"/> invites you to add Speed Dial, the
            most Seinfeld-like app on Facebook.
<fb:req-choice url="http://www.facebook.com/add.php?api_key=$APP_API_KEY&next=
            $sNextUrl" label="Add Speed Dial" />
FBML;
?>


<fb:request-form type="Speed Dial" action="http://apps.facebook.com/speed-dial"
            content="<?=htmlentities($invfbml)?>" invite="true">
  <fb:multi-friend-selector showborder="false" actiontext="Invite your friends
            to use Speed Dial."  exclude_ids="<?=$exclude_list?>">
</fb:request-form>
```

Part IV
The Part of Tens

The 5th Wave

By Rich Tennant

"I wrote my entire cookbook in a Facebook app. The other apps I saw just didn't look fresh."

In this part . . .

You see the number ten everywhere — in the Bible with its Ten Commandments, on TV with the "Late Show with David Letterman," and even in the movies with Bo Derek and Dudley Moore (okay, I admit, a dated example). Well, not to be outdone, even *For Dummies* books get into the act with the Part of Tens.

In this part, you get tips and techniques on a variety of development issues, including architectural strategy, privacy issues, killer Facebook apps, and promoting your app. Oh yeah — all these techniques are provided in lists of ten!

Chapter 13

Ten Strategies to Exploit the Power of the Facebook Platform

*B*efore you complete the development of your Facebook application, you'll want to consider a few additional strategies to make your app complete. In this chapter, I introduce you to ten additional tips and techniques that you can help you exploit the features of the Facebook application. In several cases, these techniques involve additional parts of the Facebook API and FBML that I do not touch upon elsewhere in the book.

Optimizing Your Facebook App

Potential users are a picky bunch. Yes, they'll use your app if it is useful. But they also want it to perform like Speedy Gonzales. They don't want to get stuck staring at their browsers while your app is busy behind the scenes. Therefore, after you have your Facebook application developed, your next step is to see what areas of the app can be optimized to speed up overall performance.

Here are several suggestions to consider when looking to speed up your application:

✔ Reduce the total number of server calls that you need to make from your application by using FQL queries over standard Facebook API calls.

✔ When you need to make several API calls at one time, use the `batch.run` method to combine up to 20 calls into a single request to the Facebook server.

✔ Use FBML canvas pages rather than iframe pages. According to Facebook, FBML pages are faster.

✔ Move JavaScript and CSS code to external files and then import them into your pages. Facebook caches these files the first time they are accessed and stores them indefinitely.

✔ Use the `fb:ref` element to store FBML content, particularly when you need to publish to multiple profile boxes. Facebook caches `fb:ref` references, making them quickly accessible on future usage. (See Chapter 10 for more info on the `fb:ref` tag.)

✔ Because most Facebook apps call `friends.get` at some point during their operation, consider making this call during your initial app load to minimize server requests.

✔ As in any Web application, keep your canvas pages manageable in length. If you are displaying multiple rows of data, divide your content over a series of pages. Consider, for example, how the Photos app handles this when viewing an album.

✔ Use AJAX when refreshing page content, limiting the page refresh to part of a page rather than the entire page.

Going Mobile with Your Facebook App

The Facebook Platform allows you to "go mobile" with your application by enabling your app's profile box and canvas pages to work on `m.facebook.com`, the Facebook mobile site.

In order to enable your app to go mobile, you need to use the `fb:mobile` tag. This FBML element is much like the mobile equivalent to the `fb:narrow` and `fb:wide` tags (see Chapter 10). Just like `fb:wide` renders content only when the profile box is in a wide state, so too the `fb:mobile` tag only displays its content when viewed from `m.facebook.com`. For example, consider the `fb:mobile` tag being added to a routine that publishes a user's profile box:

```
function republish_current_user_profile() {
  $fbml = <<<EndHereDoc
<fb:wide>
<p>W I D E  C O N T E N T</p>
</fb:wide>
<fb:narrow>
<p>NarrowContent</p>
</fb:narrow>
<fb:mobile>
<p>mobile_content</p>
</fb:mobile>
EndHereDoc;
  $facebook->api_client->profile_setFBML(null,null,$fbml);
}
```

To display your application's canvas pages on the mobile platform, you need to enclose the entire FBML canvas page content inside of an `fb:mobile` element. When you do so, Facebook adds an XHTML frame when the page is rendered, which is needed for `m.facebook.com`.

If you need to determine whether the user is accessing your app from a mobile device, you can analyze the `fb_sig_mobile` POST parameter. If Facebook believes that the client is likely a mobile device, this parameter returns a `1`. You could then dynamically provide a simplified mobile interface to the user.

If you are going to create a mobile version of your app, keep in mind that the user interface needs to be relatively simple. Avoid FBJS, AJAX, and some of the more advanced FBML elements.

Working with Attachments

One of the capabilities in the Facebook Platform that often causes confusion for developers is the idea of creating attachments. An *attachment* is a button-like extension that is displayed under the wall compose box. When a user clicks the link, a dialog box is displayed, enabling the user to add customized content to his or her message composition box. A user can then post the attachment content by clicking the standard Post button.

To add a PHP-based attachment, follow these steps:

1. **Go to www.facebook.com/developers/apps.php.**

   Your applications are displayed.

2. **Select your app on the left column.**

   The app is selected in the main part of the page.

3. **Click the Edit Settings link for your app.**

4. **In the Integration Point section, locate the Attachments section.**

5. **Type the text caption in the Attachment Action box.**

   You'll want to enter a command-based caption that appears as the link.

   In my case, I enter **Send iRecipe Card**.

6. **Enter the URL in which to obtain attachment content in the Callback URL box.**

   See Figure 13-1.

Figure 13-1:
Adding an
attachment
to an app.

7. **Click the Save button.**

   Your setup is now completed. Now you are ready to code the attachment.

8. **Create a source file to handle the attachment request.**

   In my case, I am creating an `attach.php` file.

9. **Type the source code for the file.**

   Here's the sample code I am using:

```
<?php

// Called when user clicks the attachment link
if ($_POST['message_sent'] < 1) {

  // Required - tells Facebook the callback URL for generating the attachment
             content
  echo '<input type="hidden" name="url"
            value="http://www.richwagnerwords.com/facebook/attach.php" />';

  // UI for selecting or composing content
  $recipe_name = htmlspecialchars($_POST['recipe_name']);
  echo '<fb:editor-text label="Recipe" name="recipe_name" value="' .
            $recipe_name . '" />';
  echo '<br />';
  echo '<fb:editor-textarea label="Contents" name="contents" />';

} else {

  // Called when Attach button is clicked in the attachment dialog box
  $recipe_name = $_POST['recipe_name'];
  $contents = $_POST['contents'];
  echo "<strong>$recipe_name</strong><br /> Contents: $contents<br />";
}

echo '<br />';

?>
```

Modify the code as desired to meet your specific needs.

The routine serves two functions. The `if` block is called when the link is clicked to obtain user input. The `else` block is called when the user clicks the Attach button in the attachment dialog box. (The line break added onto the end is added because Facebook has trouble rendering the content without it appended to the end of the source code.)

  10. **Save your file to the callback URL you specified.**

Figures 13-2, 13-3, and 13-4 show the attachment in action.

Send iRecipe card link

Figure 13-2:
Attachment
link displayed
on the wall.

Figure 13-3:
Specifying
the
attachment
content.

Figure 13-4:
Content is
rendered
in the
message
post box.

Keeping Track of the Session Key

In order for your application to communicate with the Facebook Platform, you need to establish a session using the API. But, as you see in this book, sessions are usually a non-issue when working with standard Web-based Facebook apps — either FBML or iframe. The basic rule of thumb is that after a user adds you application to his or her profile, you have an infinite session. You do need to add the appropriate call to `facebook.get_loggedin_user` to ensure that the user is logged into Facebook. However, after users are logged into Facebook, your application has full access to Facebook data.

However, suppose that you need to perform a backend process when the user is not logged in. In such a case, you do need access to the user's session key. In order to get that key, you have to go back to when a user first adds your app to his profile and accepts the terms of service. Facebook returns them to your callback URL and appends a session key, typically in the form of the following:

```
http://www.myfacebookapp.com/index.php?auth_token=dcf320
```

You want to capture this token using something like

```
$auth_token = $_GET['auth_token'];
```

After it's captured, you can store the token in your app user database for future usage when you need to perform an action when the user is not logged in.

Making Canvas Pages Accessible to Non-Facebook Users

Although a Facebook application is naturally oriented toward logged-in Facebook users, you want the ability to present your application to people who are not logged into Facebook itself. Not only does this broaden the scope of people who can check your app out, but it also permits search engines to index your application.

You don't have to do anything at all to make the page itself presentable to non-users. However, you need to account for non-Facebook users in your application. Here are some tips to keep in mind:

✔ Canvas pages are accessible to both users and non-users. All FBML tags are functional either way, but `fb:if` and `fb:else` blocks are important when rendering content for each party.

✔ The `fb:is-logged-out` tag is your best tool that you can use to render content specifically for non-Facebook users.

✔ `fb:name` displays as a first name only for non-users.

✔ `fb:profile-pic` is replaced with a question mark if a user's picture is not publicly visible.

✔ `fb:friend-selector` is replaced with a Facebook registration link. When a user joins Facebook, the application is automatically added during the registration process.

Handling Unique Browser Needs

If you have been around the world of Web development for long, you probably know all too well the quirks, idiosyncrasies, and bugs that Web browsers have in rendering pages, supporting scripting, and so on. To deal with these browser-specific issues in your Facebook canvas page or profile box, you can use the fb:user-agent tag. The basic syntax is

```
<fb:user-agent includes="match-list">
Custom content
</fb:user-agent>
```

The includes parameter is required and consists of a comma-separated list of strings that are looked for in the HTTP request's user-agent string. If a match is found, the FBML content inside of the element is displayed. There is also an optional excludes parameter that contains a comma-separated list of strings that should not be in the user-agent string. If a match is found, the content does not appear. For both parameters, the strings are not case-sensitive.

Table 13-1 lists some of the most common browser user-agent strings.

Table 13-1	Common User Agent Strings
Browser	*String*
Microsoft Internet Explorer 6.0	Mozilla/4.0 (compatible; MSIE 6.0; Windows NT 5.2)
Firefox (Windows)	Mozilla/5.0 (Windows; U; Windows NT 5.1; en-US; rv:1.8.1.12) Gecko/20080201 Firefox/2.0.0.12
Safari	Mozilla/5.0 (Macintosh; U; Intel Mac OS X; en-us) AppleWebKit/523.15.1 (KHTML, like Gecko) Version/3.0.4 Safari/523.15
Firefox (Mac)	Mozilla/5.0 (Macintosh; U; Intel Mac OS X; en-US; rv:1.8.1.2) Gecko/ 20070219 Firefox/2.0.0.2

The following example renders different content according to the user-agent match:

```
<fb:user-agent includes="msie">
  Welcome Internet Explorer user.
</fb:user-agent>
<fb:user-agent includes="firefox">
  Welcome Firefox user.
</fb:user-agent>
<fb:user-agent includes="firefox,mac">
  Welcome Firefox for Mac user.
</fb:user-agent>
<fb:user-agent includes="msie" excludes="msie 6.0">
  You are using Internet Explorer, but not version 6.0.
</fb:user-agent>
```

Integrating with Google Analytics

Facebook provides an `fb:google-analytics` tag to enable developers to monitor app usage using Google Analytics, a leading Web statistics service. In order to track a Web site, you normally need to add script code to the bottom of each Web page you wish to track.

```
<script src="http://www.google-analytics.com/urchin.js" type="text/javascript">
</script>
<script type="text/javascript">
_uacct = "UA-000000-0";
urchinTracker();
</script>
```

However, you can use `fb:google-analytics` on canvas pages and enable FBML to do the work for you. The basic syntax for the tag is

```
<fb:google-analytics uacct="UA-000000-0"/>
```

A host of optional attributes exists that you can add to the tag declaration for campaigns and other special case situations. For details, visit `wiki.developers.facebook.com/index.php/Fb:google-analytics`.

For more details on Google Analytics or to sign up for the free service, go to `www.google.com/analytics`.

Handling Redirects

If you need to redirect your Facebook app to a new URL within the canvas page, use the `fb:redirect` tag. The syntax is shown below:

```
<fb:redirect url="http://myboldandnewdomain.com/page2.php" />
```

Working with Cookies

The Facebook API has two methods that you can use to get and set cookies for your application: `data.setCookies` and `data.getCookies`.

The `data.setCookies` call sets a cookie for a given user. In PHP, the syntax is as follows:

```
$facebook->api_client->data_getCookie($uid, $name, $value, $expires, $path)
```

There are several parameters to define:

- ✔ `$uid` specifies the user associated with the cookie.
- ✔ `$name` defines the name of the cookie.
- ✔ `$value` provides the cookie's value.
- ✔ `$expires` provides an optional expiration date for the cookie.
- ✔ `$path` supplies a path (relative to the callback URL) for the cookie. If not specified, the value is `/`.

The `data.getCookies` call gets cookies for the specified user. Here's the call in PHP:

```
$facebook->api_client->data_getCookie($uid, $name)
```

The `$uid` parameter specifies the user ID of the person to get the cookies. The `$name` parameter is used optionally if you want to get a specific cookie value. If `$name` is not provided, all of the cookies are returned.

Integrating with Marketplace

If you would like to extend your application to integrate into the Facebook Marketplace, you can take advantage of several API calls (shown in Table 13-2).

Table 13-2	Marketplace API Calls
API Call	**Description**
`marketplace.createListing`	Creates or updates a Marketplace listing
`marketplace.getCategories`	Retrieves Marketplace categories
`marketplace.getListings`	Retrieves Marketplace listings based on listing ID or user
`marketplace.getSubCategories`	Gets subcategories for a specified category
`marketplace.removeListing`	Deletes a listing
`marketplace.search`	Searches marketplace listings

To retrieve all of the categories and subcategories and place them into a nested list, you could use `marketplace.getCategories` and `market place.getSubCategories` together, such as in the following PHP code:

```
$categories = $facebook->api_client->marketplace_getCategories();
echo "<h3>Display Categories and Subcategories</h3>";
echo "<ul>";
foreach ($categories as $category)  {
  echo "<li>{$category}</li>";
  $subcategories = $facebook->api_client-
            >marketplace_getSubCategories($category);
  echo "<ul>";
    foreach ($subcategories as $subcategory)  {
      echo "<li>{$subcategory}</li>";
    }
  echo "</ul>";
}
echo "</ul>";
```

The results are shown in Figure 13-5.

To get specific listings based on listing ID or user ID, use `marketplace.getListings`. Here is a PHP-based example:

```
echo "<h3>Display Listings</h3>";
$listings = $facebook->api_client->marketplace_getListings( array(10261371778,
          10276855753), null);
echo "<a href=\"{$listings[0]['url']}\">{$listings[0]['title']}</a><br/>";
echo "<a href=\"{$listings[1]['url']}\">{$listings[1]['title']}</a><br/>";
```

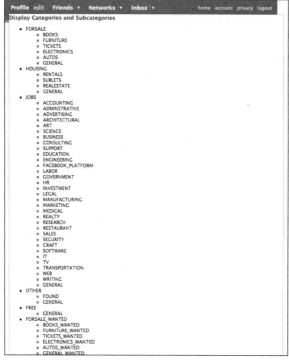

Figure 13-5:
Accessing
the
Marketplace
using the
API.

The results are rendered as a links.

To search for specific listings based on a query, you can use the market place.search call. For example, the following PHP code searches the marketplace listings for any listing with the string iphone in it:

```php
echo "<h3>iPhones and iPhone-related items for sale</h3>";
$category = 'FORSALE';
$subcategory = 'ELECTRONICS';
$query = 'iphone';
$listings = $facebook->api_client->marketplace_search($category, $subcategory,
          $query);
echo "<pre>";
print_r( $listings );
echo "</pre>";
```

The results are output into my test page as an array.

Chapter 14

Ten Killer Facebook Applications to Explore

- -

- -

Not all Facebook apps are created equal. Although thousands of Facebook apps are available, many of these are either little used or have little practical usefulness. Still, many of them take advantage of the Facebook environment and provide an added value to a person's Facebook experience. In this chapter, I select ten that I would argue are "killer" apps and help demonstrate the power of the Facebook Platform.

The criteria I generally followed were as follows:

✔ **Social app:** Some Facebook apps may tie into the platform, but never really interact with it in a meaningful way. A killer Facebook app leverages the Facebook social network and integrates it into the core of its functionality.

✔ **Limited scope:** Some Facebook apps are very useful, but they are so packed with features that they offer too much, providing functionality that most people don't have use for. The best Facebook apps have a limited scope, clear purpose, and intuitive interface. They also work well within the real estate constraints of the Facebook environment.

✔ **Repeated usage:** The best Facebook apps provide functionality that keeps people coming back to Facebook to use.

✔ **Extension of an existing service:** Some of the best Facebook apps extend the capabilities of an existing Web application by making it even more useful by integrating it with Facebook's social network. However, the smart apps do not force Facebook users to create an account on a third-party site, but merely integrate with an existing account if a user has one.

Local Picks

http://apps.facebook.com/localpicks

Developed by the popular travel review site Tripadvisor.com, Local Picks (see Figure 14-1) allows you to write and get personalized recommendations for restaurants — in your area or around the world. Tripadvisor.com offers restaurant reviews on its home site, but what makes Local Picks a killer Facebook app is that it combines that functionality with the networking strengths of Facebook. As a result, you can share reviews with your Facebook friends as well as get reviews from other Facebook members or Tripadvisor contributors.

Figure 14-1:
Local Picks
from
Tripadvisor.

iLike

http://apps.facebook.com/ilike

iLike.com is a "social music discovery service" in which you can listen and recommend music to others as well as connect with your favorite artists. iLike's

Facebook app offers this type of functionality inside Facebook itself. You can add music and videos inside a profile box (see Figure 14-2), get concert and album info on your favorite artists, share playlists, dedicate songs to your friends, and more. In sum, iLike does a great job of merging music sharing with social interaction.

Figure 14-2:
iLike's
profile box.

Attack!

http://apps.facebook.com/attackgame

Attack! is a Facebook app that I just had to include on this list. Not only is it a good representation of a Facebook-based game, but I am also personally addicted to it! Attack! is an online version of the classic board game Risk. But what makes it special is that your opponents can either be friends or other Facebook members with actual names, rather than anonymous nicknames like Spiraljoe3100 that you usually find with other online games. With a live chat box, Attack! lends itself to a strong community element, playing with friends and getting to know other Facebook members you normally would never interact with (see Figure 14-3). I've made friends with several people through a good Attack! game.

If you are not a Risk player, I also recommend Scrabulous (http://apps.facebook.com/scrabulous). Scrabulous is an online Scrabble game inside Facebook that you can play with your friends.

Figure 14-3:
Conquer the world with Attack!

iRead

http://apps.facebook.com/ireadit

iRead is the most popular book-focused app available on Facebook. Using iRead you can share reading lists, recommendations, and reviews with your friends. But you can go beyond the circles of your friends as well by finding and interacting with other iRead users who have similar reading interests as you do and get their recommendations. Figure 14-4 shows the iRead profile box.

Figure 14-4:
Share your book lists with others.

Quizzes

http://apps.facebook.com/quizzes

Quizzes could be described as a "social mixer app" — it exists purely as a vehicle for friends and others to interact with each other online. You can set up an online quiz that your friends can take about you or whatever topic you want. Here's a random sampling: *How well do you know Justus? What type of cheese are you? Do you know New Zealand?* Figure 14-5 shows a popular quiz.

Figure 14-5: Quiz your friends.

Where I've Been

http://apps.facebook.com/whereivebeen

Where I've Been is a travel app that allows you to display a map of the world, showing where you have lived (red), visited (blue), or would like to visit (green). You can share your world map and travel diary entries with your friends. The interactive world map is enjoyable to work with and can be displayed in a profile box or in a full-screen window (see Figure 14-6).

Flixster

http://apps.facebook.com/flixster

Flixster is the movie equivalent of iLike. The heart of Flixster is the ability to interact with your friends on movies. You can share movie lists, recommendations, and reviews with your friends. You can also take movie quizzes and share results with your friends. However, Flixster borders on trying too hard by offering movie trailers, show times, and other general movie info that has little to do with Facebook's social network.

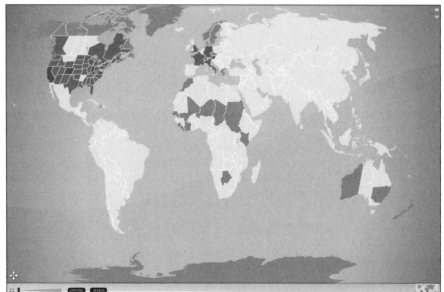

Figure 14-6:
Where I've been or want to go.

Top Friends

http://apps.facebook.com/topeight/?whoson=1&ref=sidenav

Top Friends is one of the most popular of all Facebook apps. Its purpose is very simple — display your favorite friends in a profile box on your profile page. In this way, you can make your best friends happy and your lesser friends quite unhappy. Although that functionality hardly qualifies it as a "killer app," Top Friends also provides a practical benefit: You can quickly poke or write a message to a friend through a single click.

Introplay's Workout Olympiad and Runlicious

http://apps.facebook.com/introplay

http://apps.facebook.com/runlicious

Introplay's Workout Olympiad and Runlicious (see Figure 14-7) are two Facebook apps that enable you to track your athletic workouts on Facebook, compare your progress with others, and monitor the progress of your friends. Although Introplay allows you to track workouts in dozens of activities, Runlicious is geared only toward runners.

Figure 14-7: Track workouts with Runlicious.

Appsaholic

http://apps.facebook.com/appsaholic

For Facebook developers, Appsaholic is a "killer app" simply because it tracks how users are using applications. You can use it to monitor the usage of your own app or track other third-party apps of interest. You can also buy Facebook advertising directly from within Appsaholic.

Chapter 15

Smashing Successes: Ten Tips for Making Your Application Popular

In This Chapter

▶ Avoid bad user experiences

▶ Brand your app effectively

▶ Avoid bombarding your users with meaningless drivel in their News Feeds

▶ Be visible and respond to your user base

▶ Promote your application on Facebook

*I*f you have worked through this book starting at Chapter 1, you have probably already designed, developed, debugged, and optimized your Facebook application. However, just because you have created a great app doesn't mean that anyone is actually using it. Given that harsh reality, after you have your app finished, you need to set your energies and attention to achieving success within the Facebook social network.

In this chapter, I explore ten proven tips that you can follow to help make your app a smashing success.

Avoid Social App Faux Pas

Perhaps the most important thing is simply avoiding the no-nos that instantly turn people off to your app. Facebook has, for example, cracked down on apps leading users to dead-ends — a page in which you force users to invite friends before being able to continue using the application. You can read about other practices that Facebook now prohibits at `wiki.developers.facebook.com/index.php/Platform_Policy`. Obviously, you want to avoid these major faux pas. However, apps that are successful over the long-term stay well clear of the Land of Bad User Experience.

The install base of social apps grows exponentially as users invite their friends to join them in using an application. But the key to successful growth is balancing your desire for user invitations with the need to be low-key and non-intrusive in your requests. If you go overboard with requests, users will throw your app overboard.

Think Social, Act Social

Application developers over the past 15 years have had to react to a constantly shifting environment in which they develop and deploy their apps. Stand-alone apps suddenly looked outdated in a networked environment. Desktop apps quickly were deemed "old-fashioned" in an online world. The fundamentally social nature of the Facebook Platform requires that Web developers embrace the Social Graph and make it work for them.

You've probably heard the phrase, "Think global, act local." Perhaps Facebook developers are better off with a more tunnel-vision mantra — "Think social, act social." Your app will be more successful if you follow this guideline. Therefore, always consider how your users can involve and engage their friends through your app. Always consider how you can publish interesting stories about users that their friends will want to read.

Brand Your App Effectively

Give considerable attention to the name and overall branding of your application. Too many names are either obtuse or are so generic that they are completely forgettable. Although Facebook application URLs (`apps.facebook.com/your_app`) are unique, the application name does not need to be. You might encounter half a dozen countdown timer apps, all with very similar names. As a result, it becomes harder for users to distinguish one from another. To avoid the pitfall of having users confuse your app with someone else's, choose a name that is original, yet descriptive.

If your Facebook app is linked to an outside app, you will want it to be identical or similar to your existing branding. iLike is a good example of this common naming and branding across implementations. Trip Advisor's Local Picks takes a different approach. Although its name is distinct, the overall look and feel of the Facebook app reflects Tripadvisor.com.

Communicate Wisely with Your Users

Effective communication with your users is essential to successful, viral growth. If you never publish stories to the News Feed, you risk your app becoming ignored. But, at the same time, if you communicate too much or do it in a clumsy manner, your news stories will quickly be voted down by your users. The key is a modest amount of well-crafted communication.

All too often, app developers come up with flimsy excuses for making contact with their users. Do your best to do just the opposite — make your stories a value-add to users, and something worthwhile or interesting to read.

Engage Potential Users with Your About Page

By and large, people decide whether to add an app based on friends' recommendations. *If your friend likes it, you may too.* On the other hand, if you want your app to be discovered by a potential user browsing the app directory, you have work to do. In these cases, your app's name, popularity, and About page become all-important.

The About page of an application is much like the back cover blurb of a book — people read it to determine whether to read the book. In the same way, users being introduced to your app for the first time will likely make their install-or-no-install decision based on your About page.

Man Your Discussion Board

Most users never take the time to post comments — positive or negative — on your discussion board. But those who take the time to do so usually fall into two categories — they are enthusiastic or they are experiencing problems. Either way, play an active role on your board. When you are visible to your user base, they know you are listening and paying attention. But, if you are never heard from, your users will soon ignore you and go somewhere else.

Pay Attention to User Reviews and Feedback

Be sure to be responsive to the feedback you are receiving. Respond to bugs quickly and look to add feature requests from users. If you do so, you build a highly enthusiastic user base that goes out of its way to encourage people to use your app.

Promote Your App on Facebook

Facebook offers many ways in which you can promote your app within the Facebook environment. If you have a budget, you can run an advertising campaign on Facebook through banner ads or a sponsored story appearing in the News Feed. Go to www.facebook.com/ads for more info.

If you don't have much money to spend, you can seek out other cost-efficient ways to promote your app on Facebook. For starters, you can become actively involved with Facebook groups that are related to the domain of your application. For example, if you have a stock tracking app, you could participate in stock-related groups. When you are regularly active in the group, you have the "street cred" to engage people in a positive manner without sounding like a used car salesman.

You can also partner with other application developers who have apps that complement your own to cross-promote your respective applications. This promotion can be done through the UI itself or through cross-pollinated News Feed stories.

React Quickly to Platform Changes and Enhancements

The Facebook Platform is quite literally a moving target in these early days of third-party development. As a result, you need to stay on top of the latest changes and enhancements in the platform and react accordingly. For example, I recently wanted to add a countdown timer to a Facebook page I developed. However, only one countdown timer could be added to a page instead of a profile. There were no technical reasons why the other timers could not be added, but the apps were not updated to react to this change in capability.

React Quickly to User Growth

If you are able to achieve that dream of all app developers — rapid, out of control, viral growth in the user base of your application, you need be able to respond quickly to the increased scale. Consider the capabilities of the Data Store API (`wiki.developers.facebook.com/index.php/Data_Store_API_documentation`) for a scalable storage solution. Also, consider the options you have available on your ISP. If your app hits the big time, your user base expects you to have performance in the league of the "big boys" and quickly grows frustrated with consistently slow performance.

Index

• *O* •

• *P* •

NESS, CAREERS & PERSONAL FINANCE

Fundraising
FOR DUMMIES

0-7645-9847-3

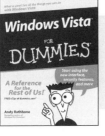

Investing
FOR DUMMIES

A Reference for the Rest of Us!

Eric Tyson, MBA

0-7645-2431-3

Also available:
- Business Plans Kit For Dummies
  0-7645-9794-9
- Economics For Dummies
  0-7645-5726-2
- Grant Writing For Dummies
  0-7645-8416-2
- Home Buying For Dummies
  0-7645-5331-3
- Managing For Dummies
  0-7645-1771-6
- Marketing For Dummies
  0-7645-5600-2

- Personal Finance For Dummies
  0-7645-2590-5*
- Resumes For Dummies
  0-7645-5471-9
- Selling For Dummies
  0-7645-5363-1
- Six Sigma For Dummies
  0-7645-6798-5
- Small Business Kit For Dummies
  0-7645-5984-2
- Starting an eBay Business For Dummies
  0-7645-6924-4
- Your Dream Career For Dummies
  0-7645-9795-7

E & BUSINESS COMPUTER BASICS

Laptops
FOR DUMMIES

0-470-05432-8

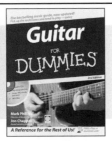

Windows Vista
FOR DUMMIES

A Reference for the Rest of Us!

Andy Rathbone

0-471-75421-8

Also available:
- Cleaning Windows Vista For Dummies
  0-471-78293-9
- Excel 2007 For Dummies
  0-470-03737-7
- Mac OS X Tiger For Dummies
  0-7645-7675-5
- MacBook For Dummies
  0-470-04859-X
- Macs For Dummies
  0-470-04849-2
- Office 2007 For Dummies
  0-470-00923-3

- Outlook 2007 For Dummies
  0-470-03830-6
- PCs For Dummies
  0-7645-8958-X
- Salesforce.com For Dummies
  0-470-04893-X
- Upgrading & Fixing Laptops For Dummies
  0-7645-8959-8
- Word 2007 For Dummies
  0-470-03658-3
- Quicken 2007 For Dummies
  0-470-04600-7

D, HOME, GARDEN, HOBBIES, MUSIC & PETS

Chess
FOR DUMMIES

0-7645-8404-9

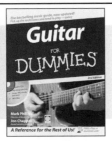

Guitar
FOR DUMMIES

Mark Phillips
Jon Chappell

A Reference for the Rest of Us!

0-7645-9904-6

Also available:
- Candy Making For Dummies
  0-7645-9734-5
- Card Games For Dummies
  0-7645-9910-0
- Crocheting For Dummies
  0-7645-4151-X
- Dog Training For Dummies
  0-7645-8418-9
- Healthy Carb Cookbook For Dummies
  0-7645-8476-6
- Home Maintenance For Dummies
  0-7645-5215-5

- Horses For Dummies
  0-7645-9797-3
- Jewelry Making & Beading For Dummies
  0-7645-2571-9
- Orchids For Dummies
  0-7645-6759-4
- Puppies For Dummies
  0-7645-5255-4
- Rock Guitar For Dummies
  0-7645-5356-9
- Sewing For Dummies
  0-7645-6847-7
- Singing For Dummies
  0-7645-2475-5

ERNET & DIGITAL MEDIA

eBay
FOR DUMMIES

Marsha Collier

A Reference for the Rest of Us!

0-470-04529-9

iPod & iTunes
FOR DUMMIES

Tony Bove
Cheryl Rhodes

A Reference for the Rest of Us!

0-470-04894-8

Also available:
- Blogging For Dummies
  0-471-77084-1
- Digital Photography For Dummies
  0-7645-9802-3
- Digital Photography All-in-One Desk Reference For Dummies
  0-470-03743-1
- Digital SLR Cameras and Photography For Dummies
  0-7645-9803-1
- eBay Business All-in-One Desk Reference For Dummies
  0-7645-8438-3
- HDTV For Dummies
  0-470-09673-X

- Home Entertainment PCs For Dummies
  0-470-05523-5
- MySpace For Dummies
  0-470-09529-6
- Search Engine Optimization For Dummies
  0-471-97998-8
- Skype For Dummies
  0-470-04891-3
- The Internet For Dummies
  0-7645-8996-2
- Wiring Your Digital Home For Dummies
  0-471-91830-X

WILEY

SPORTS, FITNESS, PARENTING, RELIGION & SPIRITUALITY

0-471-76871-5

0-7645-7841-3

Also available:

- Catholicism For Dummies
  0-7645-5391-7
- Exercise Balls For Dummies
  0-7645-5623-1
- Fitness For Dummies
  0-7645-7851-0
- Football For Dummies
  0-7645-3936-1
- Judaism For Dummies
  0-7645-5299-6
- Potty Training For Dummies
  0-7645-5417-4
- Buddhism For Dummies
  0-7645-5359-3

- Pregnancy For Dummies
  0-7645-4483-7 †
- Ten Minute Tone-Ups For Dummies
  0-7645-7207-5
- NASCAR For Dummies
  0-7645-7681-X
- Religion For Dummies
  0-7645-5264-3
- Soccer For Dummies
  0-7645-5229-5
- Women in the Bible For Dummies
  0-7645-8475-8

TRAVEL

0-7645-7749-2

0-7645-6945-7

Also available:

- Alaska For Dummies
  0-7645-7746-8
- Cruise Vacations For Dummies
  0-7645-6941-4
- England For Dummies
  0-7645-4276-1
- Europe For Dummies
  0-7645-7529-5
- Germany For Dummies
  0-7645-7823-5
- Hawaii For Dummies
  0-7645-7402-7

- Italy For Dummies
  0-7645-7386-1
- Las Vegas For Dummies
  0-7645-7382-9
- London For Dummies
  0-7645-4277-X
- Paris For Dummies
  0-7645-7630-5
- RV Vacations For Dummies
  0-7645-4442-X
- Walt Disney World & Orlando
  For Dummies
  0-7645-9660-8

GRAPHICS, DESIGN & WEB DEVELOPMENT

0-7645-8815-X

0-7645-9571-7

Also available:

- 3D Game Animation For Dummies
  0-7645-8789-7
- AutoCAD 2006 For Dummies
  0-7645-8925-3
- Building a Web Site For Dummies
  0-7645-7144-3
- Creating Web Pages For Dummies
  0-470-08030-2
- Creating Web Pages All-in-One Desk
  Reference For Dummies
  0-7645-4345-8
- Dreamweaver 8 For Dummies
  0-7645-9649-7

- InDesign CS2 For Dummies
  0-7645-9572-5
- Macromedia Flash 8 For Dummies
  0-7645-9691-8
- Photoshop CS2 and Digital
  Photography For Dummies
  0-7645-9580-6
- Photoshop Elements 4 For Dummies
  0-471-77483-9
- Syndicating Web Sites with RSS Feeds
  For Dummies
  0-7645-8848-6
- Yahoo! SiteBuilder For Dummies
  0-7645-9800-7

NETWORKING, SECURITY, PROGRAMMING & DATABASES

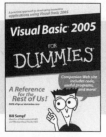

0-7645-7728-X

0-471-74940-0

Also available:

- Access 2007 For Dummies
  0-470-04612-0
- ASP.NET 2 For Dummies
  0-7645-7907-X
- C# 2005 For Dummies
  0-7645-9704-3
- Hacking For Dummies
  0-470-05235-X
- Hacking Wireless Networks
  For Dummies
  0-7645-9730-2
- Java For Dummies
  0-470-08716-1

- Microsoft SQL Server 2005 For Dummies
  0-7645-7755-7
- Networking All-in-One Desk Reference
  For Dummies
  0-7645-9939-9
- Preventing Identity Theft For Dummies
  0-7645-7336-5
- Telecom For Dummies
  0-471-77085-X
- Visual Studio 2005 All-in-One Desk
  Reference For Dummies
  0-7645-9775-2
- XML For Dummies
  0-7645-8845-1

-7645-8450-2

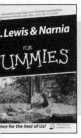

0-7645-4149-8

Also available:

Bipolar Disorder For Dummies
0-7645-8451-0

Chemotherapy and Radiation
For Dummies
0-7645-7832-4

Controlling Cholesterol For Dummies
0-7645-5440-9

Diabetes For Dummies
0-7645-6820-5* †

Divorce For Dummies
0-7645-8417-0 †

Fibromyalgia For Dummies
0-7645-5441-7

Low-Calorie Dieting For Dummies
0-7645-9905-4

Meditation For Dummies
0-471-77774-9

Osteoporosis For Dummies
0-7645-7621-6

Overcoming Anxiety For Dummies
0-7645-5447-6

Reiki For Dummies
0-7645-9907-0

Stress Management For Dummies
0-7645-5144-2

ATION, HISTORY, REFERENCE & TEST PREPARATION

. Lewis & Narnia

-7645-8381-6

0-7645-9554-7

Also available:

The ACT For Dummies
0-7645-9652-7

Algebra For Dummies
0-7645-5325-9

Algebra Workbook For Dummies
0-7645-8467-7

Astronomy For Dummies
0-7645-8465-0

Calculus For Dummies
0-7645-2498-4

Chemistry For Dummies
0-7645-5430-1

Forensics For Dummies
0-7645-5580-4

Freemasons For Dummies
0-7645-9796-5

French For Dummies
0-7645-5193-0

Geometry For Dummies
0-7645-5324-0

Organic Chemistry I For Dummies
0-7645-6902-3

The SAT I For Dummies
0-7645-7193-1

Spanish For Dummies
0-7645-5194-9

Statistics For Dummies
0-7645-5423-9

Get smart @ dummies.com®

• **Find a full list of Dummies titles**

• **Look into loads of FREE on-site articles**

• **Sign up for FREE eTips e-mailed to you weekly**

• **See what other products carry the Dummies name**

• **Shop directly from the Dummies bookstore**

• **Enter to win new prizes every month!**

ate Canadian edition also available
ate U.K. edition also available

e wherever books are sold. For more information or to order direct: U.S. customers visit www.dummies.com or call 1-877-762-2974.
tomers visit www.wileyeurope.com or call 0800 243407. Canadian customers visit www.wiley.ca or call 1-800-567-4797.

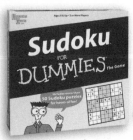